P9-CFX-566

$9.95

PROCESS EDUCATION

The New Direction for Elementary-Secondary Schools

Henry P. Cole

Process Education: The New Direction for Elementary-Secondary Schools deals with a new approach to schooling which holds much promise for increasing the quality of education in the next decade. The roots of the process education movement extend back into the late 1950s, when a United States population troubled by the Soviet Sputnik decided it was time to teach children *how* to think rather than *what* to think. This was to be achieved by methods and materials which placed major emphasis upon mastery of intellectual processes by which learning and problem-solving occur.

During the following decade large sums of money were expended by federal agencies and private foundations to fund the development of "process-promoting" curricula. The products of this activity are many major and excellent applications of recent research into the intellectual, emotive, and interpersonal skills required for effective learning and problem-solving basic to satisfying and productive living. Such programs represent a powerful new technology which, while having already made a tremendous impact on some schools, remains un-

known and unused by many in the larger educational enterprise. This book is concerned with the practical, logical, and philosophical foundations of process education as well as with the procedures used to implement the technology into widespread educational practice.

About the Author

Henry P. Cole was raised in the small town of Lebanon, Maine, where he attended the same one-room schoolhouse which served his great-grandfather. The recipient of several NSF fellowships, he completed graduate work in education and the natural sciences at Ohio State University and the State University of New York at Buffalo.

From 1968 to 1971 he worked as an educational psychologist and one of the five program directors at the Eastern Regional Institute for Education in Syracuse, New York.

Dr. Cole has taught courses in curriculum and psychology at Syracuse and Cornell universities. His earlier publications include research on human cognitive learning, creativity, curriculum design, implementation of educational innovations, and preservice and inservice teacher training designs and materials for process eucation.

Dr. Cole is presently an associate professor in the Department of Educational Psychology and Counseling at the University of Kentucky, College of Education.

TION

ion

ry Schools

PROCESS EDUCATION

The New Direction for Elementary-Secondary Schools

Henry P. Cole
University of Kentucky

Educational Technology Publications
Englewood Cliffs, New Jersey 07632

Printed in the United States of America.

Library of Congress Catalog Card Number: 79-178843.

International Standard Book Number: 0-87778-030-7.

First Printing.

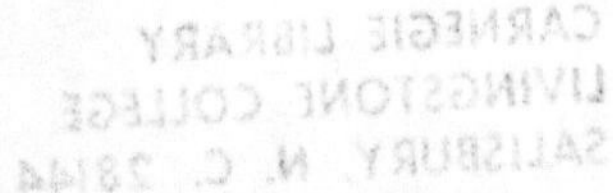

AUTHOR'S PREFACE

This book was prepared in response to program needs of the Eastern Regional Institute for Education (ERIE), which had selected as its mission the implementation of process education in elementary schools. The meaning of process, and especially the meaning of education, are extremely connotative and ambiguous. One encounters many educators who talk and write about process education but apparently have devoted little attention to either explaining what it is or how it can come about.

The book was designed to develop an explicit set of goals, definitions, assumptions, justifications, and a rationale for the practice of process education. The particular values underlying process education and derivative roles for pupils and teachers engaged in the practice of process education were also to be stated. Means for implementing the practice of process education in elementary schools through the use of existing curriculum and instructional vehicles in networks of schools and colleges such as ERIE had established were to be considered. The book was intended as a foundation document having direct applicability to ERIE program activity. It was anticipated that the book would examine, synthesize, and organize much of the philosophical, theoretical, and empirical work which underlies education devoted to the enhancement of thinking and feeling skills, as well as conditions which govern their learning. This information has been extremely useful and has greatly influenced the structure of the book.

An incomplete earlier version of the book was prepared in January, 1970. Most of the basic ideas which are found in the present volume occurred in this earlier version but were not well explicated. A large number of individuals studied this early version and made many suggestions concerning how it could and should be improved. I especially wish to acknowledge the contribution of Burton Andreas who, having earlier helped conceptualize the basic parameters for the book, read the earlier version and made detailed suggestions concerning how it could be improved. I am also indebted to Paul Nash, Florence E. Moody, Margaret Berra, Howard Stackpole, David Krathwohl, Richard Wallace, Jr., Robert Bickel, John Herlihy, Peter Dow, Anita Mishler, Eileen Simonson, Allan Hartman, William Ritz, and John Calvert for similar critical readings of the earlier version and many suggestions for revision.

The contribution of Florence E. Moody, Eileen Simonson, Margaret Berra, Robert Bickel, John Calvert, and Jim Ravencraft to the present version of Chapter 2 deserves special attention. Following study of the early version of the book, this group of individuals met with me for many hours to develop the basic statements and definitions which occur in Chapter 2 in the paradigm for process education. Members of this group also assisted in reworking and clarifying the assumptions and developing the rationale for process education, both of which are also found in Chapter 2. In addition, Florence E. Moody, Eileen Simonson, and Margaret Berra planned with me the detailed specifications for the remainder of the book.

In the writing of the present version of the book, John Calvert and Eileen Simonson assisted in identifying, studying, and organizing theoretical and scholarly references for Chapters 1 and 2. Leona Kosmac performed a similar function for Chapters 3 and 4. All three of these individuals have also acted as readers of various drafts of chapters and have made many useful suggestions which have been incorporated. Eileen Simonson's attention to matters of logical consistency and Leona Kosmac's assistance with tables, figures, and references have been particularly valuable.

Robert Bontrager, Diane King, and Susan Fox have provided editorial advice and assistance which is much appreciated. The contribution of Jo Ellen Purdy and Janelle Donigan, who have cheerfully prepared many pages of copy and many figures and tables through the multiple drafts and revisions, is especially appreciated. I am especially indebted to Mrs. Donigan, who has helped locate and check references, keep the manuscript and my notes in good order, and check and correct the final version of the work. Joan Geraci, Jean Eaton, Connie Valerio, and Jean MacAllister are also to be thanked for their assistance in typing.

And finally I an very much indebted to Sidney Archer, Milton Woodlen, and Richard Wallace, who allocated me the time and other ERIE resources needed to complete the book. It has been a most enjoyable and valuable experience.

Henry P. Cole

ACKNOWLEDGMENT

This book was begun in December, 1969. It developed out of the study of many innovative curriculum and instructional materials and related theory and research concerned with facilitating the development of thinking and feeling skills essential to adaptive and productive living in modern society. There are many individuals who have helped in the study of these materials and documents. Without their assistance it would have been very difficult to organize the huge amount of information critical to the logic and structure of the monograph. I am particularly indebted to Susan Bernstein, Albert Seferian, and Linda Kowaney. We four were members of a close-knit team which physically selected, gathered and studied many curriculum and instructional materials and their related documents. The assistance of William Ritz, Betty McKnight, Norma Reali, Eileen Simonson, and Howard Stackpole in the detailed study of particular curriculum and instructional materials was also very valuable.

The thinking and writing of Robert Gagné was exceptionally useful in helping form the basic definitions and justifications for "process" and process education. Professor Gagné met with ERIE staff members in extended conference sessions on two occasions to help more clearly explicate our thinking concerning key issues and topics. He has also personally communicated to me his recent thinking and insights relative to the nature of skills and the knowledge about means for implementing educational practice devoted to fostering a wide array of such skills.

It was anticipated that ERIE staff and members of other agencies could use the book as a base from which to plan particular implementation and evaluation strategies, design particular program activities, prepare program proposals for funding by outside agencies, and develop long-range institutional goals. Consequently, great care has been taken to document sources which have been referenced. Many times, particular page numbers have been listed, and additional notes about the source have been provided. This is done not primarily to document authoritative claims, but for the convenience of the interested and serious educator. The individual interested in learning more about the details of any of the many theoretical and empirical studies cited can easily locate the information he desires. Particular evaluative instruments, procedures, and models which may be useful to the reader are fully and completely referenced.

The book is basically a series of models which can provide direction for planning and action. Some models are very general and others are quite specific. Many have been adapted from the works of scholars such as Jacob W. Getzels, William S. Vincent, Matthew B. Miles, and Ronald G. Havelock. Other models have been developed by the author.

Chapter 1 contains a very general model in the form of the profile of the educated man. This is the end goal to be achieved by process education. It is pointed out in Chapter 1 that an adequate number and variety of curriculum and instructional vehicles have been developed which provide a basis for implementing the practice of process education. Yet, it is pointed out that these excellent educational innovations developed in the past decade have generally been used to poor effect.

Chapter 2 examines the nature of skills and the relationships among skills, processes, process, education, and process education. The empirical basis for process education and the assumptions and justifications upon which it is founded are stated and discussed. These relationships and definitions are combined in a paradigm and rationale for process education. The paradigm and rationale are conceptual models designed to establish broad parameters for thinking about knowledge, the learner, learning and the function of the school.

Chapter 3 examines the roles of pupils and teachers within the social setting of the school and society. The Getzels model of human social systems is used as the conceptual framework for considering the behavior patterns of individuals and the role expectations of institutions. The points of conflicts and barriers in social and individual behavior which have prevented the implementation of process education and other educational innovations are examined in detail. Particular attention is paid to the conflicts in values, aims, assumptions, and pupil and teacher learning roles which exist between conventional and process education. Perhaps the most important section of the book is the model provided in the last portion of Chapter 3. In Tables 5 and 6 the value positions supportive of and opposed to process education are arranged in four dimensions. The dimensions and the value positions describe four pairs of opposing views about the nature of knowledge, the learner, learning, and the function of schooling. Specific teacher and pupil role expectations are derived from each of the four pairs of value positions stated. Collectively, one set of value positions and their derivative role expectations define both quite specific objectives and evaluative dimensions for process education. The *Indicators of Quality Instrument*, developed under the direction of William S. Vincent, is another model. It shows clearly how the behavior changes expected as a result of process education can be observed and measured.

Chapter 4 is addressed to the issues which underlie procedures designed to implement change in institutional and individual beliefs and behavior patterns. Differing philosophies underlying change strategies are examined for the purpose of identifying those most consistent with the end goals of process education. The notion of temporary systems so well conceptualized by Matthew Miles is examined as a means to implement changed practices into social systems. A general model useful for implementing the value positions and pupil and teacher role expectations of process education through selected curriculum and instructional vehicles is examined. The general model described is the one developed by Ronald G. Havelock. The derivative and specific model provided incorporates the properties of Havelock's general model, Miles' conceptualizations of temporary systems, and ERIE's and the author's experience in establishing networks of schools and other educational agencies for the dissemination of new educational products and knowledge.

Chapter 5 is addressed to the problem of selecting existing curriculum and instructional vehicles appropriate to the task of implementing the new institutional and individual behavior patterns required for process education. The diverse nature and variety of curriculum and instructional vehicles is considered. The information, knowledge, or messages which curriculum and instructional vehicles contain are considered. These messages are viewed as important knowledge which can be transmitted to pupils, teachers and other members of educational agencies about how to implement process education. The fundamental elements of curriculum and instructional vehicles are noted. Procedures for analyzing and selecting vehicles for implementing particular institutional and individual behavior patterns appropriate to both process education and the needs of particular schools are provided. Finally, a number of suggestions are provided for using selected curriculum and instructional vehicles as the means to change conventional educational practice toward the general goals of process education.

This book should serve as a useful reference source of ideas to individuals involved in attempting to establish new practices and patterns of education.

THE AUTHOR

Henry P. Cole, formerly with the Eastern Regional Institute for Education, Inc., Syracuse, New York, is associate professor in the Department of Educational Psychology and Counseling, College of Education, University of Kentucky.

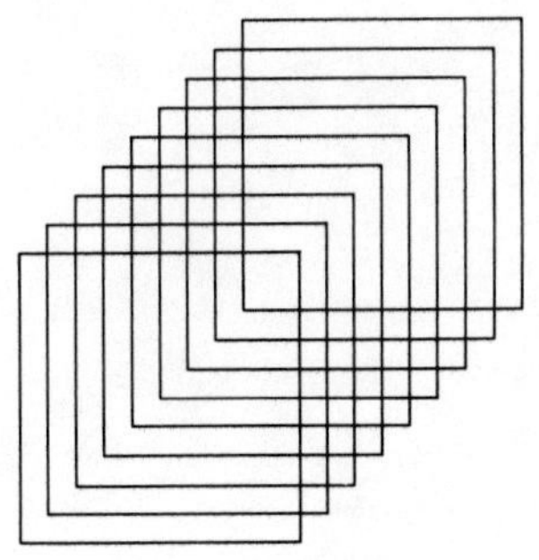

CONTENTS

PROCESS EDUCATION

The New Direction for Elementary-Secondary Schools

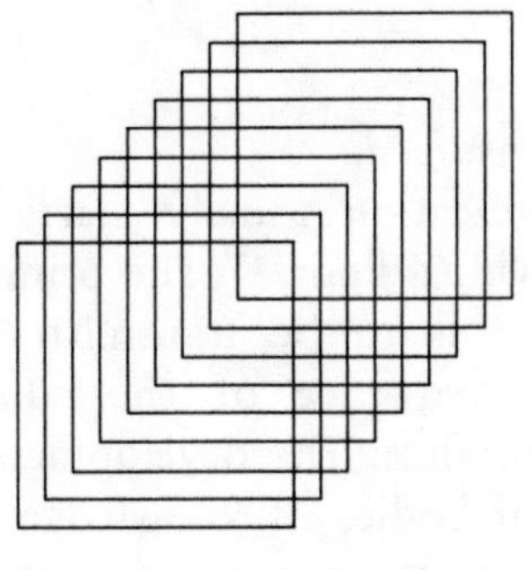

CHAPTER 1

PROCESS EDUCATION: A PRACTICAL VIEW

Process education is concerned first and foremost with the facilitation and development of skills. *Skills are organizations of behaviors which are highly transferable.* The skills which are most frequently emphasized in process education are those which relate to learning and analytic, productive, and expressive thinking. Other important skills which are less frequently emphasized are those concerned more directly with emotion, motivation, values, and interpersonal relationships.

Process versus Conventional Education

John Michaelis (1968, 1970) has pointed out that process education places a primary importance upon the fostering of skills. Acquisition of bodies of knowledge and information or content is secondary. In process education, the key question in planning the curriculum or the lesson plan is, "What skills are essential to the individual in order to make him a more effective person?" The *content* of the curriculum is selected for its utility in the facilitation and exercise of those skills. *The skills are the goals. The curriculum content is the vehicle by which the goal of skill development may be realized.*

Conventional education usually starts with the question, "What must the individual know?" The primary emphasis is upon the knowledge which is to be transmitted to the child. The *content*, scope, and sequence of the educational experience assume primary importance. The development of skills is secondary to the mastery of bodies of knowledge or information. It is assumed that mastery of the prescribed content will result in skill development.

Even conventional educational practice has recognized that some skills need special emphasis. Thus, as Heathers (1965) notes, attention to reading, speaking, writing, and mathematical skills has long been recognized as being necessary, since these skills are instrumental to further schooling and extra-school activity. However, these skills, while very important, are only a few of many known to be essential to continued learning and effective living. Process education recognizes the importance of the instrumental skills of speaking, reading, writing, and mathematics which schools have long emphasized. It would not do away with this emphasis. Rather, it would place a new and equal emphasis upon the development of many other skills which are just as important but are seldom considered so in conventional educational practice.

Process education recognizes that people live by their skills. Both the productivity and quality of life are related to the skills of the individual. Skills of learning, of relating to others, of empathy, of analyzing and synthesizing information and experience, of planning and implementing action, of conceptualizing, generalizing, expressing, and valuing are a few of those by which we live. *People do not live by information. The information is needed, but, without the skills to act on the information, the person is crippled. The power lies not so much in the information as in the skills to organize and use it, to make meaning from it.*

In the current practice of conventional education, too much emphasis is placed on information and bodies of knowledge. Too little emphasis is placed upon facilitating the skills for dealing with that information, as well as with the huge mass of information resulting from personal experience. Educational practice remains heavily fact- and information-oriented. It is imperative that formal education become oriented toward the development of skills needed for effective living in an information-rich and complex world.

Which Skills Shall Be Emphasized?

This is a difficult question to answer. As is the case with most good questions, it has no certain answer. A fundamental problem in developing and implementing process education is determining which skills should be selected for emphasis (Covington, 1970, p. 495; Cole & Seferian, 1970, pp. 34-38).

The answer requires philosophical considerations which reflect the values of individuals and society. The value positions can be used to develop a profile of that desired product of the schools, the "educated man." Given the profile, it is possible to empirically determine which skills are most important to the development and general effectiveness of such an individual.

What is the profile of the "educated man"? From the study of many statements concerning what education should be, it appears that the ideal man our schools should help develop has the following characteristics. He is a rational man skilled in reasoning and analytic thinking. He is a man who can love. He is compassionate and warm in his interpersonal relationships. He is sensitive, empathetic, and non-ethnocentric. He is an independently motivated, life-long learner. He is a problem-seeker and -solver. He is expressive and creative, both cognitively and affectively. He is flexible and fluent in his perceptions, ideas, and feelings. He is curious and an inquirer. He is a coper rather than a defender, an active seeker rather than a passive accepter. This is indeed a grand profile, and, yet, it is one which is commonly stated as a goal for education and society.

Let us assume that this is an acceptable profile of the "educated man." Now we have some options for determining which skills shall be emphasized. One of our options is to look to the work of those individuals who have pondered the problem and have subsequently recommended particular skills for emphasis in educational practice. Two books which contain the accumulated research, experience, and thinking of many scholars along these lines are *Life Skills in School and Society* (Rubin, 1969) and *Perceiving, Behaving, Becoming* (Combs, 1962). The many scholars who have contributed to these books consider a wide range of skills which collectively draw a profile of the educated man. The profile is basically the same as the one provided above.

Another option for determining which skills to emphasize involves looking to the results of behavioral research. People who have studied human behavior have learned much about the nature and utility of particular types of skills. Unfortunately, many of the tasks for which skills have been studied are peculiar to learning research and the laboratory. However, this is not always the case. Some researchers have studied the development and transfer of skills in relation to behavior and tasks more meaningful and relevant to daily life and common experience. Some of these researchers have taken an additional step. They have tried to apply the results of their own or other research to educational practice. Included in this group are Robert Gagné, Jerome Bruner, L.L. Thurstone and Thelma G. Thurstone, Marianne Frostig, David Horne, Richard Crutchfield, Martin Covington, Lauren Resnick, Paul Torrance, Elliot Eisner, Sidney Parnes, Ronald Lippitt, Robert Fox, Frank Williams, Frederick Kresse, and many more.

Consideration of the work of these individuals is particularly important. Their involvement in educational practice not only tells us which skills they judge to be important but also tells us something about means for promoting the development of such skills. The curricula and educational practices they have developed also can be used to provide empirical evidence for the effectiveness of educational practice devoted to development of skills (process education).

When one looks at the skills these researchers have emphasized, one again finds that, collectively, they cover a very broad spectrum. Many skills essential to characteristics of the "educated man" are represented, although proportionately more emphasis seems to be placed upon rational analytic-thinking and problem-solving skills than the emotive and interpersonal.

As a third option, one can, by oneself or with the assistance of others, generate a list of skills essential to the characteristics of the ideal man. One soon ends up with a huge list of skills. The relationship between them is often unclear and always arbitrary. Furthermore, when one is finished, it is next to impossible to indicate which skills are most important and deserve emphasis over others in educational practice.

The exercise of option three, though frustrating, has merit, for one is forced to the conclusion that all the skills which characterize the "educated man" are important. All the skills discussed in *Life Skills in School and Society* and *Perceiving, Behaving, Becoming* deserve attention. This is a most important conclusion. It means that, if a curriculum, a set of instructional materials, a strategy for instruction, or any other component of educational practice emphasizes the facilitation or development of *any* of these skills, it has potential for process education. It further means that the total educational setting should be concerned with the promotion of a wide variety of different skills through different curricula and educational practices.

It is virtually impossible for a given set of curriculum materials or instructional procedures to deal comprehensively with the entire range of skills. Particular curriculum developers, educators, and scholars emphasize different subsets of the skills essential to the characteristics of the "educated man." Thus, a curriculum like AAAS' *Science–A Process Approach* (AAAS, *Science–A Process Approach Commentary,* 1968b), which deals with the analytic thinking skills of scientific inquiry, should not be rejected as a useful component of process educational practice simply because it fails to emphasize affective and interpersonal skills. The processes of the AAAS science curriculum, which include observing, classifying, using numbers, measuring, predicting, inferring, formulating hypotheses, and interpreting data, are really skills. They are known empirically to be essential to inquiry, analytic thinking, and problem-solving.

Scores of recent studies in cognitive psychology confirm this (Anderson & Ausubel, 1966; Bruner, Olver, Greenfield *et al.*, 1966; Gagné, 1965a, 1968a, 1968b, 1970; Harper, Anderson, Christensen, & Hunka, 1965; Hellmuth, 1970). Furthermore, research with the *Productive Thinking Program,* an elementary school curriculum designed for the promotion of analytic-thinking and problem-solving skills, has shown that such skills can be instructed and do exhibit transfer (Covington, 1970; Davis, Manske, & Train, 1967). Certainly, such skills need to receive more, *not* less, emphasis in educational practice. Facilitating the development of these skills is required to achieve the rational characteristics of the "educated man."

There are other existing curricula and educational practices which place emphasis upon affective, expressive, and social interactive skills and which place less emphasis upon the analytic thinking skills predominant in the AAAS science curriculum or in the *Productive Thinking Program.* Three examples of curricula or instructional practices of this type are *Curriculum in the Visual Arts* developed by Elliot Eisner; *The Intergroup Relations Curriculum* developed under the direction of John Gibson; and the *Movement Education Program,* developed by Joan Tillotson.[1] The

1. For a more complete description of these programs and sources of further information, refer to *Encounters in Thinking: A Compendium of Curricula for Process Education* (Seferian & Cole, 1970).

Curriculum in the Visual Arts is designed to promote skills basic to the production of aesthetic and expressive visual forms. It is postulated that such skills enable the individual to be generally more expressive in his ideas and feelings. The *Intergroup Relations Curriculum* emphasizes social perception and social interactive skills in groups. It has as goals the reduction of stereotypic and prejudicial thinking. The human relation skills emphasized by this curriculum are postulated as basic to the healthy, effective, and rewarding functioning of the individual within the many and diverse groups of our society. The *Movement Education Program* is an unusual physical education program. It concentrates on developing skills which lead to expressive body movements and to development of the child's self-image, as well as an increased sensitivity to others. It is obvious that the skills emphasized by these three curricula are very important in process education. Education for these types of skills is strongly called for by the authors of *Life Skills in School and Society* and *Perceiving, Behaving, Becoming.* The affective, expressive, and social interactive skills emphasized by these curricula are equally important as the analytic thinking skills which are the primary concern of the *Productive Thinking Program* and the AAAS science curriculum. The "educated man" needs all these skills. All five curricula mentioned are concerned first and foremost with the facilitation of important skills through education. They all deserve a place in process education.

It is both inappropriate and impractical to attempt to structure the entire educational setting of a school around the particular schemata of skills selected for emphasis by a given curriculum, theorist, teacher educator, or scholar. Each source, of necessity, emphasizes some subset of skills it seeks to promote. Educational practice structured entirely around the analytic thinking skills of the AAAS elementary science curriculum would be woefully inadequate with respect to the development of skills of human relations and affective expression. Yet, educational practice devoted entirely to the development of affective and interpersonal skills would be equally lacking. There is no sense in saying one approach is better or more essential than the other. They are both essential. We have only to consider the student and society to see this.

Pupils have both differential needs and preferences for particular skills. Furthermore, differential roles in society and different life styles cause certain skills to be of more value and utility to some individuals than to others. Thus, while the profile of the "educated man" may include common characteristics, the emphasis upon certain of those characteristics and the proficiency in their associated skills may be expected to vary across "educated men." The engineer may be expected to value, emphasize, and show more proficiency in certain subsets of analytic thinking skills than the marriage counselor, who may value, emphasize, and show more proficiency in certain subsets of interpersonal relationship and social perception skills. Both may have proficiency in many common skills, but it is unlikely that their skill profile will be identical in emphasis and degree of proficiency. The differential demands of society, as well as differences in their individual experiences and personalities, insure this. Obviously, both kinds of individuals are needed by society. There is no moral or practical basis for attempting to produce more or fewer engineers or marriage counselors through education. There is, however, a strong moral and practical basis for providing an educational setting where both may develop their special skills according to their preferences and the needs of society and where both may also be assured adequate opportunity to become proficient to some degree in the broad array of skills which characterize the "educated man."

The ideal situation is for educational practice to make use of a wide variety of instructional materials, curricula, and personnel capable of providing a good balance for the facilitation and development of a wide array of skills. The schools must continue to emphasize what Heathers (1965) has called the instrumental skills: reading, writing, speaking, and mathematics. If process education is to be implemented, the schools must also begin the purposeful and deliberate promotion of many other skills which are generally ignored. To do this, emphasis in current educational practice on the transmission of knowledge and information to pupils must be decreased.

Is There a Sufficient Basis for the Practice of Process Education?

This question is best considered as a series of related questions. The questions are: "Can we begin to build educational practice devoted to the promotion of a wide array of skills?" "Is there both a sufficient base of experience and sufficient means for such educational practice?" "Specifically, are there a sufficient number of existing instructional systems, materials, and techniques well suited to the promotion of a wide array of skills through educational practice?" The answer to these questions is, "Yes." The answer was not arrived at casually, but from empirical findings resulting from careful planning and much study.

The activity which leads to this affirmative answer to the above questions is described in detail in "Analysis of Process Curricula" (Cole & Seferian, 1970) and numerous other ERIE documents and working papers. For convenience, major portions of this activity are briefly described below.

The task was to determine if there were a sufficient number of existing instructional systems, materials, and techniques which were suited to the deliberate promotion of a wide array of skills through formal education at the elementary school level. The search for such materials and techniques was closely guided by a detailed plan which had clearly specified objectives and procedures for obtaining those objectives.

First the plan called for the development of an "initial process list." This was a list of skills viewed as central to process education. It was the initial answer to the earlier question, "Which skills shall be promoted?" The plan also called for a set of criteria for the identification, selection, and screening of existing instructional materials, systems, or techniques appropriate to the development of the specified skills.

The initial list of skills was developed over a period of several months before the entire plan had been fully developed. The initial input to the skills lists resulted from an intensive study of the many documents affiliated or related to the AAAS *Science–A Process Approach* curriculum, the *National Schools Project* program, and the *Productive Thinking Program.* All of these programs are based on extensive research and theory. All have many documents dealing with their design, their goals, and their theoretical basis. In addition, many other articles and books which deal with the underlying skills, behaviors, and topics in these programs were reviewed. These included writings of Guilford, Torrance, Berlyne, Resnick, Russell, Bruner, Gagné, Crutchfield, Covington, and many more.

One particularly useful input to the development of the skills list resulted from interaction of ERIE personnel with the faculty and resource library of the 14th Annual Creative Problem-Solving Institute sponsored by the Creative Education Foundation, Buffalo, New York. The Institute selects as its faculty members a wide diversity of individuals who are concerned with the promotion of skills related to creative and expressive behavior, productive thinking, and problem-solving. These include, among many others, J.P. Guilford, Calvin W. Taylor, Donald W. McKinnon, E. Paul Torrance, J.H. McPherson, Sidney J. Parnes, and Frank E. Williams. The Institute library contains a comprehensive listing of research and practice related to the promotion of a wide variety of skills concerned with expressive, creative, and productive thinking and problem-solving.

Criteria for the selection of existing curricula and instructional materials having potential for process educational practice were developed. The central criterion was whether or not the materials or practice could be judged appropriate for the promotion of subsets of the skills specified on the ERIE list. It was assumed that instructional materials or other instances of educational practice *clearly* and *purposely* devoted to the development of the specified skills had utility for process education. Those materials or practices which were judged as not placing a deliberate and major emphasis upon the development of some set of the specified skills were to be excluded. In addition to determining if the materials were designed for deliberate promotion of stated skills, other criteria used in the selection procedure were concerned with whether or not the materials or techniques were available, had an evident basis in theory and research, had stated objectives, had been exposed to a systematic evaluation, were designed for use with preschool through grade six children, and had supporting documentation dealing with each of these dimensions. The purpose of these other criteria was to select those examples of instructional materials and techniques which were not only concerned with the promotion of the specified skills, but which had a sound rationale for doing so, a reality of existence, and the advantage of already having been used in actual educational practice which could provide needed information both on the means and effectiveness of such programs. Later, the initial eight criteria were expanded into a much more detailed form.

The initial process list, an early definition of process, the eight criteria for the selection of process curricula, and a statement of the procedures by which ERIE hoped to further implement process educational practice were sent to several scholars and researchers who had been engaged in the development of curricula designed to promote process skills. A few weeks after these individuals received these materials, two ERIE staff members met with them to record and discuss criticisms, recommendations, and comments. In each case, a specific agenda was prepared prior to the meetings for purposes of obtaining adequate information on each of these topics. The individuals were generally supportive of the criteria, the process list, and the ERIE definition of process. Their comments and insights were useful in refining the procedures by which ERIE intended to identify exemplary process curricula. Thus the basic tools for determining which instructional materials and practice were or were not appropriate for the promotion of process educational practice had been developed and judged appropriate to the task by an independent group of knowledgeable scholars. These tools were also soon found to be operationally useful.

A nationwide search for appropriate curricula, instructional materials, and practices which met the ERIE selection criteria was conducted. Hundreds of agencies and individuals were contacted. Of the several hundred curricular components, units, strategies, or materials identified, a few were judged to have much potential for the practice of process education. They were designed for the deliberate promotion of subsets of the highly useful generalizable skills. These materials were also found to be far more adequate on the additional ERIE selection criteria than is typically the case.[2]

Five instructional programs identified in the search activity have been installed in ERIE laboratory and network schools. There were at least three reasons for this. First, it was recognized that these programs represented the means by which an awareness of, a commitment to, and possibly the practice of process education could be facilitated in the behavior patterns of pupils, teachers, principals, professors of education, and others concerned

2. A more complete account of the search and selection activity is found in "Analysis of Process Curricula" (Cole & Seferian, 1970). The results of the search and selection activity were first reported by Cole, Bernstein, Seferian *et al.* (1969). The report was later updated and expanded as *Encounters in Thinking: A Compendium of Curricula for Process Education* (Seferian & Cole, 1970).

with education. Second, it was expected that the detailed study of these programs and their affiliated documents coupled with the opportunity to view them in actual operation in school settings would lead to a better understanding of the properties and problems of practicing process education. Third, it was expected that more could be learned about procedures for the effective and proper implementation of programs of this type in current school practice. Much progress toward these goals has been achieved.

The programs which were identified and judged appropriate for installation in schools are more than simple sets of materials. They are instructional systems designed for the deliberate promotion of skills. They frequently specify materials, activities, methods, and conditions for the interaction of pupils and teachers. Such programs are not simply statements of content to be learned or compendiums of exercises, such as 2 + 2 = 4. Perhaps an example or two will help illustrate this point.

Consider the *National Schools Project* program developed by Frank Williams (Williams, 1968a, 1970; Williams & Eberle, 1968). This program is based on a model which emphasizes eight categories of affective/cognitive processes. As is the case with the AAAS science curriculum, the processes of the *National Schools Project* are skills which are known empirically to have wide transfer to many areas of human functioning. They include skills of cognitive and affective fluency, flexibility, curiosity, imagination, preference for complexity, and tolerance of ambiguity. These processes or skills were selected for emphasis on the basis of research and empirical findings of Guilford, Torrance, Bloom, and others. The model also lists 18 teaching strategies which can be used to promote the specified skills while dealing with any subject matter area of the common elementary school curriculum, e.g., social studies, reading, mathematics, spelling, etc. The program is, in reality, a training system for teachers. It is designed to enable them to modify their usual instructional practice, select materials, and design classroom learning situations around the normal curriculum content toward the promotion of the eight categories of skills. The promotion of these skills is always attended to and consistently given primary emphasis. This approach holds much promise because it does not depend upon a particular set of materials which must be present. Rather, it depends upon the ability of a trained teacher to convert conventional classroom learning directed toward content mastery to a learning situation where facilitation of skills is the primary concern of *both the pupils and the teacher.*

Research has shown that another program for the development of skills can be used in much the same way. This is the *Productive Thinking Program.* It has also been used to focus and extend the attention of both pupils and teachers upon the importance and utility of particular problem-solving and analytic-thinking skills in the classroom learning situation (Covington, 1970; Crutchfield, 1969; Olton, Wardrop, Covington *et al.,* 1967). There is reason to believe that many of the other existing instructional materials and practices identified by ERIE could be used in a similar manner.

The *Materials and Activities for Teachers and Children* developed by The Children's Museum in Boston is another example of an instructional system which could very easily be used for broadening pupil and teacher experience with respect to changing the learning environment of the classroom toward the purposeful, mutual, consistent, and cooperative development of skills by pupils and teachers.

It is extremely limiting and inappropriate for educational change agencies or educators to think of such programs as simply sets of materials or "things" to be taught. They are a means for teacher and pupil education toward the goal of process educational practice.

The *Man: A Course of Study* (MACOS) program developed under the direction of Jerome Bruner and Peter Dow provides yet another example of an existing program which is an instructional system and not simply a set of materials. One expectation of the developers of this program was that it would change the focus of the traditional classroom upon mastery of static knowledge. A primary purpose of the MACOS program is for the pupils and the teacher to make meaning, to build knowledge and generalizations from their own unique experience and from additional experience provided by a rich array of multimedia materials which present the content of the program. The content of the program has deliberately been selected because it is in the process of being formulated by scientists. It is not presented in a final or absolute way. Rather, through carefully selected and designed materials and activities, pupils and teachers become involved in the building of knowledge and generalizations about such topics as adaptation, innate and acquired behavior, learning, social organization, dominance patterns, aggression, and culture. They soon learn that knowledge about such things is very tentative and is in the process of being created by scholars and scientists. They learn that the basic resources for creating knowledge are one's own feelings and experiences coupled with skills, such as observation, data collection, inference, hypothesis formation, and testing.[3] Knowledge about the topics of the program is presented not as something which exists in a static form but as something which is in a continual state of flux. Knowledge is shown to be something which is in a continual, dynamic process of being created. It is shown to have utility for organizing and understanding past experience, as well as having power for the prediction of future events.

The *Man: A Course of Study* program is also directly concerned with the facilitation of affective and interpersonal skills. It has as specific objectives the reduction of ethnocentrism,

3. These skills are essentially the same ones selected for emphasis in the AAAS elementary science curriculum, the *Productive Thinking Program,* the *Science Curriculum Improvement Study,* and many other curricula identified by ERIE (Seferian & Cole, 1970).

an increased awareness, and sensitivity to value systems different from one's own, both within the immediate environment of the classroom and within the broader context of ethnic and cultural differences in the local and world communities.

Certainly the existence of instructional systems of the types which have been discussed above indicates that there is opportunity to begin the practice of process education *now.* These programs and others have been designed for the promotion of many of the skills which are essential to the characteristics of the "educated man." They have been designed for the deliberate promotion of such skills. They have grown out of the theoretical and empirical work of numerous behavioral scientists who have begun to apply their findings to change conventional educational practice to what it should become—process education. To the extent that these programs can be utilized as training situations for both pupils and teachers, to the extent that they can be implemented in school settings and properly carried out, process education can be practiced today. Even one program, such as the *National Schools Project*, or *Man: A Course of Study,* has tremendous potential for developing an awareness of and commitment to a different and more appropriate practice of education devoted to the development of skills. Have these programs been used to realize that potential? If not, can they be, and how?

Have Existing Instructional Programs Been Used to Promote Process Education?

Generally, they have not. Promoting the practice of process education is not simply a matter of helping schools "adopt" the many new programs which have potential for process education. Ultimately, the practice of process education does not reside in curriculum materials, instructional systems, or programs alone. It resides more in how these materials and systems are used in the interaction among pupils and teachers in classrooms. Let us examine the basis for this position.

Beginning with the Woods Hole Conference in 1959, a great emphasis began in American education on curriculum development and innovation for the development of skills (Bruner, 1960, 1970). Initially, most of the emphasis was upon the skills of analytic and scientific inquiry which are considered to be basic tools of the scientist. As Bruner (1970, p. 66) says, the objective was to help each man be his own scientist. Later, emphasis was also placed upon other areas more directly related to affective, interpersonal, and expressive skills. During the sixties, many millions of dollars were spent developing curricula and instructional programs devoted to the facilitation of such skills. Many outstanding scholars from the academic disciplines, education, and the behavioral sciences, as well as master teachers, were involved in this development work. As Bruner notes (1970, p. 66), that which resulted was:

> . . . curricula that represent an extraordinary achievement in academic quality and in the respect they show for the nature of human thought processes.

With numerous curricula of this type available, one might assume the practice of education for the development of learning, inquiry, analytic-thinking, and problem-solving skills would be well under way by now. To what end have these many excellent curricula designed for the practice of process education been used? What has been done with them? What changes have they wrought in educational practice? Have they realized their potential? The answers to these questions are unpleasant. The curricula innovations of the sixties have been used to poor ends. Not much has been done with them. They have wrought few lasting changes in educational practice. They have *not* realized their potential. As Lippitt (1964, p. 11) observes:

> Our research is now rich with examples of opportunities provided, but nothing gained; with new curricula developed, but lack of meaningful utilization; with new teaching practices invented, but nothing spread; with new richer school environments, but no improvement in the learning experience of the child.

More recently, following an extensive survey of current educational practice, John Goodlad (1969, p. 60) concludes that the innovations of the sixties have been "blunted on the classroom door." His account of the type of educational practice he observed as the norm is shocking and disturbing. Educational practice remains much as it has been for many years–largely irrelevant to personal and social needs of the pupils, dull and boring, highly teacher-centered and -directed, structured primarily around the content of authoritative textbooks, and remarkably unconcerned with meaningful learning. Postman and Weingartner (1969) and Silberman (1970) have made similar observations. To the uninitiated, the statements made by these men about current educational practice seem extreme. To one who has observed several hundred classroom episodes within the past four years, their observations seem entirely to the point.

First-hand experience at ERIE has also shown that the practice of process education is not insured by simply arranging for excellent curricula designed for the deliberate and purposeful promotion of skills to be adopted and used in schools (Cole, 1970a, pp. 90-92). One of the basic problems appears to be that the proper and effective use of such curricula requires pupils and teachers to *consistently* play different classroom roles than is customary. In classrooms of laboratory schools where a number of programs judged appropriate to the practice of process education have been installed, it has been observed that teachers generally do not exhibit behavior consistent with the role required for the effective utilization of these programs.

A later chapter will deal more fully with the roles of pupils and teachers in the practice of process education. However, for the present, to help illustrate appropriate classroom roles for pupils and teachers, consider again the *Man: A Course of Study* program. The successful use of the program requires a different role for both teachers and pupils than is usual. Pupils must become not only more independent and self-directing but have a greater part in determining the norms for the learning activity in the classroom. The pupil's observations, ideas, feelings, judgments, and experiences must become positive and influential contributors to the interaction which occurs in the classroom if the program is to meet its objectives. Consequently, the teacher must become much less directive than is usual. The teacher must not dominate the learning activity with his experience, his ideas, and his knowledge. He must recognize that the pupils have collectively more experience, which is always personally more relevant and frequently socially more relevant to them, and that they are capable of forming ideas and generalizations equally as valid as his. He is no longer an expert in all things. He is an expert only in some things. His pupils are experts in some other things. There are times when he should look to them for directive help and times when they should look to him. It is clear from lesson plans and the many other materials prepared for teachers using the *Man: A Course of Study* program that the developers intend for teachers and pupils to behave this way. The role described above is also appropriate to the proper use of numerous other programs identified and studied by ERIE. Furthermore, the role described is one which is consistent with the recommendations of Lippitt (1966, 1970, pp. 3-5), Rogers (1967, pp. 175-177), Goodlad (1969, p. 60), and Bruner (1970, pp. 68, 78-79) relative to implementing more effective educational practice.

In addition to demanding a new role for pupils and teachers in the learning activity of the classroom, there are other problems which have tended to prevent the widespread and effective utilization of the curriculum innovations of the sixties devoted to the facilitation of important skills. Some of these are: The programs usually cost far more than schools can or are willing to pay. They frequently contain a wide array and variety of materials which not only increase the cost of the program but lead to problems related to storage of the materials and their management on both a classroom- and district-wide basis. Such programs usually require much inservice teacher education. Yet, neither adequate time nor money is commonly available to teachers for participation in this necessary inservice training. There is also an insufficient cadre of personnel who can be marshalled to provide the inservice education and supportive assistance required during the implementation of such programs. Such personnel need to be both skilled in techniques for helping teachers and pupils assume the new roles required by such programs and highly familiar with the objectives, organization, and content of the programs themselves. In short, personnel are needed who can help teachers and pupils achieve more appropriate classroom learning roles through the use of programs designed specifically for operation under those roles.

These and possibly other problems have prevented the curriculum innovations of the sixties designed for the deliberate promotion of skills essential to characteristics of the "educated man" from realizing their potential. These existing programs represent a great but latent resource for the practice of process education. Let us now briefly consider how this resource can be used. A more detailed consideration will occur in a later chapter.

Can the Practice of Process Education Be Implemented?

The answer to the question posed in the sub-heading is "Yes." The idea of process education is not new. Much of the curriculum reform movement of the past decade has been devoted to the development of instructional programs designed for the facilitation of skills for effective and productive living. Therefore, if one is to implement process education into current educational practice, it would seem most appropriate to begin with these instructional programs and with what has been learned about the practice of process education through their use. Even though that use has been limited, it provides needed experience and information which is not otherwise available.

The previous section documents the failure of such instructional programs to generally effect needed change in educational practice. This does not mean that the programs developed are impotent or inappropriate. It means, rather, that something else is needed to achieve their general, proper, and effective utilization. Implementation of the practice of process education may be considered to be primarily a matter of developing intervention procedures and tactics to insure that the many exemplary process-oriented curricula and instructional programs which have been developed can be effectively utilized both as instructional programs in their own right and as catalysts to change common educational practice in the classroom beyond their old boundaries. What has been missing is not instructional programs appropriate for process education but the techniques, procedures, and means for their proper implementation and impact.

It is beyond the scope of this chapter to discuss in detail the *how* of implementing the practice of process education—a subject to be treated in a later chapter.[4]

4. A review of products resulting from program activity shows ERIE has been concerned with the *how* of implementation. It has developed many operational implementation procedures over the past three years. See Cole, Andreas, and Archer (1969); Herlihy, Andreas, and Archer (1969); Andreas (1970); Andrulis (1970); Cole (1970a, 1970b); Cole and Seferian (1970); Mahan (1970a, 1970b); Ritz, Harty, Brown, and C. Wallace (1970); Seferian and Cole (1970); R. Wallace and Shavelson (1970).

Conclusion

Process education recognizes that the first and foremost objective of curriculum and instruction should be those skills which the learner needs if he is to acquire, organize, generate, and utilize in a satisfying and productive manner the wealth of information and knowledge available to him. These include perceptual, motor, affective, cognitive, and social interactive skills. The primary task of implementing process education is to bring schools and the educational community to the point where the learner is actively and purposely assisted in acquiring these skills.

Knowledge about which skills are central and important to effective and satisfying human functioning is at hand. Furthermore, the means to facilitate the development of a wide array of these skills exist in the form of many excellent instructional programs developed during the curricular reform movement of the sixties. In many cases, both knowledge about the skills to be promoted and the means of promoting them are based upon the study of human behavior. These instructional programs represent a largely untapped resource. They can be used not only as programs to be taught in and of themselves but as concrete experiences for pupils, teachers and other educators in a more appropriate practice of education. They can become the focal points for activity designed to implement the general practice of process education.

The problem of implementing the practice of process education through the selective use of existing instructional programs is primarily one of developing intervention procedures and tactics to insure the widespread and effective utilization of such programs both in their own right and as catalysts to change educational practice generally.

The nature, meaning, merit, and goals of process education are sufficiently clear and well-defined that the job of transforming current educational practice toward those goals is eminently possible. It would indeed be foolish and wasteful to ignore those goals and means already formulated by numerous curriculum developers who have developed and tested instructional programs well suited to the practice of process education. It is essential that the further delineation of process education, its goals, and its operational means be forged in the context of the experience gained from the implementation and study of numerous existing process-oriented programs and practices in actual school settings. If the existence of these programs is ignored, much of the accomplishment in curriculum design in the sixties will be wasted. The foundation for the practice of process education has been laid. It is time to build upon that foundation.

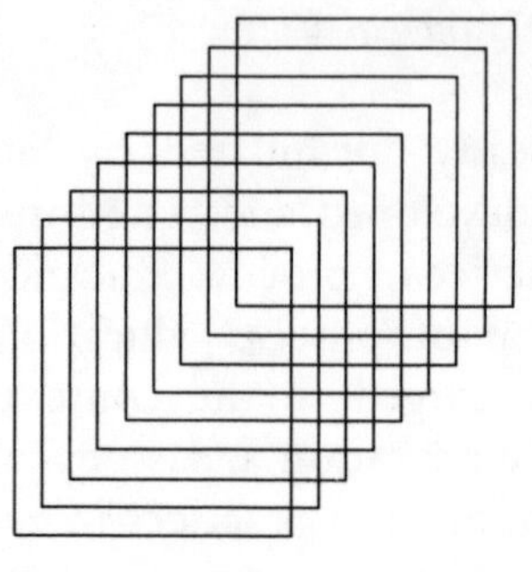

CHAPTER 2

PROCESS EDUCATION: A CONCEPTUAL VIEW

Process education recognizes that the first and foremost objective of curriculum and instruction should be the facilitation of those *skills* which are needed by the learner if he is to acquire, organize, generate, and utilize information and knowledge in a satisfying and productive manner. These include the individual's perceptual, motor, affective, cognitive, and social interactive skills. First priority should be given to the development of those skills which are known from experience to be central and important to human functioning in the reality of the present decade. As noted in Chapter 1, many skills of this type have been identified, and means have been developed for their facilitation through education.

What Are Skills?

Skills may be considered to be behavioral control systems which incorporate, select, and direct different response patterns and attitudinal and behavioral tendencies and capabilities in a series of actions toward some goal. In skilled behavior, responses are not simply "acquired," but are selected and constructed by the individual toward the attainment of some goal within a plan of action for attaining that goal. The skill is the plan, the program for action, the means by which behavior (action) is organized and directed toward goal attainment. Different goals may be obtained by the same skill. Different behaviors (actions) may be incorporated into attaining a particular goal on different occasions or under different conditions. Perhaps an example will help illustrate these points.

Consider a skill frequently called "inferring" which is emphasized by a number of existing instructional programs. Suppose a child is given the specific task of inferring the shape of a small object inside a completely closed cigar box. He is not to open the box. There is no way to see or probe into the box. With these restrictions operating, his skill at inferring may lead him to shake the box to obtain auditory and kinesthetic information about the size, shape, and weight of the object. He may tip the box carefully back and forth, first in the transverse, and later in the lateral plane, while being attentive to tactile and auditory stimuli which his previous experience would allow him to categorize as resulting from a sliding or a rolling object. If the object slides in one plane and rolls in the other, he might reasonably infer it has a cylindrical shape. If it rolls in both planes, he might infer its shape to be spherical.

Let us consider a variation of this problem. Suppose the object is now placed within a clear plastic box which has been completely lined with one thickness of ordinary white paper. The box is suspended one foot above a table on a support. Again the box is completely closed and may not be opened or probed. In addition, in this problem, the box may not be touched or moved in any way. In this new situation, the child must use a different series of behaviors to make the inference. He must draw on other response patterns and capabilities resulting from other experiences. If he has had experience with the translucent properties of paper, light sources, and shadows, he may obtain a flashlight and shine it on first one side of the box and then on the others, each time observing the projected shadow on the opposite surface of the box. From the shape of the shadows in the various planes, he may reasonably infer the shape of the object.

Let us consider still a third situation. Suppose this same child is at a party at the home of a friend. He is last to arrive and is curious about who arrived first. It is winter time. As his host hangs his coat in the closet, he observes many empty hangers to the left. His host takes his coat, places it on a hanger, and slides it all the way to the right until it is touching the previous coat. There are seven other children at the party, and seven other coats in the closet. The child may assume that, if his host's "coat hanging" behavior was consistent, the person whose coat is farthest to the right was the first to arrive. He has again made a reasonable inference, this time in an entirely different context and drawing upon a different set of behaviors and experiences. If this child continued to make logical inferences in many other varied situations, we could reasonably assume he was skilled in the activity of inferring.

Skills by their very nature are *not* task- or problem-specific. They are generalizable ways of dealing with a multiplicity of different situations and events. As Bruner (1970, p. 67) says:

> In broad outline, skilled action requires recognizing the features of a task, its goals, and means appropriate to its attainment; a means of converting this information into appropriate action; and a means of getting feedback that compares the objective sought with the present state attained.

Skills, Processes, and Process Education

Skills are frequently referred to as "processes" by the

behavioral scientists who have studied the functioning of adaptive human behavior and by developers who seek to promote such behavior. As noted in Chapter 1, the "processes" of the *Productive Thinking Program,* the AAAS *Science—A Process Approach* program, the *Minnesota Mathematics and Science Teaching* program, the *National Schools Project,* and many other existing curricula are really skills or categories of skills. It is from this reference to skills as "processes" that process education gets its name.

The use of the term "processes" for skills is quite appropriate in terms of the denotative meaning of the word "process." According to the *American College Dictionary* (1964), "process" is "a systematic series of actions directed to some end." *Webster's Dictionary* (1967) defines "process" as a "series of actions or operations definitely conducing to an end . . . " In the present context, "process" is a systematic series of actions (behaviors) directed toward goal achievement by the individual. The systematic series of actions (behaviors) employed are skills. Skills are also called processes. Education directed toward the purposeful and deliberate promotion and facilitation of such skills or processes is process education.

The Empirical Basis for Process Education

Behavioral scientists have studied human learning, adaptive behavior, and problem-solving, and have conceptualized categories of skills or processes to explain these behaviors. The study of skilled behavior and the delineation of skill categories or processes has been and remains a concern for many scholars, as evidenced by their research and writing. Let us consider a few of the scholars and the terms they use to describe the skills they have studied. Gagné has referred to them as "learned capabilities" (1968a, p. 181), "intellectual skills" (1968b, p. 8), statements of "what the individual can do" (1968b, p. 8), "intellectual operations" (1968b, p. 10), and "processes" and "intellectual activities" (1965b, p. 4). Newell, Shaw, and Simon (1958) call them "processes" and equate them to Bruner's strategies (Bruner, Goodnow & Austin, 1956; Bruner, Olver, Greenfield *et al.,* 1966). Bruner also calls them "skills" and "intellectual habits" (1968, pp. 34, 95, 99; 1970, pp. 67-68). Crutchfield (1969) calls them "skills." Andreas refers to them as "psychological processes" (1968). Skinner (1968) calls them "self-management behaviors." Williams (1968a, 1969, 1970; Williams & Eberle, 1968) has called them "processes." They are also the "process competencies" which underlie Heathers' (1965) "process goals." They are Worthen's "processes in education" (1963). They are the "affective and social interactive processes and skills" essential for learning and problem-solving that are discussed so frequently by Rogers (1961, 1962), Combs (1962), Kelley (1962), Maslow (1962), Bettelheim (1969), Brandwein (1969), Fox, Lippitt, and Girault (1969), Lippitt, Fox, and Schaible (1969), Meade (1969), Rubin (1969b, 1969c, 1969d), and Lippitt (1970). They can be considered the taxonomic categories of cognitive functioning of Bloom, Englehart, Furst, Hill, and Krathwohl (1956) or the categories of affective functioning of Krathwohl, Bloom, and Masia (1964). They may also be considered the "operations" of Guilford (1967), the "logical operations" of Piaget (Inhelder & Piaget, 1958; Flavell, 1966), and the "abilities in thinking" of Russell (1956). These and many other researchers have studied, enumerated, and discussed skills and processes in relation to education for effective living.

As noted previously, many of these scholars named above have begun to operationalize process education. They have been directly involved in the development of instructional materials and programs for pupils and teachers designed to promote the behaviors they have empirically identified as having utility for transfer of training and problem-solving. Many of these programs and materials have been and are currently being evaluated in actual school settings. This has resulted in additional, more direct evidence for the value of educational practice devoted to the promotion of such skills (AAAS Commission on Science Education, 1968a; Kresse, 1968; Hanley, Whitla, Moo, & Walter, 1970a; 1970b).

Justifications for Process Education

The justifications for educational practices devoted to the deliberate and purposeful promotion of skills stem from the realities of a satisfying and productive life in the present world. The justifications have been stated by many. Earlier and somewhat less comprehensive listings of conditions which justify the practice of process education may be found in statements by Bloom, Engelhart, Furst *et al.* (1956, pp. 39-43) and Cole (1969, pp. 245-247). The justifications which follow were prepared after a study of many documents and after interaction with a number of scholars concerned with process education.

1. *The world of the eighth decade in the 20th century is changing so fast that it is impossible to predict what knowledge and information individuals will need in just a few years.* While some individuals attempt to minimize this problem by noting that change has always been present, it must be realized that the *rate* of change is fantastically greater than ever before. This reality is made alarmingly clear by the observations of Bennis (1966, 1969, 1970), Bennis and Slater (1968), E.J. Meade (1969, pp. 35-38), and Postman and Weingartner (1969, p. 10). It is vital that education be concerned with helping individuals to acquire the generalizable and adaptive skills which have the power to serve them well in new situations.

2. *The store of knowledge is so vast that it is impossible to instruct the student in anything but a small portion of what is*

known. The only feasible approach is to help the student acquire some of the more relevant and central information and those skills which will enable him to adapt and expand this limited knowledge acquired through his formal education.

3. *The acquisition of skills insures an individual who can successfully solve problems, and this leads to a healthy and productive personality.* This, in turn, tends to foster a healthy and productive society. Failure to achieve skills needed for coping with life leads to mental and physical illness which results in maladaptive and destructive behavior.

4. *Skills are more widely applicable than knowledge and information.* If we wish that the student learn to exhibit broad and useful transfer to all realms of his experience, then by definition, we must be concerned with the promotion of generalizable behavior patterns or skills.

5. *Skills are more permanent than other types of learning.* It has repeatedly been demonstrated that information which is learned is subject to rapid extinction but that skills are frequently life-long in nature.

6. *Information is easily obtained when needed, but skills cannot be "looked up."* Information can be and usually is physically recorded somewhere. This means that information can be "looked up" or retrieved and, hence, be easily acquired when it is needed. However, generalizable behavior patterns or skills are not so easily acquired. Since they are dynamic processes, they cannot be physically stored and later retrieved for use. It should be noted that, with the advent of the computer program, some types of logical "skills" can be stored and retrieved at will. However, it seems unlikely that computer programs can be expected to replace man's skills. Rather, the computer, like other tools man has developed, has awesome possibilities for extending human skills.

7. *An emphasis on skills in educational practice is needed to prevent academic isolationism and social irrelevancy.* There is a

tendency for human knowledge to become isolated into conceptually distinct disciplines. This tends to focus educational activity around the static conceptual products of the minds of men from other times. It is this compartmentalization which has caused the content of curriculum and instruction in our schools to be largely irrelevant to the world of the here and now. Educational practice devoted primarily to promoting the understanding of the content and structure of the disciplines frequently leads to cultural lag and stagnation. This cannot be tolerated in our "temporary society." This is not to say that there is not much knowledge which is useful. Great stores of knowledge exist and must be drawn upon in the solution of new problems. However, such knowledge alone is not sufficient for problem-solving activity. Neither is it the private possession of any single discipline. As both Roberts (1966, p. 354) and Tanner (1966, p. 363) have noted, educational practice must be interdisciplinary not only with respect to knowledge and content common to the disciplines but also with respect to the *behaviors* common to the pursuit of knowledge in *any* discipline. These are the generalizable and adaptive behavior patterns or skills previously discussed and with which process education is concerned.

8. *Skills are required for learning to occur through formal education.* The first major problems the child must cope with outside his immediate home environment are primarily encountered in his school experience. When the child begins school, a tremendous increase occurs in the number of learning and problem-solving tasks set for him. These problems span virtually the entire spectrum of human functioning, including the interpersonal, cognitive, perceptual, motor, emotional, moral, and spiritual. The child's success for further learning and his capacity to develop into an effective problem-solver who can cope with this diversity of problems are largely determined by his repertoire of skills already established by preschool and early-school experience. Educational practice cannot afford to underestimate the impor-

tance of purposeful and deliberate attention to the facilitation and development of skills. This is a major justification for process education in the pre-primary and early-school years.

9. *Skills are required for man's peaceful coexistence with others of his species.* The survival of the human species is dependent upon man's ability to understand and tolerate the many and diverse value systems which lead to different assumptions, beliefs, behaviors, and cultural practices. In former times, there were fewer people in the world and less opportunity for them to be in contact with one another. During the last 50 years, the world has been torn by nearly continuous warfare waged by men against men frequently because of differences in their value systems and ideologies. The advanced technology of this decade with its rapid transportation and instantaneous communication helps to bring diverse beliefs and values into more frequent direct conflict. If individuals are not taught to accept and analytically consider the existence of values and practices which conflict with their own, we can almost certainly expect more violence and warfare, both internally as a nation and internationally as a species. In speaking about this problem, E.J. Meade (1969, p. 36) notes that contemporary society is a very primitive problem-solver. He goes on to express the belief that this need not be the case. To the extent that humans can learn to cope with the moral and value problems which divide the modern world, the technological problems can be solved. All our pressing social problems which may appear to be of a technological origin have deep underlying moral issues which must be resolved. Educational practice must be concerned with promoting those skills which can help us to cope with moral and value issues. To the extent that process education is concerned with the promotion of such skills, it is certainly justified.

On the basis of these or similar realities of the present century, many scholars have argued the need for educational practice to be directly committed to the development of skills

(Rogers, 1961, 1967; Worthen, 1963; Heathers, 1965; Torrance, 1965; Bruner & Dow, 1967; Covington, Crutchfield, & Davies, 1967; Cronbach, 1967, p. 28; Andreas, 1968; Bower, 1968; Bruner, 1968, pp. 34, 35, 38, 95, 99; Michaelis, 1968, 1970; Segal, 1968; Clark, 1969).

Basic Assumptions for Process Education

The assumptions which follow concern the nature and activity of *knowledge, learning,* and the *learner.* The last assumption concerns the role of *formal education* in these activities. The assumptions stated are intimately and logically related to one another. Collectively, they represent a position on the nature and purpose of education. They have been derived following much study of recent attempts by scholars and educators to formulate a philosophy and practice of process education.

1. *Knowledge is an organized but tentative and arbitrary collection of changing and expanding information which each individual adapts and uses to make meaning from his unique experience.* The content of both the academic disciplines and common-sense experience is knowledge. In both cases, this knowledge is invented. It represents not "truth" but pragmatically useful means for explaining and sometimes predicting perceived reality. Some knowledge is more widely applicable, useful, and stable than other knowledge. Certainly educational practice should strive to transmit such useful knowledge from one generation to the next. However, such knowledge *should not be transmitted as a static body of "truths"*! Let us consider an example.

The very useful and highly generalizable concept that "all matter is particulate" should be taught. However, it is almost universally taught as an absolute truth or law. This is most inappropriate. It is not absolute. It is only one of several alternative conceptualizations which is useful in explaining the interaction of matter and energy in many cases. In other cases, it fails entirely as an adequate explanation or is irrelevant.[5]

Educational practice which causes the individual to accept knowledge made by other minds from other times as absolute and inviolate is most inappropriate. Rather, knowledge should be presented as something which is tentative and arbitrary and which is best utilized by bending, changing, or expanding it to one's own needs and purposes. Knowledge arises from the activity of meaning making and has as its primary utility further meaning making.

It appears that the best way to insure a population of knowledgeable individuals is not by direct instruction in knowledge but by education for skills related to curiosity, problem-seeking and -solving, creative production and expression, and self-initiated learning. Studies of creative individuals who are also capable problem-solvers have shown they have acquired huge stores of knowledge. Such individuals are avid seekers of knowl-

5. The field of classical thermodynamics is a good example of a case where this conceptualization is irrelevant. All the basic theory was derived without the assumption that matter existed as particles. Another example is modern chemical bonding theory, which finds it more convenient to conceptualize matter as consisting of probability distributions of energy fields rather than as particles. Physical scientists have learned it is necessary to hold alternate conceptualizations of matter and energy. Sometimes it is more useful to consider both matter and energy as discrete particles and, at other times, as continuous energy distributions. Even the notion of a dichotomy of matter and energy is not a truth but a convenient and sometimes useful conceptualization (Holton & Roller, 1958; Kemeny, 1959; Blackburn, 1966; Heisenberg, 1966). As Kemeny points out, laymen often impart an absolute and prescriptive quality to scientific laws. They feel that scientific laws dictate reality and cannot be defied. This is really very humorous if one realizes that a scientific law is simply a concise statement of human experience with the behavior of matter and energy. Scientific laws have predictive utility in certain situations but are in *no way prescriptive, absolute, or true.* There are no truths. There are only arbitrary but useful organizations of human experience which occur at different times and places and under different conditions.

edge, always adding to their store (Torrance, 1965; Williams, 1968b). Therefore, if educational practice becomes more concerned with promoting the skills basic to learning and building knowledge (meaning making), children can be expected to demand, seek, and create more and more information and knowledge as they continue to engage in the thrill and adventure of meaning making.

2. *Learning is a natural and creative activity by which each person organizes and makes meaning (knowledge) from his experience toward fulfillment of his needs.* The view that learning involves the creative organization of the culture's knowledge with the individual's experiences to produce a new and unique perception of the culture by the learner is common to many behavioral scientists (Parnes, 1967, pp. 2, 3, 5; Anderson, 1968; Crutchfield, 1969, pp. 55-57; MacKinnon, 1969; Woodruff, 1969). Even a "fact" in becoming learned becomes a part of a new structure which is re-created or at least reorganized by the learner (Crutchfield, 1969, p. 55). The equilibration theory of Piaget also corresponds with this viewpoint (Flavell, 1966; Piaget, 1967). Piaget assumes that a child conceptualizes the world through the assimilation of information derived from experience into "his" previously existing logical schema. However, the logical schema, which is never adequate for the assimilation of the new experiences the child continually encounters, is forced to accommodate itself to include this new information. Thus, the child's perception of the world at any given instant consists of a series of "creative products" which have resulted from the interaction of the existing schemata of the child with the stimuli of the environment. Since both the child's schemata and experiences are unique, the "creative products" of each child are also unique. In a discussion of learning by discovery, it has been noted that the "creative products" of the learner may consist of either the minor discoveries which can be assimilated within the learner's existing schemata or major discoveries which require that he restructure his

thinking in a much more thorough manner (Shulman & Keislar, 1966, pp. 29-30).

There is also evidence to indicate that there exists a primary and universal need to make meaning. Berlyne's work (1960, 1963, 1965, 1966) suggests the existence of a strong need to explore, to seek the novel, complex, and unusual for the intrinsic satisfaction of organizing that experience. Humans seem to have a natural propensity to engage in exploratory behavior, to seek new experience, and to make meaning from that experience.

Learning can be considered a creative activity any time that anything is learned. Learning is an act of "meaning making" (Postman & Weingartner, 1969). This applies to the learning of "Who am I?" and "What is my worth and purpose?" of which Rogers (1961, 1962), Combs (1962), Kelley (1962), MacKinnon (1969), Maslow (1962), and many others have spoken. It also applies to the learning of tying one's shoes, the multiplication tables, Archimedes' principle, and the Newtonian synthesis. Furthermore, when the child learns a method of tying his shoes, Archimedes' principle, or the Newtonian synthesis, they become *his* method, *his* principle, and *his* synthesis. All of these meanings which he has made have been derived in a large part from his cultural milieu, but they are internalized as his own personal organizations of personal experience. Ultimately, they are *his* meanings.

3. *Needs are the basis of the affective commitment which makes possible both the task of meaning making (learning, building knowledge) and the retention of the meaning made (knowledge).* The solving of any problem requires the learner to have an emotional commitment to the solution of the problem. Likewise, learning cannot occur without the affective involvement of the learner in what is to be learned. The question of whether or not something to be learned is relevant to the child is really a question of whether or not the child feels *a need* to learn the "something." If the "something" is personally relevant for him, a

need exists and insures his emotional commitment to the task which makes possible both the learning activity and the retention of what is learned. Affective commitment arising from needs is necessary for what Rogers has called "significant learning" (1961, 1967). Significant learning occurs when goals and standards for the learning activity are largely intrinsic rather than predominantly extrinsic. Intrinsic goals are possible when what is to be learned has personal relevance to the learner. Personal relevance is determined by the needs of the individual learner. This assumption is made by Snygg and Combs (1949, pp. 208-212), Rogers (1961, 1962, 1967), Combs (1962), Kelley (1962), Maslow (1962), and Williams (1969) based upon their research and experience. In addition, many studies have shown that the process of arousal which precedes learning activity, problem-seeking, and problem-solving requires the emotional or affective commitment of the learner (Berlyne, 1960, 1965; Haber, 1967; Hunt, 1967).

It is the failure of conventional educational practice to establish personal relevance for what is to be learned which leads to the "ho-hum," boring classroom which lulls so many pupils and teachers into a state of near sleep.

Goodlad (1969) reports from his extensive observations that such "ho-hum" classrooms are more typical than atypical. Beatty (1969) also comments extensively on this problem in "Emotion: The Missing Link in Education." Andreas (1968) notes the problem by referring to pupils as the "bored of education." Certainly, significant learning cannot occur in classrooms where such a negligible emotional commitment to the learning activity exists. If educational practice is to be personally relevant, *it must relate to and build upon the needs of the pupil.*

As noted in Assumption Two above, a primary need is the need to engage in the activity of meaning making. This need to seek and organize experience insures that learning will always occur with or without formal provision for education.

4. *The process by which individuals make meaning (learn,*

build knowledge) from their experience is equally as important and more stable and lasting than either that experience or the meaning made (knowledge). Process is commonly defined as a systematic series of actions directed toward some end. In this case, it is an organized sequence of behaviors (actions) directed toward the end of rendering one's experience comprehensible, which is needed to solve one's problems and meet one's needs. This dynamic and creative activity of organizing and making meaning from experience results in numerous "products."

The "knowledge," "content," and "structure" of the "disciplines" are all products of creative human activity. These products include such things as works of art, organizational schemas, concepts, and principles. Anderson (1968) points out that the products of creative human activity exist only in the past. Once a creative mind has produced, recorded, and communicated a product, it becomes a static and historical part of the cultural system. Given this assumption, all knowledge and the structure of the disciplines must be viewed as static products which have been created in an arbitrary fashion by individuals for use as temporary and partial solutions to problems encountered. As useful means for dealing with present needs and realities, such products usually become quickly outdated. Therefore, there is no utilitarian structure for reality other than the creative organizations of experience made by the learner. Coping with the world requires that the individual be able to create such structure (Bruner, 1960, 1969) or "viable meanings" (Postman & Weingartner, 1969). He must make his own meaning. This does not mean that the past products of creative human activity, which include the acquired information, knowledge, generalizations, feelings, and attitudes of a culture, are not useful to the learner. They are necessary but are not sufficient for learning and problem solution. Thus, as Anderson (1968, p. 37) says, "The body of science is the residue of the repeatable of man's creative moments." However, the residue is static and historical. It becomes dynamic and contemporary only when it is assimilated, accommodated, and applied to learning and problem-solving by the individual in relation to meeting his needs. The assimilation, accommodation, and application of such previously existing creative products is in itself a creative activity which results in "new" creative products which have a new utility as partial and temporary solutions to contemporary problems. To learn is always to create meaning from previous experience and knowledge. To solve a problem is always to create a solution.

Unlike the static, created products of other minds from other times which usually comprise the content of the curriculum, the dynamic and creative process of meaning making is quite similar among different people, while the products it produces are extremely diverse in nature. This process is, in reality, what the person must do to produce the products which may be concepts, generalizations, feelings, hypotheses, or anything else that organizes information resulting from experience. The basis for this process of meaning making is those skills which have been discussed previously. Unlike the meanings they make (products), skills are frequently retained life-long and have an indefinite utility.

5. *Skills are the basis for the process of meaning making and all adaptive, productive, and satisfying behaviors.* Skills have been extensively discussed both in Chapter 1 and the present chapter. In summary, skills essential to the characteristics of the "educated man" have been noted. The empirical evidence for the importance of such skills in adaptive and productive behavior has been considered. The existence of instructional programs and techniques designed to facilitate the development of skills has been mentioned. Evidence for the effectiveness of such programs has been cited. Additional means for promoting educational practice for the facilitation of skills have been suggested. Skills have been defined and justifications for educational practice concerned with facilitation of skills have been stated.

Skills are in fact *processes,* and they collectively comprise the *process* of meaning making. As noted earlier, they are behavioral control systems which incorporate, select, and direct organized series of behaviors toward goals. They are the means by which responses and purposeful actions toward the goal of meaning making are constructed by the individual. It is assumed that skills are the generalizable action programs which are required for productive and adaptive behavior in an environment in a state of constant change. Individuals live by their skills which enable them to deal effectively with experience and information through the process of meaning making.

6. *Freedom to creatively apply skills to the process of organizing and making meaning (learning, building knowledge) from experience results in seeking, finding, and solving problems.* Earlier assumptions state that the individual has a need to seek experience and to explore for the purpose of organizing that experience in order to make meaning. Acceptance of these earlier assumptions requires that the individual be allowed much freedom. Significant learning occurs when the individual is provided with a rich and varied environment and is allowed the freedom and autonomy to make his own meanings from that experience.

Problem-seeking and -solving is dependent upon the freedom to engage in the creative activity of meaning making. To solve a problem is to create a solution. This is true even if the solution involves only the selection of a previous solution which is judged to be reasonably appropriate to a new situation following some modification. If the choice of a solution requires no selection, judgment, or modification, there is no problem. Problem-solving as a form of learning involves the creative activity of meaning making. It enables the individual to cope with, rather than defend against, the problems he must and does encounter (Bruner, 1968, pp. 129-148). Coping behavior is required for a healthy and productive individual and society.

The acceptance of the learner's need to explore and create his own meaning, as well as the observation that he must be allowed much freedom to do so, is an assumption made by many who have studied human behavior and have become involved in education (Dewey, 1944, pp. 69-76; Rogers, 1961, 1962, 1967; Combs, 1962; Kelley, 1962; Maslow, 1962; Montessori, 1965; Torrance, 1965; Taba, 1967; Anderson, 1968; Bettelheim, 1969; Crutchfield, 1969; and MacKinnon, 1969). The assumption is derived in large measure from the research of these individuals and their colleagues. Still other research indicates that highly directive teacher influence may restrict learning and produce less desirable attitudes in children toward learning (Flanders, 1965; Amidon & Flanders, 1967; Amidon & Hough, 1967). Other evidence which tends to support the assumption that learning may be made more effective by increasing the autonomy of the learner may be found in the research concerning "learning by discovery" (Gagné, 1966; Shulman & Keislar, 1966; Wittrock, 1966).

Allowing the learner a great deal of freedom to create his own meanings—build his own knowledge—insures that he will commit errors. He will sometimes build unsound generalizations, reach "wrong" conclusions, and fail to organize his thinking in accepted ways. However, as Bruner has pointed out, such errors in learning are not only to be expected, they are to be valued, for they are frequently most instructive in the business of learning how to make meaning (Bruner, Goodnow, & Austin, 1956; Bruner, 1960). Such a viewpoint embodied in educational practice produces individuals skilled and highly motivated in the great adventure of problem-seeking and -solving which lies at the heart of all discipline inquiry or meaning making.

7. *Schools can provide the setting for individuals to develop and use those skills needed to freely build and make use of knowledge.* Schools can and should be utilized to purposely and actively facilitate the development of skills essential to the characteristics of the "educated man." This is an assumption held in the face of evidence that schools do not typically function very

effectively in this role (Goodlad, 1969; Postman & Weingartner, 1969; Silberman, 1970). However, as pointed out in Chapter 1, it is an assumption held by many contemporary educators and researchers as evidenced by their attempts to develop curricula and instructional practices for the promotion of such skills within the school setting. As was also pointed out in Chapter 1, the involvement of these individuals in changing educational practice toward the development of important skills provides information on both the means and effectiveness of such practice. This information, coupled with the existing procedures for further implementing the practice of process education, makes this a reasonable assumption.

Positions, Relationships, Definitions, and Rationales Basic to Process Education

The next section of this chapter consists of a series of statements, definitions, and illustrations which collectively present a value position concerning the nature of learning and human activity. The paradigm presented is based upon the preceding assumptions and is consistent with the justifications which have been stated for process education. The statements *collectively* describe this value position. The definitions *collectively* comprise a glossary of key terms used throughout this and other chapters. The illustrations provide a small sample of the infinity of observations that could be made relative to the behavior under consideration.

The paradigm is a logical system. It was developed over a period of several weeks by six ERIE staff members. It is intended to provide the context for fundamental conceptualizations for activity in curriculum development, teacher education, and the development and study of other aspects of educational practice designed for process education.

Following the paradigm is a section which deals with educational intervention for the development of skills. In this section, statements which represent logical and studied considerations are made. The statements made deal with the possibility, need, resources, and procedures for implementing the practice of process education. A rationale supporting each statement is provided.

The paradigm and the intervention section should be studied in the order they appear. Jointly, they tie together many of the ideas, observations, and statements made in the previous sections of Chapters 1 and 2.

A Paradigm for Process Education

Statement	Definition	Illustration
Needs are the basis for purposeful and goal-directed behavior.	*Need* = A condition which motivates behavior toward some goal. This includes both basic physiological needs and acquired needs (wants).	a. Need to explore, to structure experience. b. Need for parental approval. c. Need for acceptance by peers.
	Goal = A condition or end to be achieved toward the fulfillment of a need.	a. "Where does this trail go?" b. "Get a high grade on my social studies test." c. "What are the norms for acceptance by my peers?"
	Behavior = An action, a series of actions. The action has emotional, cognitive, and psychomotor aspects. The action can be observed directly only in part. It can be inferred from its results or the changes it brings about in the environment or the individual.	a. Walking along a trail, wondering and hypothesizing where it leads. b. Reciting the names of countries and their major cities, exports, and industry. Developing associations between these facts which will aid recall. c. Asking questions to find out how your friends feel about an issue

A Paradigm (cont.)

Statement	*Definition*	*Illustration*
What an individual does to meet needs is in essence *process.*	*Process* = A systematic series of actions directed toward some end, in this case, those collections or series of actions (behaviors) continually employed to direct behavior toward the fulfillment of needs.	Organizing behavior, perception, and feeling in an exploratory manner for purposes of seeking the goal, "Where does this trail lead?"
		Organizing behavior such that factual relationships may be learned and recalled for a test.
		Organizing behavior to be attentive to cues from others in order to determine how they feel.
Process, the organization of behavior toward goals, occurs through the use of *skills.*	*Skills* = Behavior control systems which integrate differential response patterns into goal-directed behavior. Skills are also referred to as processes.	Skills include such things as inferring, algebraic factoring, hypothesizing, reading comprehension, running and walking, speaking, social perception of when to laugh and when to be serious, proving that 9 x 7 = 63 or 2 + 2 = 4 without resorting to the authority of tables, inductive and deductive reasoning, seriation, or ordering of any series on the basis of the relative magnitude of some property such as size, weight, color intensity, etc. Sometimes skills are organized into broader conceptual categories such as perceptual, cognitive, psychomotor, affective, and social interactive.

A Paradigm (cont.)

Statement	*Definition*	*Illustration*
Skills articulate *differential response patterns* into sequences of efficient and purposeful goal-directed behavior.	*Differential response patterns* = Intermediate units of behavior resulting from experience. These units comprise an individual's repertoire of actions from which larger goal-directed behavior patterns may be developed by the control systems called "skills."	The alphabetic sequence of letters or numeric sequence of numbers; position learning including up-down, left-right, back-front, and compass coordinates. Common and acceptable ways of greeting and responding to others such as, "Hello, how are you?" and "Fine, thank you." The multiplication tables; the rules for conduct in a library; the sequence of musical notes in a tune; the sequence of steps in balancing a chemical equation.
	Attitudinal and behavioral tendencies and capabilities = Predispositions to ways of feeling, perceiving, and responding which cause perception to be selective and set limits upon behavior. The tendencies and capabilities are both acquired and innate. These tendencies are referred to as primary skills by Rubin (1969c, p. 19).	An acquired behavioral capability is the visual discrimination of small changes in the shape, orientation, and size of printed symbols which makes reading possible. An innate behavioral capability is the physiological construction of the eye which makes such fine visual discrimination possible.

A Paradigm (cont.)

Statement	*Definition*	*Illustration*
		An acquired attitudinal tendency is the fear or anxiety aroused by persons of a particular race, spiders, fire, or any other stimuli which have been *learned* to be aversive. An innate attitudinal tendency is anxiety resulting from pain, loud noise, or loss of support.
		The reduction of prejudice or the development of any motivation is primarily a task of changing existing attitudinal tendencies and capabilities which limit behavior and learning. Teaching a non-swimming child frightened of water to swim requires changing his attitudinal tendency. His anxiety when in the water must be changed toward a feeling of pleasure and control. If this occurs, his behavioral capability can be changed, and he can become a swimmer. Teaching a child to be a good reader means a positive attitudinal tendency toward the reading activity must first be established.

A Paradigm (cont.)

Statement	*Definition*	*Illustration*
Although attitudinal and behavioral tendencies are both innate and acquired, response patterns and skills are predominantly learned.		
Skills direct behavior toward the activity of *meaning making.*	*Meaning making* = The act of applying one's skills to the organization of information, experience, and behavior; the use, adaptation, or creation of knowledge by the individual. Manifestations of meaning making include organizing experience, learning, and problem-solving.	Examples of the act of meaning making include exploring; experiencing; problem-seeking, -finding, and -solving; "contenting" and "knowledging" (building content and knowledge about experience); willing; expressing; imaging; ikonocizing; and creating.
	Knowledge = Organized bodies of information and conceptual relationships created by the culture and the individual through shared and individual experiences.	
	Problem-solving = Skilled behavior directed toward the attainment of goals established by needs.	

A Paradigm (cont.)

Statement	*Definition*	*Illustration*
	Learning = The act of meaning making or forming organized bodies of information. When an individual repeatedly structures his experience to make meaning, he is also learning a skill. He is structuring his experience about how he acts to learn; i.e., he learns about how he makes meaning. Response patterns and attitudinal and behavioral tendencies and capabilities are also learned from organization of perceptions, feelings, and experience.	
The need to make meaning is primary and universal for all men.		Most work as well as most play seems to be directed toward the end of creating order, structure, relationship or developing skilled behavior by which to better organize and control some aspect of one's environment.

A Paradigm (cont.)

Statement	*Definition*	*Illustration*
Since the need to make meaning is primary and universal, learning occurs with or without formal provision for education.	*Education* = "Educing" or bringing out of that which is potential or latent within the learner. Activity designed to begin with the experience and meanings already accrued to the learner for the purpose of stimulating him to actively extend, modify, and reorganize his experience, meanings, and skills.	
Formal provision for *process* education can facilitate the development of skills essential to a satisfying and productive life.	*Process education* = Formal intervention toward the facilitation and development of skills essential to dealing effectively with information and experience for the purpose of meaning making and obtaining goals.	

Educational Intervention for the Development of Skills Through Process Education

Statement	*Rationale*
Educational practice can be designed for the promotion of skills.	Educational intervention is possible because attitudinal and behavioral tendencies and capabilities, as well as response patterns and skills, are all influenced by experience. They may be facilitated or inhibited.
It is imperative to intervene with educational practice designed for the facilitation and development of skills.	Education for skills has frequently been ignored (see Chapter 1). Education for skills is justified in terms of what is known about significant learning and the realities of the present world (see Chapter 2). Calling attention to skills and the capability for skilled behavior results in individuals both more motivated and competent in the structuring of experience or meaning making (see Chapter 2). A formal educational setting can provide numerous opportunities to increase the normal range of experience encountered by the individual. It can, therefore, provide the setting where he can acquire, test, and modify a wide array of skills and response patterns essential to characteristics of the "educated man" (see Chapter 1).
Adequate knowledge and resources are available for educational practice designed for the purposeful facilitation of skills.	Many behavioral scientists have studied skilled behavior and its development (see Chapters 1 and 2). These scholars have developed a conceptual universe of skills which can be broadly categorized into perceptual, psychomotor, cognitive, affective, social interactive, and interpersonal skills. From this universe of skills (the process bag), different scholars, theorists, researchers, educators, and curriculum developers have sampled particular subsets of skills for emphasis. Many objectives, instructional materials, teaching strategies, and learning experiences have been designed by these individuals for the facilitation of subsets of these skills (see Chapter 1). Collectively, these educational practices deal with the promotion of a wide array of skills essential to the characteristics of the "educated man." Although they have

Educational Intervention for the Development of Skills (cont.)

Statement	*Rationale*
	received only limited use, such educational practices have already demonstrated their ability to facilitate the development of important skills (see Chapter 2).
Procedures are available for the more effective utilization of existing resources for the practice of education devoted to facilitation of skills.	Generally, the educational practices which have been designed for the facilitation of skills have not been used widely or effectively (see Chapter 1, pp. 18-22). A number of operational procedures designed to implement existing instructional programs and resources appropriate for the facilitation of skills for moving current school practice toward the goals of process education have been developed (see Chapters 4 and 5). Further refinement of these curriculum and instructional vehicles and their implementation holds much promise for developing an educational practice generally concerned with the facilitation of a wide array of skills essential to the characteristics of the "educated man."
Criteria needed for the selection of curriculum and instructional vehicles appropriate to the facilitation of skills have been and can be further developed.	Criteria have already been developed and used to select existing instructional materials, curricula, and programs concerned with the promotion of skills (see Chapter 1 and Cole & Seferian, 1970, pp. 26-34). Educational practice may be considered to consist of several components: objectives for the learning activity; content and materials of the learning experience; and teaching-learning or instructional strategies. Criteria, derived from the assumptions and justifications for process education, as well as other sources, can be developed and used to select from among existing educational innovations those vehicles appropriate to implementing the practice of process education (see Chapter 5).

Summary

The nature of skills has been discussed. It has been pointed out that education directed toward the purposeful and deliberate facilitation of skills is process education. The empirical basis for process education as derived from both behavioral research and the actual study of particular instructional programs in actual school practice devoted to the development of skills has been listed. The basic assumptions which underlie a commitment to process education have been provided. Hopefully, all of this leads to an understanding of the conceptualization of process education presented. Perhaps the following remarks can help communicate some additional feelings and ideas which stem from this view of education.

Epilogue

"Process"

Process is the way we be
Process is the way we see,
We touch, we think, we feel
We fear, we love, we hate.
We need, we will, we choose
We live and die and wait.

Ever changing, never stable!
That's reality whatever label
Is selected by the being
To describe it as his fable.

Not to know this is to be
Out of touch with reality.

For static things do not exist
In any place or time.
They never have, they never will
Except in one strange place . . .

Sometimes, that process which is *minding* is considered to be a static thing, the "mind." The mind does not exist. However, the minding process does things. It is the way in which each person builds from his own experience. His experience, like his minding, is not a thing but a process. When a person organizes and makes meaning from his experience, he is engaged in learning. Learning, too, is a process and results in the *process of knowledge.*

Many have assumed that knowledge is something other than process. But knowledge is in no way static. It is a collection of ever-changing and expanding information about the meaning individuals and societies have constructed from their singular and collective experiences. It always has ill-defined boundaries, no limits on its extension, and exists only in a continual state of flux. It must be considered process and not a static entity.

If knowledge, the "mind," learning, and virtually everything in the universe are in a continual state of ebb and flow, where can one turn for a sense of organization and stability?

The most stable reality seems to be the *ways* in which people build meaning from their experience. It appears that nature has equipped the human organism's *minding process* with a series of skills, processes, action programs, sub-routines, strategies, or whatever which have great utility for repeated use in an ever-changing world. For convenience, let us simply call these programs "skills." These skills, which are plans for actions or programs, are used again and again by the individual to organize and make meaning from an infinite number of events and a huge array of situations encountered in the flow of his experience. In all this ebb and flow—this continual sea of change—that which is most constant are those skills by which individuals use, change, and create knowledge or any other product.

Products of the process of minding include ideas, generalizations, works of art, and anything which is created, visualized, conceptualized, or even willed or felt. Products are frequently solutions to problems. The creative products of men's minds vary tremendously. However, the process of minding in the creation of products is remarkably constant in many respects across different individuals. Certain skills seem to form the basis for highly useful approaches to the problems of creating products, organizing experience, and making meaning. The ways in which people use these skills are equally as important as the events of their experience.

A condition essential to the process of minding and meaning making is the freedom *from* restrictions and the freedom *to* create. This freedom, coupled with the necessary skills, the experience, and the meaning made from that experience, results in a person who expressively changes and expands knowledge while seeking, finding, and solving problems.

Yet, paradoxically, most education is predicated on the view that knowledge is something other than process, that it is stable and unchanged over long periods of time. The process of minding has been considered best achieved by the largely passive acquisition of static "knowledge." The "mind" has been considered as an object receptive to the acquisition of information rather than as a process for using, creating, and changing knowledge. The need of the individual to expressively and creatively organize and make meaning from his flow of experience has been largely ignored, and his freedom to do so has frequently been denied. His opportunity for problem-seeking, -finding, and -solving has been interfered with. He has been taught that, in school and by implication in society generally, he is not to be a creator and changer of knowledge. Process education rejects this conventional and traditional approach to education.

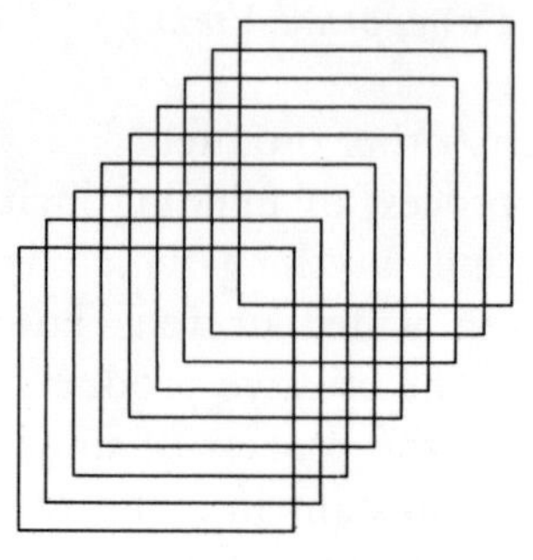

CHAPTER 3

ROLES IN PROCESS EDUCATION

It was noted in Chapter 1 that process education is not insured by simply arranging for excellent curricula designed for the deliberate and purposeful promotion of skills to be adopted and used in schools. The proper and effective use of such curricula requires pupils and teachers to consistently exhibit different classroom behavior than is customary. It is known that teachers, and subsequently the pupils whom they instruct, frequently fail to adopt behavior patterns essential to the practice of process education.

This chapter examines pupil and teacher roles within the context of the school as a social institution. The Getzels model for the interaction of institutional role expectations with individual personality need-dispositions is discussed and used to note points of conflict between current educational practice and process education. Values and institutional role expectations critical to process education are stated and contrasted with existing value positions and expectations which govern current educational practice.

Throughout the chapter particular words from the jargon of social psychology are used in consistent denotative ways. The reader is cautioned to interpret these terms as they are *technically defined* in the chapter rather than in a general or common usage sense. The language of Chapter 2 as defined in the paradigm for process education is also retained in the present chapter.

Roles in Social Systems

The school may be considered an institution and the pupil and teacher as role incumbents within that institution. The concept of a role within such a social system is more complex than is usually recognized in educational literature, where roles are usually characterized simply as behavior patterns. Such interpretations usually fail to recognize the importance of the interaction among the pupil and teacher role perceptions, the institutional role expectations, and the individual personalities of these role incumbents.

Roles and Behavior Patterns

Although roles may be simply considered to be consistent patterns of behavior, this is not wise for our purposes. Indeed, teacher roles have been defined this way by Wallen and Travers (1963, p. 451) who suggest the phrase "pattern of behavior" be substituted for the term "role" to avoid the additional connotations attached to "role" in the jargon of social psychology. Wallen and Travers define a behavior pattern as follows:

> . . . an identifiable grouping of behaviors which occur in the same teacher.

In the jargon of social psychology the term "role" involves concepts of self-other perception and mutual expectancy in social interactive behavior. As used by Wallen and Travers, a role or behavior pattern is simply an identifiable pattern of teacher (or pupil) behavior with no element of expectancy or social reciprocity. The advantage of this definition is that it considerably simplifies the task of dealing with classroom roles. One can list general categories of teacher or pupil behavior which are patterns of appropriate outcomes to some set of educational goals or particular aspects of educational practice.

Patterns of behaviors among pupils, teachers and other individuals in the school do exist: they can be observed and described. Furthermore, ideal patterns of behavior for achieving specified educational goals can be stated as well as operationally defined. However, it is important to realize that these or any other patterns of behavior occur within a social context. The connotations attached to the term "role" by the social psychologist deal with important additional factors which always operate at the cultural, institutional, and individual levels to determine these patterns of behavior. It is the problems in the lack of congruence between the values and ethos of the culture; the expectations and roles of the schools versus curriculum developers and change agencies; and the personality and need-dispositions of the individuals who socially interact in the schools that result in conflicts which prevent innovative curricula and practices from being properly implemented. Consequently, while Wallen and Travers' concept of "patterns of behavior" is useful and will be used in this and later chapters, it is an inadequate conceptualization for dealing with many of the problems involved in implementing the practice of process education in the schools. Therefore, let us consider a more complex but also more adequate model in which the term "role" retains its social-psychological connotations.

Getzels' Model for Roles Within Social Systems

The model about to be described was developed by Jacob W. Getzels (1952, 1963). It is a general model for examining interpersonal or social behavior within the context of a social system. A schematic of the model is provided in Figure 1. For convenience and clarity, key terms used in the model are defined in Table 1. It may be helpful to examine the definitions and the schematic of the model before reading further.

The Getzels model has been used by many scholars in conceptualizing and studying the behavior of educators and pupils within schools. It seems most appropriate to a consideration of roles and existing role conflicts in the practice of process education.

The basic assumption of the model is that interpersonal or social behavior always functions within a social system. A social system may have as its focus a single classroom, a peer group, a school, a school district, a community, an educational laboratory, or any other purposeful and organized collection of individuals. It is further assumed that any social system involves two dimensions of possible activity. These are "the publicly mandatory and the privately necessary" (Getzels, 1963, p. 310). These two activity dimensions arise from two "conceptually independent but phenomenally interactive" components in the model.

The first component of the model consists of the institution, role, and expectation which are collectively referred to as the nomothetic dimension of the social system. For example, the institution might be a school. The role might be that of principal, teacher, pupil, janitor or school nurse. The role is defined by the normative expectations for the particular position or role in the institution. Different rights, privileges, and obligations exist for different roles within the institution. These define and limit the behavior patterns which are acceptable for pupils, teachers, principals and others in the school. Thus, the principal must attend board of education meetings, has free access to the public address system, and may leave early or arrive late. This is not true for pupils and teachers, who must be present during the normal school day schedule, ask and receive special permission to use the

Figure 1

Getzels' Model for Interpersonal Behavior Within Social Systems[6]

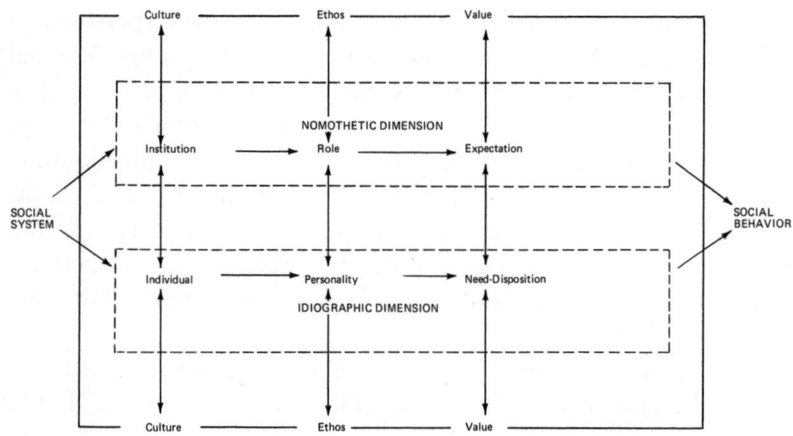

6. Adapted with permission from Getzels, Jacob W. Conflict and role behavior in the educational setting. In W.W. Charters, Jr. & N.L. Gage (Eds.), *Readings in the social psychology of education.* Boston: Allyn & Bacon, 1963, pp. 311-312.

Table 1

Definitions for Key Terms in the Getzels Model[7]

SOCIAL SYSTEMS—Structures where cultural ethos and values impinge upon the idiographic and nomothetic dimensions to produce social behavior.

Nomothetic Dimension—Normative dimension of activity in a social system. Consists of three conceptual constructs: institution, role, and expectations.

Institutions—*Agencies established to carry out* functions for the social system.

Roles—*Dynamic aspects of position and status* which are *defined by the institutional expectations.*

Expectations—The institutional *rights, privileges, and obligations to which any incumbent of the role must adhere.* The normative standard for the behavior of the individual within the institution. This standard reflects values of the culture.

Idiographic Dimension—Personal dimension of activity in a social system. Consists of three conceptual constructs: individual, personality, and need-disposition.

7. These definitions were taken in part from pages 310-311 of Getzels, Jacob W. Conflict and role behavior in the educational setting. In W.W. Charters & N.L. Gage (Eds.), *Readings in the social psychology of education.* Boston: Allyn & Bacon, Inc., 1963. The passages drawn from the Getzels article are italicized. The remaining definitions have been added by the present author. The substance of several of these were taken from the *Random House dictionary of the English language.* Unabridged edition. New York: Random House, 1966.

Table 1 (cont.)

Individuals—Persons with unique personalities and need-dispositions who inhabit the social system as members with roles in institutions.

Personality—*The dynamic organization of those need-dispositions within the individual that govern his unique perceptions and reactions to the environment and to its expectations.*

Need-Dispositions—*Individual tendencies to orient and act with respect to objects in certain manners and to expect certain consequences from these actions.*

SOCIAL BEHAVIOR—Behavior patterns resulting from the interaction of roles and expectations of institutions and personalities and need-dispositions of individuals.

Behavior Patterns—Identifiable and consistent acts of individuals operating in a social system and resulting from the interaction of the idiographic and nomothetic dimensions.

CULTURE—The sum total of existing social systems and all their components.

ETHOS—Prevailing moral views of a culture which describe characteristics of the ideal man (i.e., the "educated man" of Chapter 1). The cultural ethos are ideals or goals which characterize and direct both institutional roles and individual personalities.

VALUE—An ideal, belief or custom of a culture toward which its members have an affective regard. The regard toward a particular value can be either positive or negative.

public address system, and are seldom required to attend board of education meetings.

The second component of the model consists of the individual, his personality, and his need-dispositions, which are collectively referred to as the idiographic dimension. This is the personal dimension of the social system. As an example, a given individual pupil, principal or teacher within the social system of a school has a personality and a need-disposition which may or may not be congruent with institutional roles and expectations. If, for instance, in a given school the institutional expectation for the teacher role calls for dominant, didactic, and authoritative behavior in dealing with pupils, an individual teacher having personality and need-disposition characteristics similar to these normative institutional standards will function effectively. The same teacher in a different school where the norms call for accepting, non-directive, and dialectic behavior in dealing with pupils will no longer be effective. The reverse is, of course, also true. Similar examples can be enumerated which further illustrate the interaction of the personality and need-dispositions of individual pupils, principals, or janitors with the institutional norms for their various roles.

The behavior patterns of which Wallen and Travers (1963) speak are simply the outcomes of the interaction between the institution and the individual in the social context. The Getzels model, therefore, not only includes these behavior pattern outcomes, but helps interpret their formulation as well as diagnose situations where behavior patterns are inappropriate or non-functional within existing institutional norms. This is a most important property of the model.

Behavioral pattern outcomes for any given institution, such as a school, are not, however, solely determined by the interaction of the individual and the institution. At any given time an individual is always simultaneously a member of many social systems, both large and small, superordinate and subordinate, compatible and incompatible, and related and unrelated. Social systems, through their diverse individual members—and sometimes more directly through institutions such as the family, the corporate factory, the classroom, the school district, the state education department, the church, and the federal government—affect and influence each other. All these institutions, roles, and expectations collectively combine to form another pervasive dimension which interacts with both particular individuals and particular institutions. This is the cultural dimension to the Getzels model. It provides the matrix in which particular institutions and their individual members interact socially in multiple social systems.

As an example of the influence of the culture upon the interaction of the institutions of schools with their pupils and teachers, consider the recent changes in institutional expectancies for the grooming and attire of pupils and teachers. Specifically, a few years ago institutional expectancies in our schools called for skirts to be long and male hair lengths to be short. Pupils who did not conform to these standards were expelled or otherwise "disciplined." Teachers who did not conform were not granted tenure or were fired. But there are many social systems in society other than schools to which pupils and teachers belong. Furthermore, many of these are more sensitive, susceptible, and responsive to changing cultural ethos and values than are schools. Consequently, the normative standards governing both male hair length and female skirt length began to change in the various extra-curricular youth and peer group social systems of both pupils and younger teachers. The standards were also changing in many of the various social systems to which parents of elementary school children belonged. Subsequently, the combined influence of this cultural pressure for longer hair for men and shorter skirts for women was transmitted to the school through the modification of many of its individual members' perceptions of what was appropriate and acceptable behavior within their multiple institutional roles. A more direct influence was exerted on the schools by those other social institutions which manufacture, distribute, and market women's clothing. Until the recent advent of the midi and maxi skirts, it has been difficult for girls and young women to obtain long dresses and skirts. Likewise, a male is currently confronted with barbers eager to trim and make his hair neat but reluctant to cut it very short. Thus, changes in cultural values have combined through many social systems to change aspects of certain role expectations for pupils and teachers within a particular social institution. The behavior patterns of pupils, young teachers, many middle-aged teachers, and some older teachers have subsequently been modified.

Other situations involving changes in the curricular content and related role expectations for pupils and teachers can be cited as examples of how ethos and value changes in the cultural milieu affect school practice. Some high schools now have student lounges where pupils may relax without supervision, or even smoke. In many schools, drugs, alcoholism, the moral issues of United States military involvement in Southeast Asia, and many other current social problems are no longer taboo topics. Rather, they are discussed openly, seriously, and with strong feeling by pupils and teachers in their classrooms.

Utility of the Getzels Model for Process Education

The Getzels model is a useful analytic tool. It can be used to interpret existing behavior patterns of pupils and teachers in schools in terms of the interaction of established institutional roles and expectations with individual personalities and need-dispositions of pupils and teachers in the context of prevailing cultural ethos and values.

In Chapter 1, while reviewing the observations of John Goodlad, Ronald Lippitt, Neil Postman, and Charles Weingartner, as well as the experience of the Institute staff, it was pointed out that the numerous and excellent curriculum innovations of the sixties have had little effect upon improving educational practice. To repeat Goodlad's (1969, p. 60) cogent observation, these innovations have been "blunted on the classroom door."

It has been pointed out elsewhere (Cole, 1970a) that those curriculum and instructional innovations which are most appropriate to the practice of process education and most complete in their design may be the very ones most likely to be improperly used or even rejected by the administrative and teaching staffs of many schools. This can be understood in terms of the Getzels model. In many cases, the agencies which have developed these new process curricula have been attuned to different values within our culture than have the schools. Therefore, role expectations for pupils and teachers according to the developers of these innovative process curriculum and instructional methods have frequently been in opposition to those established role expectations in the schools. Consequently, when such programs have been installed they have tended to be used within the institutionally sanctioned and established behavior patterns in the schools. The new and different behavior patterns essential to the proper functioning of these programs and methods were not designed to operate under the old and prevailing behavior patterns of the schools. Therefore they have been frequently operationally nonfunctional and ineffective.

There are five related and key questions which can be asked concerning the failure of the many excellent process curricula and instructional methods, developed in the sixties, to be widely and properly implemented in elementary schools. These are:

1. *Are there conflicts* between existing school behavior patterns of teachers and pupils and the expectancies of the developers of process programs?

2. *Where are the conflicts* and points of incongruity between the values and expectations for these new programs and existing school norms for teacher and pupil behavior patterns?

3. *What* are the key *values and expectations,* which *must be changed* in the institution, the school, to achieve the goals of new process curricula and process education generally?

4. *In what directions* must existing values and expectations be changed to insure the desired behavior pattern outcomes for pupils and teachers for process education?

5. *How can* the critical *values, expectations,* and *need-dispositions* once identified *be changed* to promote behavior pattern outcomes desired as goals for process education?

The first and prerequisite question has already been answered in Chapter 1. Obviously, such conflicts do exist. They have prevented the effective adoption and use of many excellent process programs. The fifth question will be dealt with in a later chapter concerned with means for implementing the practice of process education. Questions 2, 3 and 4 will be dealt with in the remainder of this chapter. The Getzels model has a utility not only in formulating these questions but in providing a logical framework from which to proceed to their answers. They are critical questions since they approach the role of the pupil and teacher in process education within their institutional and cultural contexts. One cannot profitably conceptualize the behavior patterns of the teacher and the pupil as if they existed in isolation within the classroom. Their roles are determined in large part by the press of the institution and culture in which the classroom exists. Changing the existing classroom roles of teachers and pupils to be more appropriate to the practice of process education realistically requires an understanding of the current and prevailing forces which cause the conflicts which now exist.

Conflicts Between Process Education and Current School Practice

There are many points of incongruity between the expectations of the developers of process curricula and existing school norms for teacher and pupil behavior. The origin of these conflicts lies in opposing values which exist simultaneously in our culture. The problem is that frequently communities, schools, and educators subscribe to a different set of values than the change agency or curriculum developer who advocates process education.

Conflicting Values

In Chapter 1 a profile of the educated man was drawn. For convenience, it is repeated here.

> . . . the ideal man our schools should help develop has the following characteristics. He is a rational man skilled in reasoning and analytic thinking. He is a man who can love. He is compassionate and warm in his interpersonal relationships. He is sensitive, empathetic, and non-ethnocentric. He is an independently motivated, life-long learner. He is a problem-seeker and -solver. He is expressive and creative, both cognitively and affectively. He is flexible and fluent in his perceptions, ideas, and feelings. He is curious and an inquirer. He is a coper rather than a defender, an active seeker rather than a passive accepter.

The above profile represents an ideal sought only by *some*

members of our society. For them it embodies values which they seek to translate into the roles and expectations of institutions, such as the school, in order to foster the personality and need-disposition patterns in children consistent with the ethos of the "educated man." However, there are others in our society who regard this ideal of the "educated man" as foolhardy and an abomination. Specifically, some of these groups and individuals in our society seek to develop individuals who *are* ethnocentric, who *are* passive and submissive, who have both the desire and the need to be told what to believe, what to do, and when and how to do it. Furthermore, they believe that learning does not occur best through independent motivation and intrinsic guides but that extrinsic pressures must be applied to *make* the individual learn, act and generally "behave himself." These two sets of conflicting beliefs are represented not only within different groups of society but also as ambivalent feelings within each individual personality. This condition is the fundamental cause of the conflict which underlies the common failure of process programs in the schools.

While ambivalence may exist in both groups and individuals with respect to these sets of opposing values, the fact remains that each usually has a consistent predisposition toward one set of values as being more important and generally positive, while the other set is viewed as less important and generally negative. In the framework of the Getzels model, these predispositions for the social group or institution are the role expectations. For the individual they are the personality need-dispositions.

Conflicting Aims

An excellent statement of these two conflicting value positions as they relate to educational aims has been made by Carl Rogers (1967). These are reprinted in Table 2. As Rogers notes, the aim which deals with the transmission of knowledge is the one which has an historical tradition in education. It is also currently the prevalent aim which dominates ongoing educational practice.

It should be pointed out that each educational aim is functional under different cultural conditions. Thus, as Rogers notes, the aim dealing with the transmission of knowledge has been valuable in that it has enabled societies to amass and transmit information and skills for dealing with a relatively unchanging world. However, a new aim concerned with the "process of discovery" is more appropriate to the present world situation in which we live.

This question of which aim is more appropriate to this society is not primarily a moral or ideological question. It is, rather, a question of practicality with strong empirical underpinnings. The question to be asked is, "Which educational aim is better suited to the present conditions and demands of society?" The answer is clear. Given the tremendous and ever accelerating rate of change in all facets of life in the present world, the functional aim must concern the nurturance of the process of discovery, learning, and meaning making. This was the conclusion previously reached in Chapter 2, where the justifications for process education were explained. The justifications are, in reality, conditions of the modern world which demand process aims in education. Yet, it is obvious that current educational practice, while paying lip service to process aims, is operationally concerned with transmitting knowledge and nurturing not discovery, self-directed learning, and independent thinking, but deference, submissiveness, passive conformity, and undue reliance upon authority and tradition.

Conflicting Assumptions

There is an unstated set of assumptions which underlies much current educational practice in the schools. These assumptions

Table 2

Two Possible Aims for Education[8]

To Transmit Stored Knowledge

For the most part, the current educational system is geared to the aim of inculcating in the young the stored knowledge already accumulated, together with the values which have guided men in the past. *Its natural product is the informed, essentially passive conformist.*

Historically, there has been much to be said for this point of view. Because of a recent visit in Australia, I have been reading and hearing about the Australian Aborigine. For twenty thousand years he and his kind have survived in a most inhospitable environment in which modern man would die. He has survived by passing on every bit of knowledge and skill he has acquired about a relatively unchanging world and frowning upon or tabooing any new ways of meeting the relatively unchanging problems. This has been the description of American education goals as well.

To Nurture the Process of Discovery

But modern man is face to face with a situation which has never before existed in history. The world—of science, of communication, of social relationships—is changing at such a pace that the knowledge stored up in the past is not enough. The physicist cannot live by the stored knowledge of his science. *His confidence, his basic trust, is in the process by which new knowledge is acquired.* In like fashion, if society is to be able to meet the challenges of a more and more rapidly changing world—if civilization is to survive—people *must be able increasingly to live in a process manner.* The public, like the physicist, will have to put their trust in the process by which new problems are met, not in the answers to problems of the past.

This need implies *a new goal for education. Learning how to learn, involvement in a process of change*—these become the primary aims of an education fit for the present world. *There must evolve individuals who are capable of intelligent, informed, discriminating, adaptive, effective involvement in a process of change* . . . the ability to face the new appropriately is more important than being able to repeat the old.

8. From Rogers, Carl R. The facilitation of significant learning. In L. Siegel (Ed.), *Instruction: some contemporary viewpoints.* San Francisco: Chandler Publishing Co., 1967, pp. 173-174.

have been independently noted by Rogers (1967, p. 174) and Postman and Weingartner (1969, p. 20). They include:

> The student cannot be trusted to pursue his own learning.
>
> Presentation equals learning.
>
> The truth is known.
>
> The aim of education is to accumulate brick upon brick of factual knowledge.
>
> Constructive and creative citizens develop from passive learners.
>
> The voice of authority is to be trusted and valued more than independent judgment.
>
> Feelings are irrelevant in education.
>
> Discovering knowledge is beyond the power of students and is, in any case, none of their business.
>
> Passive acceptance is a more desirable response to ideas than active criticism.

Operation of many schools based upon these assumptions is evident from direct observation of educational practice. Based upon much experience with classroom as well as general school organization and activity, the findings of both Goodlad (1969, p. 60) and Silberman (1970) clearly indicate that schools do indeed operationally subscribe to such assumptions. That educational practice based upon such implicit assumptions is the antithesis of process education is a certainty. The assumptions for process education stated and discussed in Chapter 2 may be found in

Table 3. The conflict between the assumptions for process education and the operational assumptions which underlie school practice is incredible!

Strangely, practicing educators do not usually recognize the real assumptions which underlie their practice. As Goodlad (1969, p. 61) points out, most teachers have a favorable image of what they are doing in the classroom.

Many teachers and principals can read the assumptions stated for process education and with much apparent feeling and extensive verbalization "dedicate themselves to these ideals" and yet continue to deal with their students in ways completely inappropriate to the ideals. The reason for this is that, for practicing educators, the goals, assumptions, and justifications for process education remain as simple slogans. Many of them are not even new slogans. Slogans serve a useful function. They can mobilize people and create a sentiment which seeks change and improvement. But slogans which remain as empty and unfilled promises are frustrating and dangerous. In education, slogans have traditionally been substituted for solutions. Consequently, those involved in educational practice have found that slogans should be stated, shouted, and pledged allegiance, but that they have little or no relation to the operational activity of the school and the classroom. Therefore, there exists a second set of *operational* assumptions and rules for the "actual" education of the child in the "real situation" of the classroom. These operational assumptions dictate that most school and classroom practices be directed toward managing the child to *make him learn and make him do what is prescribed for him by the teacher, the curriculum, and the authoritative textbook.*

The idea that the child must be *made to learn* and *made to do* is very central to most educational practice. The idea is based upon the notion that children generally have a tendency to avoid learning and to "misbehave." Since a significant number of the learning tasks set for students in the classroom are not related to

Table 3

Assumptions for Process Education

- Knowledge is an organized but tentative and arbitrary collection of changing and expanding information which each individual adapts and uses to make meaning from his unique experience.
- Learning (meaning making) is a natural and creative activity by which each person organizes and makes meaning (knowledge) from his experience toward fulfillment of his needs.
- Needs are the basis of the affective commitment which makes possible both the task of meaning making (learning, building knowledge) and the retention of the meaning made (knowledge).
- The process by which individuals make meaning (learn, build knowledge) from their experience is equally as important and more stable and lasting than either the experience or the meaning made (knowledge).
- Skills are the basis for the process of meaning making and all adaptive, productive, and satisfying behavior.
- Freedom to creatively apply skills to the process of organizing and making meaning (learning, building knowledge) from experience results in seeking, finding, and solving problems.
- Schools can provide the setting for individuals to develop and use those skills needed to freely build and make use of knowledge.

their experience, are dull and boring, and are concerned primarily with the rote and associative learning of facts, pupils do, indeed, frequently try to avoid the prescribed learning and have a quite natural tendency to be more interested in things other than the learning tasks set for them. This pupil behavior provides teachers with reinforcement for their ideas on the need to force the child to learn and to make him behave acceptably. Thus, most teachers press on, viewing themselves as subject matter specialists and perceiving the "forced" transmission of the body of information and "truth" of their specialties or disciplines to their students to be the first and, in most cases, the only matter of importance, despite lip service paid to other views. This attitude is especially widespread among secondary school and college teachers and is frequently emulated by elementary school teachers. Curriculum developers, state education departments, and textbook publishers have also made a large contribution to this most unfortunate attitude. As Roberts (1966, p. 353) notes, many "innovative" curricula have been designed for the purpose of cramming more information into students. The same thing may generally be said about state education department curriculum guides. Every year, they seem to get thicker, and the list of what the student is supposed to be *made* to "know" grows longer and longer.

In most operational aspects of current educational practice, little emphasis is placed upon objectives and procedures dealing with assisting the learner in the motivation for learning, discovery, acquisition, organization, and application of information—all of which are important considerations under process education. In short, conventional educational practice is too caught up with the static content of the "disciplines" which is so readily prescribed as an essential body of knowledge for the learner, while ignoring the question of *why he needs it* or *what he and the teacher must do* to help him acquire, organize, and utilize that information.

In terms of the Getzels model, it is apparent that there are conflicting value positions represented by the ethos of the process educated man and the more traditionally educated man. These two value positions are expressed as conflicting aims in education. The primary aim for process education is the development of skills by which new knowledge is acquired, invented, and used. The primary aim for traditional education is the transmission of existing knowledge. In the framework of the Getzels model the operational assumptions which underlie current educational practice are really institutional expectancies which largely define the role of the pupil and the teacher. These assumptions are expressed in role expectancies which conflict with the role expectations held for teachers and pupils by the developers of process curricula and other advocates of process education.

Existing Role Conflicts

Under the current conditions of educational practice there are serious role conflicts for both teachers and pupils which adversely affect teaching and learning. Attempts to implement the practice of process education through new curriculum materials or methods will certainly be affected and likely impeded by these existing conflicts.

Locus of Role Conflicts

As was noted earlier, the two different and opposed belief patterns which have been discussed in the previous sections are represented not only within different groups of society but also as ambivalent feelings within individual personalities. It was also noted earlier that while ambivalence in commitment to these two belief patterns may exist for both institutions and individuals, each usually has a consistent predisposition toward one set of values, aims, and assumptions as being generally more important and positive, while the opposing set is generally viewed as less important and negative. It seems likely, however, that the institutional role expectations of the schools are far less ambivalent than the personality need-dispositions of the incumbents of the teacher and pupil roles.

Those implicit assumptions which Rogers as well as Postman and Weingartner have identified are summarized in Figure 2. These statements do in fact operationally define the acceptable role for the pupil and the teacher within the institutional expectations of the school. Furthermore, these implicit assumptions, or operational role expectations—whichever we choose to call them—are in direct conflict with the values underlying the ethos of the process educated man. Rather they are in support of values which call for the ideal man to be informed; accepting of the absolute nature of knowledge and the traditional means by which it has been developed; and a passive conformist within existing social systems. In short, the implicit assumptions that underlie school practice operate as role expectations which serve the interest of a stable social institution that is resistant to change and concerned with the preservation of its *status quo* and longevity. The implicit and operational assumptions governing current educational practice are designed to protect and serve the bureaucratic institution, the school.

There is evidence which indicates that many teachers, at least initially, have ideals, personalities, and need-dispositions which conflict with the institutional bureaucratic roles prescribed for them by the implicit but operational assumptions. Furthermore, many of those who remain in teaching may *not* resolve this conflict. It is also clear that pupil ideals and needs, the role expectations held for them by their peer groups, and the conditions favorable for learning, inquiry, and meaning making conflict with the prevailing institutional role expectations of the schools.

Figure 2

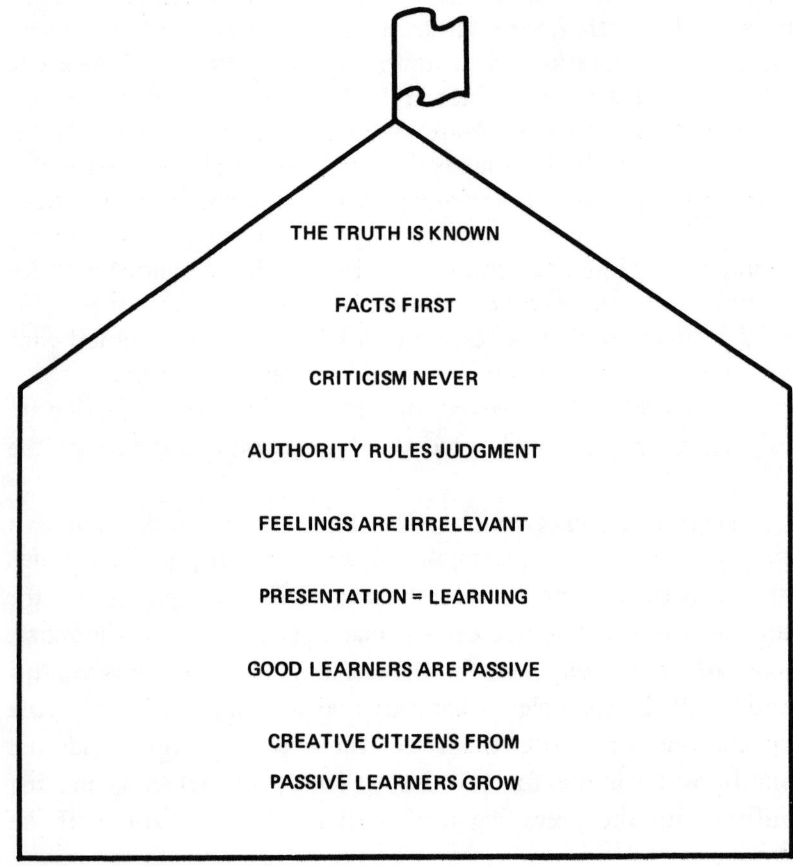

THE TRUTH IS KNOWN
FACTS FIRST
CRITICISM NEVER
AUTHORITY RULES JUDGMENT
FEELINGS ARE IRRELEVANT
PRESENTATION = LEARNING
GOOD LEARNERS ARE PASSIVE
CREATIVE CITIZENS FROM
PASSIVE LEARNERS GROW

Schools as Bureaucracies

In a recent article titled "Professional Role Discontinuities in Educational Careers," Herbert J. Walberg (1970) uses Weber's theory of "bureaucracy" to examine the adjustment of individual careers to educational institutions. Walberg observes, from his own observations and those of others, that schools tend to be "bureaucracies." As bureaucracies, they are organized hierarchically in a series of roles or positions where each lower position is controlled and supervised by a higher one. A set of practical rules is formulated as the normative standards or institutional expectations which govern behavior patterns of role incumbents within the institution. Bureaucracies tend to be rational and efficient organizations within the rules that govern their organization and operation. The bureaucratic organization of an institution may also help it use efficient means to meet its ends and thereby contribute to the survival of the institution. Furthermore, the normative standards for the roles of individuals within the institution help members of the system to move successfully through their "careers" in the system. Under bureaucratic control, roles for dealing with the social system and its members are well defined, and a participant member knows what is expected of him and will be rewarded for behaving consistently with that institutional expectation. However, he may personally disagree with the institutional expectation. He may not wish to behave in the prescribed manner. If this is so he will undergo a role conflict.

Walberg points out that a problem with bureaucratically organized institutions is that as they gain power and establish a tradition, they may come to emphasize the means which resulted in institutional stability rather than the original ends. In the case of the school, the original client, the child, is replaced by a new client, the school organization itself. Subsequently, the role expectations for pupils and teachers come to serve and protect the stability and longevity of the school as a social institution. This is the function served by the previously stated implicit assumptions which govern the operational practices of schools.

Bureaucratically organized institutions frequently lag behind the rapidly changing society in which they find themselves. Their procedures are frequently insensitive to changing values and ethos in the culture. Consequently, they are not able to cope effectively with many of their problems because of the "force of ingrained habits which are no longer adaptive" (Walberg, 1970, p. 410). This observation seems to be particularly appropriate to educational institutions, given the failure of most schools to cope with current educational problems. It is precisely the assumption that schools have become such self-preserving, unresponsive, non-adaptable, change-resisting bureaucracies that underlies the criticism of current educational practice by many scholars.

It should be pointed out that if indeed schools are change-resisting bureaucracies, the ideals and related role expectations for process education cannot be acceptable to them. For such a bureaucracy the ethos of the process educated man is inappropriate. Rather, the individual to be desired is the informed, passive conformist who will accept both the established order of the social system and the established knowledge which has been accumulated through traditional means. Such individuals will add to the stability and longevity of the bureaucratically organized institution. They will not "rock the boat."

Personality-Role Conflicts for Teachers

In reviewing a number of empirical studies concerned with the personality need-dispositions of preservice teachers, Walberg (1970, pp. 413-414) notes that prospective teachers have needs to identify and associate with children. They tend to have empathy for children and be generally child-centered rather than teacher- or institution-centered. The studies reviewed specifically indicate that student teaching and first teaching experiences tend to (1) reduce the satisfaction derived from teaching, (2) deflate the professional self-image of the teacher, (3) lead to self-depreciation on intellectual mastery, (4) lead to lower expectation for pupil behavior, (5) lower aspirations for self in the role of a teacher, and (6) lead to less rapport with children. It is noted that these findings have been replicated across several studies. Walberg interprets the findings as a result of a conflict between the prevailing institutional role expectations of the schools and the personality need-disposition characteristics of beginning teachers.

Similar observations about the role conflicts encountered by beginning teachers are made by B.O. Smith (1969) in his chapter titled "The Teacher as a Dropout." Smith points out that teachers are burdened with extra classroom responsibilities and problems which have little to do with teaching or learning and with which the beginning teacher is frequently unable to cope. The teacher, unlike other professionals, has almost no power in making decisions and formulating policies which relate to his role and his working conditions. Therefore, Smith *et al.* (1969, pp. 25-26) conclude:

> . . . the impotence of the teacher in his own job and his own profession often leads to intense dissatisfaction and in some cases ultimately to his departure from teaching.

It has been empirically shown that beginning teachers are frequently child-centered. They view the child as the client to be served by the school and themselves. However, experienced teachers tend to think of the client as the school or the larger social system, the community. Seldom do experienced teachers see themselves serving pupils. A recent study by Hoy (1970) documents this transition as a function of initial teaching experience. There is an interesting corollary to this situation.

An article by Daniels (1969) titled "The Captive Professional: Bureaucratic Limitations in the Practice of Military Psychiatry" deals with the role conflicts faced by military psychiatric personnel. Psychiatrists, as are teachers, are trained to be client-centered. Unlike teachers, psychiatrists do, in their normal practice, deal directly with and serve the client. They are normally "free" professionals. However, psychiatrists are sometimes inducted into the armed forces. At this point the professional psychiatrist has a new client to serve. The client becomes the bureaucratic social institution of the military. The conflicts in the psychiatrist's personality need-dispositions and in the institutional expectations are frequently severe. Daniels (1969, p. 255) hypothesizes that:

> When a member of one of the "free" professions becomes an employee of a bureaucratic organization, the organization often supersedes the ultimate control and authority normally invested in his professional colleagues, and the professional thus becomes a "captive."

It is apparent both from the direct observation of the operation and organization of schools and from numerous studies of experienced teachers that the teacher is a captive professional and consequently suffers much role conflict. Unlike the psychiatrist, he cannot easily remain in the profession and be "free" to directly serve the child as a client.

It is reasonable, as Walberg (1970, p. 414) concludes from his review as well as his own studies (Walberg, 1968; Walberg, Metzner, Todd, & Henry, 1968), that the individual personality-institutional role conflict causes beginning teachers to move away from a child-centered approach to teaching and learning. For beginning teachers, the client is the child. For experienced teachers, the client becomes the institution. It appears that novice teachers may resolve the conflict either by leaving the profession or by staying and adopting a teaching approach in which the bureaucratic management of the child serves the institution that becomes the new client. It appears that the conflict tends to be most severe for those who are potentially the best teachers. These individuals may be driven away by the existing bureaucratic expectations for teacher and pupil roles which are expressed in the implicit assumptions for school practice. Those who remain tend to become "captive professionals" who fulfill the acceptable institutional roles.

The attrition rate among new teachers is extremely high compared to other professions. In discussing this problem, Greenberg (1969, pp. 106-107) informs us that of the approximately 200,000 new teachers entering public schools each year 140,000 are replacement teachers, and that ten percent of the total teaching profession in any given year is new to the field. As Smith observes, many female teachers who leave after the first year do return to teaching after they have raised families. However, the attrition rate is much higher than can be accounted for by pregnancy of female teachers. It seems reasonable to believe that personality-role conflicts are a major causal factor.

The usual source of conflict in the form of the implicit assumptions which govern school practice are aggravated for the beginning teacher. Beginning teachers are generally poorly trained in the planning and management of instructional and classroom activity (Smith *et al.,* 1969, p. 24). The novice teacher, of all staff members in a school, is typically in most need of assistance with his many classroom, instructional management, and other institutional responsibilities. However, in the typical bureaucratic structure of the school hierarchy, the role for the beginning teacher is one more appropriate for exploitation than assistance. Consequently, it is the beginning teacher who usually receives the least desirable working conditions and duties, the problem students, the largest classes, and so forth (Smith *et al.,* 1969, pp. 24-25; Greenberg, 1969, pp. 110-111). There is ample evidence that these factors combine to force beginning teachers to either flee the profession or to be socialized to the bureaucratic institutional role expectations.

Selection and Socialization of Teachers to Bureaucratic Roles

In a study involving 328 graduate education students who were presumably individuals who had been involved in teaching for some time and had been socialized to the role of teacher or principal within the school, Spindler (1955) found that the majority were opposed to many of the values central to the ethos of the process educated man. Specifically they tended to devalue characteristics of independence, high intelligence, high academic ability, and creativity. The same group tended to value characteristics of sociability, popularity, conformity, and *average* intellectual and academic ability. In a later study, Guba, Jackson, and Bidwell (1959, 1963) found experienced teachers to exhibit a set of needs characteristic of a "meek" personality structure well suited to the subservient role of the teacher in the bureaucratic mode of the typical school. A sample of 366 public school teachers from 24 schools in nine counties in the Midwest was the focus of the initial study. It was determined that these teachers generally had high needs on the dimensions of deference, order, and endurance, and low needs on the dimensions of heterosexuality, dominance, and exhibition. The authors note that the needs of achievement, interception, and nurturance—all of which might be expected to be high for teachers—are conspicuously absent from this group.[9]

9. The personality instrument used was the *Edwards Personal Preference Schedule.* The six dimensions are defined as follows: *Deference*—to yield to the leadership and judgment of others. *Order*—to organize one's work and personal life systematically. *Endurance*—to work at a task until it is completed. *Achievement*—to accomplish demanding tasks, to be able to do

In another series of informative studies Guba, Jackson, and Bidwell (1959, 1963) compared the need characteristics of the 366 experienced teachers with education students attending a number of private and state universities and colleges. They found that college students at teacher colleges exhibit personality profiles closely resembling those of experienced teachers. University students were shown to have need patterns differing from experienced teachers. Upon entering teaching, however, the differences between the university and college preservice teachers disappear. University students, either through attrition or role socialization, also adopt the typical need-disposition profile of the experienced teacher.

Additional analysis of the data from these studies by Guba, Jackson, and Bidwell (1963, p. 278) showed that "teachers who have personalities like that of the veteran teacher are valued" by the principal. The paradox is, however, that the more closely an individual teacher in a school resembles the typical teacher in terms of need structure, the less likely he will be satisfied, feel effective, or have confidence in the principal's leadership. Guba, Jackson, and Bidwell (1959, p. 27) hypothesize:

> . . .the deferent, orderly, enduring teacher is a boon to the administrator, an asset to someone who is concerned with the effective functioning of a social institution. Yet these very attributes might be linked with a rather negative self-image . . .It might also be conjectured that the data reflect a real change in satisfaction, effective-

---

things better than others. *Intraception*—to observe and analyze the behavior of one's self and of others. *Nurturance*—to show sympathy and generosity toward those who are in trouble. *Heterosexuality*—to be interested in the members of the opposite sex and in the subject of sex. *Dominance*—to lead; to make decisions and influence others. *Exhibition*—to talk cleverly for the sake of impressing others; to be the center of attention.

ness, and confidence as the teacher realizes more and more how far from ideal everyday teaching practices and school procedures really are.

It would seem that the role conflicts which exist for teachers not only cause many to leave after the initial school experience, but add to a loss of esteem and satisfaction and contribute to feelings of inadequacy in many of those who remain.

It seems reasonable to suppose that the implicit assumptions stated by Rogers as well as Postman and Weingartner, which are summarized in Figure 2, are role expectations which arise from the bureaucratic nature of the schools. Virtually every one of these implicit assumptions, both as they are stated and as they are practiced, is directed toward making school operation more predictable, functional, and rational from the standpoint of the organization. These implicit, but operational, assumptions serve to insure the order and welfare not of the child, but of the school system itself. Under such an arrangement principals, teachers, and other members of this social system are selected or socialized to serve the institution. As Walberg's (1970) review and his own studies show, it is the administrator and teacher exhibiting behavior patterns consistent with the bureaucratic institutional role expectations who are promoted and rewarded. However, it would appear that many veteran teachers cannot completely resolve the conflicts between institutional expectations and their own ideals.

The Teacher as All Things to All Men

Another source of role conflict of somewhat different origin from those previously discussed exists for teachers. The institutional role expectation for teachers tends to be that any individual teacher will perform a huge array of diverse tasks and activities. As

Smith *et al.* (1969) note, the notion of *a* teacher role is archaic. There are multiple roles and responsibilities for the teacher within any school.

Historically, differentiation of the teaching occupation has been lacking. Not many years ago the teacher in the one-room school house was the janitor, nurse, administrator, and teacher for eight grade levels and several different subjects, as well as director of physical education and recreation. More recently with the rise of large centralized school districts, additional differentiation of teachers by grade level, subject matter area and area of special school service (nurse, reading specialist, speech teacher, librarian) has become common. However, as Smith points out, most rank and file teachers continue to be trained for their profession by very global programs in the expectation that they have both the inclination and capability to perform the very wide array of duties that await them. Smith *et al.* (1969, pp. 31-39), Allen and Hawkes (1970, pp. 7-8), Olivero (1970) and many others have suggested that differentiated teacher roles and differentiated staffing of schools are more realistic approaches to the effective performance of the multiple responsibilities of teachers within schools. Gradually it is becoming recognized that the operation of a classroom requires not a single teacher but an instructional team working toward common educational ends. It seems likely that members of the team should include pupils, teacher aides, teacher specialists, and other individuals who are not teachers in the usual sense. These could include instructional planners, developers, and evaluators responsible for aspects of designing, staging, and assessing the classroom learning production.

The usual attempts at differentiated staffing through "team teaching," "departmental" organization, and similar popular approaches, although intended as steps in the right direction, are typically inadequate or inappropriate to the problem. Such approaches usually recognize only the traditional differences among subject matter area, grade level, and "slow" and "fast" learners. Other more important reasons exist for differentiation of teacher roles.

One reason for the existence of multiple roles for teachers within the school arises because there are different types of learning which require different conditions of instruction. For example, some teachers enjoy drilling pupils in basic information and response patterns. While such drill is often boring and dull to pupils, some skilled teachers can make this activity enjoyable and humorous. Such teachers are probably more effective than a "canned" programmed learning sequence, since their zest and humor is contagious and helps create favorable attitudes toward both the drill activity and the content which is being drilled. There are other teachers who cannot stand repetitive drill activity. It bores them. They become irritable and impatient with pupils. They almost certainly communicate their displeasure with the activity and are likely to create negative attitudes toward both the drill activity and its content. However, such teachers may prefer and be skilled at teaching children to engage in speculative and imaginative thinking. In short, some teachers are more interested and capable of supervising one type of learning than other types. To expect a teacher who hates drill work to teach children to enjoy drilling is "a bit much." Conversely, to expect a teacher who is strictly and expertly a "drill master" to instruct pupils in divergent and speculative thinking is also unrealistic. Both teachers can serve different and needed functions. Pupils have similar differences in their preferences, styles, and needs for structure and routine. Matching appropriate teaching personalities and styles to the particular conditions of learning tasks and the particular learning needs of pupils may be a most important differentiation of teaching staffs which is usually ignored.

As educational media, materials, and techniques continue to become increasingly diverse, further differentiation of teacher roles will almost certainly be required. Many instructional systems now exist which are carefully and well designed to teach particular response patterns. Some of them are so intricate that they require a teacher-specialist to be properly utilized. It seems reasonable for a teacher to master a wide variety of these techniques but not *all* of those needed to insure optimum learning for the many different pupil needs present in the classroom.

Role Conflicts for Pupils

The bureaucratic organization of schools also leads to role conflicts for pupils. There are at least two major dimensions of conflicts for pupils. The first concerns the failure of the role expectations for the pupil as defined by the social institution, the school, to correspond with the role expectations for the pupil as defined by other social systems to which the pupil belongs. The most influential of these other social systems and the ones which result in the most conflict with established school norms are the various peer groups which exist both in and outside of all schools and which influence the behavior patterns of all pupils. The second dimension concerns the conflict in the typical roles called for by the school for pupil behavior and those behavior patterns required as conditions for higher order learning activity concerned with inquiry, problem-solving, and meaning making. Each of these conflicts will now be considered in turn.[10]

10. Undoubtedly these same conflicts exist for teachers, and are especially a problem to beginning teachers. However, they probably exist to a lesser degree for teachers than pupils, since as pointed out previously, teachers may and do leave teaching when the conflict is too great. Pupils do not have that option, at least before age 16. The peer group expectations of the adult teacher also tend to be congruent with the traditional school pattern, since teachers who remain are socialized to the institutional norms. Again, this is not the case for pupils.

Peer Group Versus School Expectations

The often discussed and very important issue of relevancy in education revolves around the conflicting expectations of student controlled social systems, such as peer groups, and the institutional expectations of the school which are controlled largely by administrators and teachers who have been socialized to the institutional norms. The two social systems exist simultaneously but they are incompatible in many ways because each subscribes to a different set of values. They also exert influence upon one another but are not related in a superordinate-subordinate manner. An example of different values and resulting role expectations subscribed to by schools and student peer groups has been presented in an earlier section. It may be recalled that the example dealt with the differential expectations of pupil peer groups and the institution, the school, regarding male hair and female skirt lengths.

As a bureaucratically operated and stable institution the school is far less able to incorporate changing ethos and values in the culture than are student peer groups. The school is, rather, a perpetuator of a relatively stable body of knowledge and values. It is slow to respond to change. The social institution, the school, may be characterized as *traditional*. On the other hand, the social systems of peer groups for a particular generation of students are of much more recent origin. Unlike schools they do not have a well organized, rational, and efficient bureaucratic structure. They are, instead, organized more along the opposite dimension referred to by Weber as the "collegium" mode. They have not existed long enough to develop a tradition and do not exist long enough to become bureaucratized. Therefore, student peer groups and similar "temporary" social systems are more culturally malleable. They are much more sensitive to the changing ethos and values than are the schools. Consequently, the pupil peer group social system may be characterized as *emergent*.

The emergent nature of peer group social systems and the

traditional nature of the school and other stable social systems in society are the sources of the often mentioned "generation gap." As has been observed by many, the generation gap has always existed. However, it is unlikely that it has ever been as severe a problem as it is currently. And indeed it is likely to become even worse. The reason for this is simple. Never before in the history of man has the *rate* of change in knowledge, values, skills, and capabilities been as great as it is today. Twenty years ago a "cultural lag" of 10 or 15 years in the knowledge and values being taught by the schools did not matter very much. In the present world and near future a "cultural lag" of this magnitude perpetuated by the schools could be devastating. At the very least a lag of this size is guaranteed to create even greater problems of the social and personal relevance of schooling for students of all ages from kindergarten through graduate school.

As has been recognized by Ronald Lippitt and his colleagues, the role expectations of the peer group greatly affect the classroom learning activity (Lippitt, 1970; Schmuck, 1968; Lippitt, Fox, & Schaible, 1969; Chesler & Fox, 1966; Fox, Luszki, & Schmuck, 1966; Schmuck, Chesler, & Lippitt, 1966). This series of publications referenced in the preceding sentence deals specifically with the classroom learning and management problems which arise from pupil-peer group norms which conflict with the expectations of the school and the teacher. A series of teacher resource books concerning social relations and learning has been developed by this group. The series provides explicit procedures designed to assess the role expectations held by both pupils and teachers for their classroom learning activity toward the end of developing congruent expectations and need-dispositions. The most interesting aspect of the series is that both the teacher and pupils are taught how to assess the institutional expectations for the learner and teacher in their classroom. The objective is to change both the expectations of the institution (in this case the classroom) and the peer group expectations in a way that learning will be maximized. Needless to say, for such a program to work, the values, perceptions, and behavior patterns of both the teacher, who represents the institution, and the pupils must be modified. It is not a case of simply socializing pupils to accept the teacher's values and standards. The teacher or institutional expectations must also be modified to be more congruent with the pupil peer groups.

Programs of this type involving social relations as they affect learning activity would appear to be most promising in effecting needed changes in behavior patterns for both pupils and teachers, as well as changing the institutional role expectations of administrators and schools for pupils and teachers. Similar procedures can be used on a larger scale with entire schools and school districts. This topic is dealt with in Chapter 4. Such an approach is consistent with the Getzels model. It can, if effectively applied, help reduce many of the existing role conflicts which prevent institutional administrator-teacher and teacher-pupil cooperation needed to maximize learning.

Conditions for Learning Versus School Expectations

The implicit assumptions which govern the practice of education in the schools may be well suited to the operation and maintenance of the school as a bureaucratic institution, but they are very poorly suited to establishing and maintaining important conditions for the learning activity.

If allowed the opportunity, children are active, avid seekers of knowledge and creative explorers of their world. They are, by their very nature, learners and problem-solvers. It is known that the preschool years of the child provide opportunity for, and usually result in, great amounts of learning. The learning which is accomplished during both preschool and school years can be greatly accelerated and broadened through guidance in multiple and carefully constructed learning sequences with definite objectives set in an environment rich in diverse materials, ideas, people, content, and experience. The schools in our society are financially and technically in a position to provide this ideal environment needed for significant learning, yet they seldom do.

Many studies have shown that the schools typically tend to inhibit and destroy the attitudinal tendencies associated with the child's natural curiosity and tendency to learn through exploratory and creative interaction with his environment (Torrance, 1965, 1968a, 1968b; Strang, 1968; Williams, 1968c; Silberman, 1970). Even in the areas of reading, writing, and computation, where the schools have been most systematic in attempting to foster response patterns and skills instrumental to further learning, they have frequently failed because the child's will to learn has been inhibited. There is no better example of this than in reading. How can a child—or an adult, for that matter—be said to be a reader if he hates reading? Undoubtedly, many persons who once had the capability to become fluent readers did not become so because their intrinsic motivational commitment to the task was not cultivated or was destroyed. In the language of Chapter 2, the attitudinal tendencies of the pupil, which are prerequisite to the development of response patterns and skills required for effective reading, were inhibited.

This unfortunate condition of schools preventing learning is not apt to change through the addition of more and better instructional materials to classrooms, the development of individualized learning programs, the clear statement of educational objectives, or any other technological or curricular innovations. The simple but seldom recognized fact is that the implicit assumptions, which govern the operation of the school and determine the prevailing pupil and teacher roles within schools, generally have prevented and may continue to prevent these innovations from being used toward ends concerned with improved learning. New means have been and undoubtedly will be used toward old ends.

The existing business of education as practiced in countless schools is not primarily concerned with learning. It is concerned with providing for and maintaining institutions called "schools." It is assumed that, if schools are maintained, the education of the pupil will occur. This is a most doubtful assumption.

Think for a moment about the primary concerns of boards of education, administrators, and teachers. Consider the problems they discuss at their meetings, the issues that lead to teacher strikes, and the way the money is spent in school budgets. The practice of education is preoccupied with finances, transportation, classroom schedules, bond issues for new buildings, furniture, discipline, rules and regulations, selection of "new" instructional materials from the limited type and variety available, report cards, attendance forms, school lunches, vandalism, teacher benefits, building maintenance, etc. Almost never does one find a group of practicing educators who are concerned with the basic issues of learning and curriculum. Both our society and the schools tend to assume that responsibility for the education of children means providing the physical plant and affiliated support services needed to put teachers and children into rooms together with books, maps, audiovisual materials, and perhaps an innovative curriculum or two. The assumption is that this is *all* that is needed to insure learning. Present educational practice indicates that elaborate plans and expenditures are made in time, effort, and money for almost everything except the learning which is somehow supposed to automatically occur in the classroom, given a teacher, books, materials, and pupils. Note the order of these three. The learning activity of pupils is nearly always last in priority of concern in school practice.

Let us turn to a more direct consideration of conditions for learning and existing school expectations for pupils. In so far as the existing bureaucratic institutional role expectations call for the careful control and precise management of pupil activity and experience, school practice is biased toward the conditions favorable to some types of learning and unfavorable for other types. Gagné noted some time ago that there are different types of learning which require different conditions for facilitation. Specifically, it would appear that existing institutional role expectations for pupils favor Gagné's (1965a) first six types of learning but that the types of learning he once labeled "principle learning" and "problem-solving" may be discriminated against. The reason for this, as Gagné points out in a recent paper (1970a), is that the conditions for the simpler types of learning are external to the learner and may be established by the teacher or curriculum. However, the conditions for the higher order forms of learning are internal and *must* be largely established by the individual, although they can be facilitated by the school.

In his recent paper, Gagné (1970a) distinguishes three general types of learning, all of which are related to one another and all of which are essential to process education. His categories are "verbal information," "intellectual skills," and "cognitive strategies." They are roughly equivalent to the definitions for "knowledge," "response patterns," and "skills" given in the paradigm for process education in Chapter 2. Gagné suggests that knowledge (information, data, facts) and response patterns (particular common, effective, and efficient ways of processing and organizing data) are essential to the development of cognitive strategies, problem-solving, and inquiry. The school, curriculum, textbook, or teacher can and should specify, organize, and arrange for the pupil to learn this basic information and the useful and common response patterns for dealing with this and related information encountered from personal experience. For this type of learning the task of instruction is to arrange conditions external to the learner to guide him to apprehend specific information and perform specific operations. This is essentially a convergent approach and one that works well in teaching computation, decoding, and encoding of written symbols, spelling, typing, and grammatically correct sentence construction. However, "cognitive strategies"—or as they have been referred to in Chapter 2, "skills"—cannot be developed by such carefully contrived, externally controlled, convergent learning sequences. Rather they are developed slowly over a long period of time. The controls which guide this learning activity are largely internal to the learner. They require that he seek multiple and diverse experiences and problems and attempt to transfer, extend, and modify the information and response patterns in which he has been instructed for the business of inquiry and problem-solving. Gagné (1970a, p. 13) suggests that for a pupil to develop such competence there must be:

> . . .many opportunities, throughout the course of his instruction, for him to encounter, formulate, and solve problems of many varieties in his chosen field.

The control the school and teacher can exercise over this type of learning involves, first, the preparation of the pupil in the prerequisite information and response patterns and, second, the creation of a stimulating and rich learning environment where much opportunity exists for playful, exploratory, and productive thinking. Schools frequently provide the former but seldom the latter conditions. This comes about because the existing role expectations for pupils in most schools are unfavorable to establishing the learning environment necessary for the development of self-directed inquiry. Indeed, as Torrance (1968b) and many others have shown, the school experience typically leads to a decrease in creative and productive thinking in elementary school pupils. A recent study by Burns (1968) involving the analysis of instructional objectives and classroom tests has shown, as have many previous studies, that schools remain concerned primarily with transmitting verbal information and facts, secondarily with developing response patterns, and very infrequently with developing "cognitive strategies." In summary, conditions favorable to the development of cognitive strategies or skills do not usually exist in schools. Furthermore, when pupils exhibit these behaviors they are not rewarded or are even punished.

Now that some of the major points of conflict between process education and conventional educational practice have been identified, let us turn to the next question.

Values and Role Expectations Critical to Process Education

What are the *key* values and expectations which must be changed in the social institution, the school, to achieve goals of new process curricula and process education? This is a question which was asked earlier in the chapter. Before seeking the answer to this question it would be well to review the definitions for several key terms in the question. In Table 1 each of the following terms was defined as follows:

Value – An ideal, belief or custom of a culture toward which its members have an affective regard. The regard toward a particular value can be either positive or negative.

Expectations – The institutional rights, privileges, and obligations to which any incumbent of the role must adhere. The normative standard for the behavior of the individual within the institution. This standard reflects values of the culture.

Need-Dispositions – Individual tendencies to orient and act with respect to objects in certain manners and to expect certain consequences from these actions.

It should also be recalled that behavior patterns have been defined as:

> . . .identifiable and consistent acts of individuals operating in a social system and resulting from the interaction of the idiographic and nomothetic dimensions.

In the Getzels model, values of the culture are the base for institutional role expectations, which in turn are interpreted by individual personalities as guidelines for particular actions and consequences (need-dispositions) in the social system. In the framework of the model the most critical areas which must be attended to are the values which underlie the justifications and assumptions for process education. The school as an institution, and the individual principal, teacher, pupil or other role incumbent of the school, must be cognizant and accepting of the justifications and assumptions for process education. If this is the case, the values underlying the justifications and assumptions can be translated into institutional role expectations which will shape, select, and reward individual personality need-dispositions needed to produce behavior appropriate to process education.

Important, But Less Critical, Dimensions

There are other dimensions of important behaviors which may, in general, facilitate the use of existing process curricula and process education. These include the skills and competencies associated with instructional planning and management; specification of curriculum and learning objectives; selection and design of activities, materials, and tasks appropriate to objectives; use of a wide range of instructional methods, media, and technology; and the planning and evaluation of individual pupil learning sequences. These additional dimensions are very important but not unique to process education. Any type of educational practice can profit from teachers and schools highly competent in these instructional planning and management activities. However, efficiency in these activities does not insure the practice of process education.

The question to ask is, "Toward what end is all this new-found instructional technology, planning, and management to be used?" It hardly needs to be pointed out that it can be used toward the traditional aim of education: to produce an informed, passive, accepting individual who learns by being told what to study, how much to study, when to study, and toward what end. In fact, much of the new educational technology has been used to "prescribe" learning sequences for pupils. Such sequences are almost always characterized as being predominantly convergent toward goals predetermined for the learner, and as offering very limited options for individual pupil needs and preferences apart from the rate of learning a particular series of particular tasks in a particular order. Educational programs which consistently identify the problems to be solved, as well as the tasks to be completed, the method, and steps to solution, can be expected to teach the pupil that it is his responsibility *not* to seek and solve his own problems and create his own meaning. Rather, he learns that he is to follow in the footsteps of the curriculum developer or some other external authority to recreate meaning already made. He is taught that the answers are known, that problems have known solutions, and that his task is primarily one of converging toward those predetermined "truths." This is simply because such programs typically have little concern for, and are inadequate in, providing the conditions for the development of higher order learning activity involved in the development of "cognitive strategies," or what has been referred to as "skills" in Chapter 2. Such carefully designed and well structured learning sequences can be particularly well suited to transmitting to pupils certain needed information and response patterns. However, if learning materials and methods are used exclusively to this end they will only accomplish more efficiently what schools already can do, and not correct what schools presently fail to do.

This is not to say that recent advances in instructional

planning, management, and technology are in opposition to process education. They are not. They are simply means—not ends. They may be used toward ends consistent or inconsistent with values underlying process education.

Far more important than how skilled teachers and schools are in instructional management and technology is how they perceive the nature of *knowledge* and *learning*, the role of the *learner*, and the function of the *school*. It is in these areas that critical differences exist between those committed to process education and those committed to other types of educational practice.

Critical Dimensions

The assumptions and justifications for process education may be grouped around four logically related value positions. The value positions focus on the nature of *knowledge, learning,* the *learner*, and the function of the *school.* The opposing value positions are stated succinctly in Table 4. Each value position gives rise to a different and opposed set of institutional role expectations for the teacher and pupil. To the extent that teachers and pupils perceive and accept the institutional expectations as guidelines for their actions, the institutional expectations will be reflected in the behavior pattern outcomes. However, if the pupils and teachers fail to perceive, or reject the institutional expectations, role conflicts will occur, and the resulting behavior patterns will not clearly and consistently represent either the institutional role expectations or the individual personality need-dispositions.

In Tables 5 and 6 the four pairs of opposing value positions are more fully stated, and derivative institutional role expectations for both the pupil and teacher are enumerated.

It is best to think of the four opposing pairs of values as representing extremes on a continuum rather than as dichotomous classes. As noted earlier, individual teachers and pupils all exhibit

Table 4

Opposed Value Positions Underlying Process and Conventional Educational Practice[11]

Knowledge is	- absolute and true. ↓ + tentative and arbitrary.
Learning is	- unnatural and difficult. ↓ + natural and enjoyable.
The *Learner* is	- a humble and passive recipient of knowledge and experience. ↓ + an aggressive and active seeker of knowledge and experience.
The *School* is	- the authoritative transmitter of established values and knowledge. ↓ + the setting for emergence of values and knowledge through inquiry.

11. The value positions consistent with the justifications and assumptions of process education are indicated by a plus (+) sign. The opposed and prevailing value for current educational practice is indicated by a minus (-) sign. The desired direction of change for the implementation of process education is indicated by an arrow.

Table 5

Values and Roles Opposed to Process Education

Value Position Concerning Knowledge (-)

Existing knowledge is organized, stable, true, and authoritative. It has utility for the individual in that it creates meaning for him.

Institutional Role Expectations for the Teacher (-)[12]

Teacher: Rejects multiple interpretations of knowledge and experience. Adopts a rigid and dogmatic approach to knowledge and problem-solving through frequent appeal to his own and other authority and convention. Presents existing knowledge as absolute and true. Clings to old and established ideas and concepts and rejects or ignores conflicting assumptions, values, and information. Rejects the value and validity of pupil experience, observations, feelings, values, knowledge, and information. Inhibits and punishes student observations or conclusions different from his own, the textbook, or established authority. Inhibits divergent interpretations and thinking in pupils while striving to have all pupils converge toward the acquisition of specific factual information and conceptual relationships.

Institutional Role Expectations for the Pupil (-)

Pupil: Respects the teacher as an authoritative source of truth and absolute knowledge. Emulates the dogmatic approach of the teacher toward knowledge and problem-solving, e.g., "It's true because the book says so!" Is afraid to question even obvious points of confusion in the values, assumptions, observations, logic, and conclusions of the teacher or other authoritative sources of knowledge; but instead, when he encounters such logical contradictions, attributes their existence to his own intellectual inadequacy. Rejects his own experience, values, feelings, observations, and knowledge in favor of the authority of the teacher, text, or another source. Consistently strives to converge on the ideas, conceptualizations, and knowledge presented by the teacher, the text, or curriculum rather than engaging in making his own meaning.

12. It should be remembered that these are institutional role expectations for teachers and pupils derivative from the stated value positions. The statements represent not preferences or modes of operations of individuals, but rather the institutional expectations for how the pupil and teacher should behave.

Table 5

(Continued)

Value Position Concerning Learning (-)

Learning is an unnatural and difficult activity for which little intrinsic motivation exists. Learning must be made to occur through extrinsic rewards and punishment.

Institutional Role Expectation (-)

Teacher: Views learning as necessary but predominantly difficult and frequently unpleasant. Does not enjoy manipulating ideas and creating new and unusual interpretations of knowledge and experience. Views the memorization of information and the mastery of the conceptual structure of particular content areas as determined by convention or authority to be the primary goal of learning and to be, when finally achieved, a rewarding experience. Believes that most pupils have a propensity for play but little inclination for disciplined study. Seeks through the application of extrinsic rewards and punishments to force the pupil to memorize critical information and procedures essential to the conventional or authoritative structure of concepts within disciplines. Seeks to identify the specific information and procedures which pupils fail to memorize or comprehend in order to drill them and help them master specific concepts, knowledge, and response patterns.

Pupil: Views the teacher as a benevolent authority figure who is trying to assist him in accomplishing a difficult task. Recognizes and accepts the need to be forced to "behave," to attend, and to study, in order to memorize and comprehend the wisdom available from the teacher, the text, and other authoritative sources. Does not usually enjoy learning but submits himself to the regime of disciplined study which is prescribed by the teacher. Derives his primary pleasure *not* from the learning activity itself but from the rewards given by the teacher when he performs in accordance to the teacher's wishes.

Table 5

(Continued)

Value Position Concerning the Learner (-)

It is the primary function of the learner to master the meanings central to the authoritative structure of the disciplines. The learner is incapable of and should be discouraged from taking license in reorganizing information and knowledge presented by the teacher, textbook or curriculum.

Institutional Role Expectation (-)

Teacher: Recognizes that he himself, as a learner, is humble before the accumulated wisdom of the culture, tradition, and scholarly authority. Strives to master the body of information and relationship central to some discipline(s) in order that he may become an effective transmitter of this authoritative knowledge. Does not, himself, take license in speculating about other values, assumptions, logic, information and, consequently, very different organizations and interpretations of the body of knowledge within his chosen content area or discipline. Recognizes his inadequacy at formulating knowledge and making meaning. Rather, he seeks to learn and improve his mind by studying the products of great minds and conventional wisdom. Consequently as a teacher he expects his pupils to be humble and awed before his wisdom and authority which he has derived from his study of authoritative sources. Expects that pupils should seek to learn the knowledge which he will present to them. Discounts their competence to question the values, assumptions, logic, or organization of the knowledge presented. His objectives for instruction are definite and consistent in that he expects pupils to value, feel, and think about the content presented in precisely the way he does. Expects pupils to arrive at their knowledge through his direct mediation. Discourages direct pupil-pupil interaction and exchange of ideas as it tends to generate diverse views and prevent congruence toward the established and predominant value, feeling and knowledge patterns he seeks to establish in all pupils. Rewards pupils who strive to learn what he, the teacher, values, how he feels, and what he thinks and who exhibit proficiency in converging toward these preferred patterns on examinations and assignments. Inhibits and punishes students who question his authority, seek other viewpoints, and offer divergent interpretations of the knowledge presented.

Table 5

(Continued)

Pupil:	Emulates the learning behavior of the teacher. Discounts his own and his peers' experience and competence in building knowledge and making meaning. Is humble before the authoritative knowledge of the teacher. Seeks to please the teacher and educate himself by determining the values, feelings, and thinking of the teacher relative to the knowledge presented and by adopting those preferred patterns. Rejects the leadership of other pupils in the class relative to the learning activity and seeks the teacher's direction. Avoids direct interaction with peers in relation to establishing information or interpretations different from those presented by the teacher. Works with other pupils only on specific tasks specified and mediated by the teacher.

Table 5

(Continued)

Value Position Concerning the School (-)

The school should be organized efficiently and authoritatively toward the primary end of transmitting to the learner a specified portion of the established information, knowledge, and values of the society. A secondary end concerns the facilitation of particular response patterns and instrumental skills needed to master the information and knowledge presented (*i.e.*, reading, writing, and arithmetic).

Institutional Role Expectation (-)

Teacher: Is primarily a passive and accepting implementer of the knowledge, skills, and response patterns selected for emphasis by the curriculum developer, the curriculum guide, or the textbook. Is also a passive and accepting implementer of the conditions, rules, regulations, and arrangements which are established for classroom instructional activity and school management. Has and seeks no major role in establishing policy relative to the content or management of instruction. Views as his client the institution and its authoritative representatives including the principal, curriculum coordinators, and administrative-clerical personnel. Views as his major responsibility the impartial execution of institutional, instructional, and management preference, policy, and procedure. Expects pupils to comply with institutional values, preferences, policies, and procedures concerning the content of instruction and the method of the learning activity. "Disciplines" pupils who deviate from the acceptable institutional patterns. Drills pupils in prescribed response patterns and information to produce mean performance acceptable within the institutional standards.

Pupil: Is a passive and accepting subject who carries out the activities prescribed by the school through the teacher in accordance with established policy. Pupils are expected to vary in both their ability and inclination to perform the expected tasks. The distribution of competence in performance may be expected to follow the normal distribution of random numbers. Some pupils may be expected to excel, some to fail, and most to exhibit mediocre task commitment and performance. The pupil has and seeks no major responsibility in establishing the content, sequence, purpose or conditions for his classroom learning activity.

Table 6

Values and Roles Critical to Process Education

Value Position Concerning Knowledge (+)[13]

Existing knowledge is organized but tentative, arbitrary, rapidly changing, and expanding. It has utility for the individual only in so far as it can be adapted to his experience to help him create his own meaning.

Role Expectation (+)

Teacher: Seeks multiple and divergent interpretations of knowledge and experience. Avoids a didactic, rigid approach to knowledge and problem-solving through appeal to his own or other authority. Operates in a dialectical manner in presenting existing knowledge. Actively seeks new information for reformulation of old ideas to changing conditions. Recognizes the value, validity, and wealth of knowledge which pupils have already acquired through their personal experience. Seeks to use pupil knowledge and expertise in teaching. Seeks and encourages diverse, but rational, student observations, assumptions, and conclusions different from his own, the textbook or other authoritative sources. Expects, encourages, and accepts different values and feelings to be aroused and expressed by pupils in the learning activity. Encourages individual pupils to seek and organize their own preferred interpretations and patterns from among the multiple information sources and views presented.

Pupil: Respects the teacher as a leader skilled in the comprehension and manipulation of a wide array of experience and information into multiple conceptualizations for multiple purposes. Emulates the teacher's behavior with respect to his open and dialectic approach to knowledge. Questions the values, assumptions, observations, and conclusions of authoritative sources of knowledge. Recognizes the utility of information and knowledge in organizing experience and solving problems. Seeks to select from, modify, and reformulate the multiple ideas and conclusions presented by the teacher and the curriculum to formulate his own meanings consistent with his own observations and experiences.

13. It should be remembered that these are institutional role expectations for teachers and pupils derivative from the stated value positions. The statements represent not preferences or modes of operations of individuals, but rather the institutional expectation for how the pupil and teacher should behave.

Table 6

(Continued)

Value Position Concerning Learning (+)

Learning is a natural and creative activity motivated by an intrinsic and primary need to organize and create meaning from experience.

Role Expectation (+)

Teacher: Views learning as exciting and stimulating. Enjoys creating new and unusual interpretations based on his own observations which conflict with convention and authority. Views the creation of ideas, relationships, and feelings as the primary goal of learning. Recognizes the value of authoritative information and knowledge as being useful in formulating particular logical perceptions and interpretations. Is aware that pupils have a natural propensity for learning; that they are curious; that they constantly engage in imaginative and exploratory activity. Seeks ways to channel and further stimulate this natural desire to learn through providing the pupils with a rich and varied set of ideas, materials, and topics in relation to the content of his teaching. Seeks through given instructional situations to involve and develop individual pupil interest and commitment to any one of multiple tasks or activities. Recognizes the need for and prescribes drill in instructional sequences designed to develop memorization of particular information such as spelling or other frequently used knowledge and highly useful response patterns. However, this does not become the end to his instruction or the predominant means.

Pupil: Views the teacher as a competent, knowledgeable individual who provides many new and interesting insights, ideas, and experiences. Pursues facts and information with a zeal about topics and problems which he encounters in the classroom materials and activities. Organizes the information he gleans from his own experience, the teacher, other pupils and authoritative sources into inferences and hypotheses which he can subsequently test and match to additional experience and different interpretations by others. Derives his primary pleasure from the variety and scope of the learning activity itself as he exchanges ideas with other pupils and the teacher and discovers innumerable fascinating facts and logical paradoxes. Submits himself to drill in response patterns because he feels it is essential to his acquisition and use of information and because he enjoys memorizing large amounts of information of interest to him.

Table 6

(Continued)

Value Position Concerning the Learner (+)

A primary function of the learner is to create meaning from information, knowledge, and experience encountered in his schooling. The pupil must be encouraged and assisted in freely seeking, finding, and solving problems toward building knowledge.

Institutional Role Expectation (+)

Teacher: Recognizes that he himself as a learner is capable of noting conflicting and unaccounted-for values, assumptions, and information in the existing authoritative structure of knowledge in various disciplines. Strives to master information, concepts, and relationships which form the body of knowledge in some discipline(s) out of interest, curiosity, and the desire to be informed, experienced, and better equipped to make meaning. Seeks and enjoys finding logical inconsistencies, conflicting assumptions, values, and information between organized knowledge in an area of a discipline and his own experience and other existing organizations of that same knowledge. Enjoys and frequently engages in speculative thinking, hypothesis formation, inference, and theory building. Constantly attempts to explain his observed experiences and newly encountered information in terms of the existing structure of knowledge he has acquired. Has great respect for the utility of established conceptualizations and relationships in the disciplines for organizing experience, but also knows that they bias perception and cognition. He therefore frequently bends or accommodates the constructs of "established" knowledge to better suit his own values, needs, experience and problems. Consequently as a teacher he expects his pupils to be skeptical and questioning of both his authority and the authority of the discipline(s) with respect to the body of knowledge central to the discipline(s). He further expects and encourages the pupils to question the values, assumptions, information, logic, and organization of the knowledge presented; to seek alternate interpretations based on their own experiences, the experiences of their peers and additional information and knowledge from other sources; to consider their own feelings, observations, and judgments. His objectives are definite with respect to establishing pupil proficiency in critical attitudinal and behavioral tendencies, response patterns, and skills essential to inquiry in the discipline(s). Expects and strives to teach all pupils

Table 6

(Continued)

to develop the same vocabulary and other essential and conventional response patterns such as rules for computation, language, notation, etc., which are needed to communicate and create knowledge. Expects pupils to value, feel, and think about the content presented in ways different from himself, other pupils, the curriculum developer, or textbook author. Expects and encourages as a major learning activity direct pupil-pupil interaction without mediation through him. Recognizes that such interaction produces many new observations, ideas, and relationships which insure the existence of multiple, diverse interpretations differing in both utility and rationality. Rewards pupils who strive to acquire information and knowledge, who seek and generate divergent interpretations, and who organize this information into personal preferred logical meanings relevant to their own experience, capabilities, and needs.

Pupil: Emulates the learning behavior of the teacher. Seeks and uses his own direct experience and the experience of his peers in adapting existing knowledge encountered in the classroom to his own needs and interests, in making his own meaning. Rejects the leadership of the teacher as the final authority about knowledge in the classroom. Views the teacher as a talented and helpful resource person skilled in providing needed information, assistance, and direction in solving problems and capable of stimulating much interest and activity through a wealth of ideas, materials, and topics relative to classroom activity. Seeks the leadership and resources of other pupils as well as the teacher in learning activity. Builds multiple and preferred meanings and interpretations from the information, knowledge, and experience encountered in the classroom. Continually seeks to extend, apply, and modify these meanings both within and without the classroom.

Table 6

(Continued)

Value Position Concerning the School (+)

The school should be flexibly and practically organized toward the primary end of fostering a wide range of attitudinal and behavioral tendencies and capabilities, response patterns, and skills which underlie the process of meaning making and self-initiated and -directed learning. A secondary end is the transmission of some of a wide variety of values, information, and knowledge, which while tentative and arbitrary are particularly useful for making meaning in the present world and serve as appropriate content to be explored and processed.

Institutional Role Expectation (+)

Teacher: Is an active selector, organizer, and designer of content, knowledge, response patterns, methods, and materials. He is a leader in the design of the conditions and arrangements which govern the classroom learning activity he supervises. Plays an important and major role in establishing institutional policy relative to the objectives, content, methods, and management of instruction. Views as his client the pupil. His major responsibility is fostering the attitudinal tendencies which underlie the "will to learn"; the provision of a learning environment rich in ideas, topics, and materials; and stimulating and guiding independent pupil learning. Expects pupils to be directly involved in the establishment and maintenance of the normative standards and conditions which govern the learning activity in the classroom and school. Expects pupils to identify their own learning goals, patterns, and routes within the broad outlines prescribed by himself and the institution. Drills pupils in standard information, instrumental skills, or response patterns as a necessary condition for establishing individual pupil competence prerequisite to the performance of higher order learning activity such as problem-solving or inquiry.

Pupil: Is an active co-learner with the teacher. Looks to the teacher for leadership but is actively involved in establishing the policy and conditions which govern his classroom learning activity. Is responsible for selecting many of his own problems, topics, and patterns of inquiry from among a rich variety of materials and experiences. Pupils are expected to have different needs and talents and consequently to exhibit different interest and performance profiles across a wide array of tasks and topics. Exhibits leadership in his areas of interest, competence, and excellence for other pupils during the classroom learning activity. Accepts and seeks leadership from other pupils more competent than himself in certain topics and tasks.

some instances of each type of behavior expected by the opposing role patterns, and all schools are somewhat ambivalent in orientation toward the opposing value positions. However, it is clear that particular schools and educational agencies tend to be characterized by one or the other extreme and consequently tend to demand one or the other role for teachers and pupils.

The set of values and expectations which characterize process education represent common, long-sought and rational ideals for education. It is also clear that the opposing set of values and expectations represents more closely and accurately the present status of educational practice. Consequently, the question, "In what direction must existing values and expectations be changed to insure the desired behavior pattern outcomes for pupils and teachers for process education?" can now be answered. Obviously, the value positions and institutional role expectations must be moved along the continuum from their present position toward the ideal positions and expectations stated for process education. The arrows in Table 4 indicate the necessary direction of change.

It would appear from the previous consideration of existing role conflicts that the need-dispositions of both pupils and teachers are more inclined toward the values and role expectations which underlie process education than those opposing values which underlie current educational practice. It is evident from many empirical studies that many beginning teachers have need-dispositions consistent with the expectations for process education. It is also evident that many of these individuals leave when the conflict between their need-dispositions and the usual institutional expectations becomes too severe. There is additional evidence that many of those teachers who remain in teaching are still unhappy and troubled by institutional expectations which conflict with their ideals—which may be repressed but not forgotten.

Perhaps the last question, "How can the critical values, expectations, and need-dispositions once identified be changed to promote behavior pattern outcomes desired as goals for process education?" can best be answered through a consideration of means to modify the present bureaucratic institutional structure of schools and classrooms through multiple temporary social systems designed to change existing norms and role expectations of educational institutions. However, this is a topic of a later chapter.

Characteristic Behavior Patterns

The value positions and their derivative role expectations for teachers and pupils characterize and define the behavior patterns one would expect to see in operation in classrooms located in schools having a commitment toward either extreme on the four continua. Conversely, and more important, the behavior patterns exhibited by pupils, teachers, and other role incumbents in the school reflect the prevailing institutional values and role expectations not as they are mouthed as slogans but as they exist operationally.

Many of the behavior patterns appropriate to the goals of process education have been operationally stated in *Signs of Good Teaching* and "Indicators of Quality" (Vincent, 1967, 1969) published by the Institute of Administrative Research, Teachers College, Columbia University. Based upon a great deal of research and careful thought, William S. Vincent and the other scholars who developed *Signs of Good Teaching* identified four areas, or categories, of school quality. Each category consists of observed characteristics which are indicators of the quality of teaching and learning within the classroom. In the earlier language of this chapter, the *Indicators of Quality* are pupil and teacher behavior patterns which are stated in observable and operational terms. The four categories basic to the system are reproduced in Table 7. The 40 observational items which comprise those four categories may

Table 7

Categories from Indicators of Quality[14]

Category	*Description*
Individualization	Procedures for taking account of the fact that individuals differ in their rate and manner of cognitive development (the recall or recognition of knowledge and the development of intellectual abilities and skills), and that every child is different from every other child in background, requirements, goals, capacities, learning styles, and in most other respects.
Interpersonal Regard	General behavior reflecting warmth, kindness, respect, consideration, empathy among pupils and between teachers and pupils.
Creativity	Opportunities for pupil expression that take account of the fact that there are many methods for the expression of intelligence, many talents employed in human creativeness, and much divergence of thinking and difference of opinion in intellectual pioneering.
Group Activity	Procedures for taking account of the fact that pupils are members of groups and must be equipped to be successful members of adult groups, and that group interaction is an important instrument in learning.

14. These categories and their descriptions are taken from Vincent, W.S. (Ed.) *Signs of good teaching.* New York: Columbia University, Teachers College, Institute of Administrative Research, pp. 5-6. The categories are closely related to the four pairs of value positions represented in Table 4. However, the items in each category cut across the derivative pupil and teacher role expectations for each value position. The derivative role expectations are presented in Tables 5 and 6.

be found in *Signs of Good Teaching* (Vincent, 1969) and the *Indicators of Quality, Orientation Manual* (1968). The manual provides positive and negative statements of each of the 40 behavior pattern items, as well as a clear example of each type.

The four categories do not correspond directly to the four value positions for process education which have been stated in this chapter. However, the categories and their operational indicators are directly related to the derivative role expectations stated for each of the four pairs of value positions. It may be recalled that each of the pairs of value positions and their derivative expectations are extremes along four continua. Similarly, the operational statements or signs for observing the quality of classroom teaching-learning activity are designed to classify observable behavior patterns as being closer to one or the other end of a continuum where the extremes are represented by poor versus quality educational practice. Collectively the *Indicators of Quality* items within their four categories define behavior patterns appropriate and inappropriate to process education. It is apparent from direct observation that virtually every one of the 40 operationally stated behavior patterns, which are used to observe teachers, pupils, and teacher-pupil interaction in the *Indicators of Quality* observation system (*Indicators of Quality, Observer Instrument,* 1968), correspond directly to one or more of the derivative role expectations for pupils and teachers which have been stated in Tables 5 and 6. Furthermore, each of the 40 items used in the classroom observation instrument has a polar nature. Therefore, each item indicates toward which end of the continuum the observed behavior pattern falls—that is, toward the expectation for process education or the conflicting expectation opposed to process education.

Although virtually every one of the 40 items in the *Indicators of Quality* classroom observation instrument is appropriate to one or more of the stated pupil and teacher role expectations for process education, there are some process expectations for which no items exist.

In its present form the *Indicators of Quality* instrument is well suited to providing information concerning whether the prevailing behavior patterns in a school are congruent with or opposed to the practice of process education. Additional items could be easily developed to match role expectations not currently tapped in the 40 items which now make up the instrument. It should be a relatively simple task to translate any of the particular pupil or teacher role expectations which have been stated into operational and observable behavior pattern items. These could be assembled into other classroom observation scales similar in design and construction to the *Indicators of Quality.* Such an effort has much to recommend it, given the proven and excellent reliability of the *Indicators of Quality* instrument (Vincent & Casey, 1968; Casey, 1969).

The appropriateness of the *Indicators of Quality* instrument to determine the existing behavior patterns in schools and, consequently, to determine their ability to practice process education is not surprising. As Vincent (1967, p. 2) comments, "Virtually all research on learning is related to one or another of these four categories of teaching-learning procedure." Furthermore, the individual items within the instrument have been developed to reflect behavior patterns studied by many researchers and known empirically to be important conditions for learning (Vincent, 1967, 1970). Unlike most other existing classroom observation scales the *Indicators of Quality* scales were from the beginning designed to assess teacher roles, pupil roles and their interaction in the classroom learning activity (Vincent, 1970). A subsequent analysis of the instrument has shown that the majority of the items are concerned with assessing the classroom role perceptions and interaction/communication of teachers and pupils (Vincent, 1969, p. 86). It is apparent that the instrument is most appropriate for use within the conceptual framework of the Getzels model.

The close correspondence of the *Indicators of Quality* instrument's observational items to the role expectations for pupils and teachers under the practice of process versus traditional education helps confirm the previously stated notion that many existing ideals for education are largely process goals. Such goals have been long stated and sought but infrequently attained in educational practice. Work with the *Indicators of Quality* scale in 122 school districts from 1968 to 1970 has shown that pupils are still far from assuming the active learning role in the classroom called for by both the philosophy of process education and the conditions known empirically to be essential to self-directed learning, inquiry, and other activities of meaning making (Vincent, 1970, pp. 4-5).

Summary

This chapter consists of three parts. In the first part the roles of the pupil and teacher are defined and described within the context of the Getzels model for social systems. The relationships between cultural ethos and values, institutional roles and expectations, and individuals and need-dispositions are defined and discussed as they relate to behavior pattern outcomes of pupils and teachers. The Getzels model is presented as a conceptual framework with which to approach the problem of implementing the practice of process education. Five questions concerning conflicts between goals of process education and conventional educational practice are raised. The questions concern whether or not such conflicts exist, the points of the conflicts, key values and expectations which must be changed to resolve the conflicts, the direction in which the value and expectations must change and the means to implement the desired change. The first portion of the chapter provides the theoretical framework and conceptual tools to deal with the five questions. The remainder of the chapter seeks to answer the first four questions.

It is noted that the first question concerning the existence of conflicts in values and role expectations inhibitory to process education has been previously answered in Chapter 1. The second part of this chapter is directed toward answering question two, concerning the points of conflict between process education and conventional educational practice. Incongruency is noted and discussed between values, aims, and assumptions of process education and prevailing educational practice. Existing role conflicts for pupils and teachers are considered as another factor inhibitory to the practice of process education. The locus of role conflicts is discussed in relation to the organization and management of the school as a bureaucratic institution. The problem of personality-role conflicts for teachers is examined and discussed in the framework of the Getzels model. The problem of institutional press toward the selection and socialization of teachers to roles more appropriate for bureaucratic school management than to learning and instruction is considered. The multiple nature of the teacher's role is noted. Two points of role conflict for pupils within the social institution, the school, are identified and discussed. The first concerns the conflict between the institutional role expectation of the school and the peer group role expectation. The second concerns the conflict between school institutional role expectations and the conditions required for learning.

The third part of this chapter deals with questions three and four, which concern the identification of the key values and related role expectations for process education, their relationship to prevailing and traditional educational values and pupil-teacher role expectations, and the direction in which change must occur if the practice of process education is to be implemented. Four value positions concerning *knowledge, learning,* the *learner,* and the *school* are derived from the assumptions and justifications stated for process education in Chapter 2. Four corresponding, but diametrically opposed, value positions concerning these same topics are stated as the values underlying traditional and most current educational practice. Derivative role expectations for both pupils and teachers are stated for each of the four pairs of opposing value positions. One set of role expectations defines the ideal for process education within each of the value positions. The other and opposing set of expectations defines the pupil and teacher role at the opposite end of the continuum. It is suggested that current educational practice generally calls for pupil and teacher roles consistent with the negative ends of the four continua relative to the positive and ideal end for process education. It is noted that the implementation of process education requires changing the values and role expectations of educational agencies along each of the four continua toward the ideal process education aim.

The derivation of specific and observable behavior patterns from the positive and negative pupil and teacher role expectations is discussed. The congruence between the operationally defined behavior pattern items of the classroom observation scale, *Indicators of Quality,* and specific pupil and teacher role expectations derived from the four value positions is examined.

Thus, the first four of the five questions raised are answered. The fifth question, dealing with means to implement change in institutional values and role expectations toward the ideals for process education, is the subject of the next chapter.

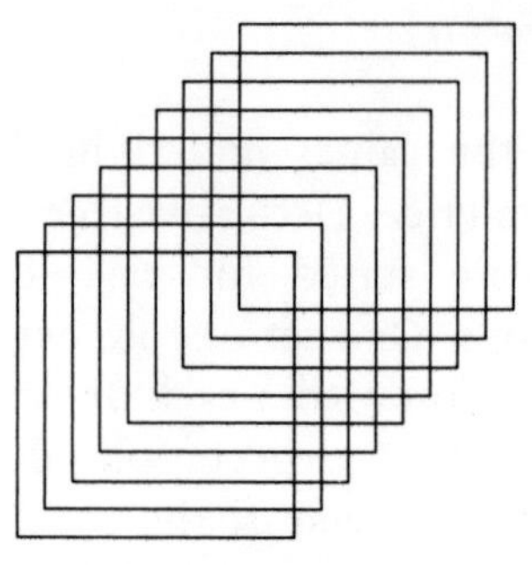

CHAPTER 4

IMPLEMENTING PROCESS EDUCATION

Before turning to the topic of this chapter it will be helpful to briefly review the major points of the first three chapters as they relate to implementation of process education. Chapter 1 concludes with the statement that there are currently available many excellent curriculum and instructional vehicles capable of facilitating the practice of process education. It is also pointed out that these programs have generally had little impact in changing current school practice. It is further stated that the primary problem involved in the promotion of process education is one of implementing existing knowledge and programs.

Chapter 2 defines the construct of process education and develops both a conceptual framework and language for dealing with the topic. The definitions, assumptions, justifications, paradigm, and rationale provided serve three functions. First, they explicate the philosophy which process education seeks to implement. Second, they provide a logical analysis of the need which exists in the modern world for the implementation of educational practice committed to this philosophy. Third, they provide insight into the knowledge base upon which the concept of process education is built.

The third chapter seeks to identify points of conflict between the philosophy, values, and roles of process education and prevailing educational practice. These conflicts are seen as preventing the implementation of process education. The school is examined as a social system consisting of an institution with roles and expectations filled by individual personalities with need-dispositions. The assumptions and justifications of process education are grouped into four basic and positive value positions which concern the nature of *knowledge, learning,* the *learner,* and the function of the *school.* Four opposing and negative value positions which characterize much current educational practice are also stated. Derivative pupil and teacher role expectations are formulated for each of the four pairs of opposing value positions. It is suggested that the implementation of process education requires changing the prevailing institutional values and their derivative teacher and pupil role expectations toward the process education end of the four value position continua. Chapter 3 concludes with a question concerning the means to implement such a change in the institutional roles of pupils and teachers.

In summary, it is assumed that there now exists knowledge in the form of curriculum and instructional vehicles appropriate for implementing educational practice consistent with the philosophy of process education. It is further assumed that by themselves these vehicles have had and will continue to have little chance to change educational practice in the direction of process education unless they are viewed as *means* to changing pupil and teacher roles and not simply as ends in themselves or *things* to be adopted. The present chapter is concerned with the question of how process education can be implemented within these assumptions. Philosophical, theoretical, empirical, and practical knowledge about change strategies and their appropriateness to the task of implementing process education is considered.

An important question concerns *what* is to be implemented. Is it particular curricula or sets of instructional materials? No, it is not. Rather, it is the new role expectations and value positions for process education described in Table 6 in Chapter 3. The many excellent existing curriculum and instructional vehicles, while seen as being justified in their own right as programs to be adopted by schools, are viewed as having a larger purpose. They provide the focus and part of the means to implement change in schools toward the goals of process education.

Changing Social Systems

Implementing process education is primarily a task of bringing about change in the schools. Both the nature and direction of the change have been stated in Chapter 3. Fortunately, the process of implementing change in human social systems has been a topic of much attention and study in the past few years. Recently Havelock (1969) identified, studied, and organized more than 4,000 empirical studies, theoretical writings and case studies which deal with the implementation of change in human social systems toward the dissemination and utilization of knowledge for improved institutional practice. Havelock's *Planning for Innovation Through Dissemination and Utilization of Knowledge* is an exceptionally complete compilation and interpretative organization of the theoretical and practical knowledge of the process of implementing change in social systems. His derivative *A Guide to Innovation in Education* (1970) is a very comprehensive and detailed set of procedures for implementing change in school practice. In addition, unlike most other sets of change procedures for education, it is firmly rooted in the exhaustive theoretical and empirical base provided by the literature review in the former report. Collectively, these two volumes tell much of what is known about how to implement changes in institutions and individuals in social systems. Needless to say, they contain information concerning the implementation of institutional role expectations critical to the practice of process education. Much attention will be paid to the findings of Havelock and his colleagues throughout the remainder of this and the next chapter. The reader interested in pursuing the topic of implementation of educational innovations is well advised to study the two Havelock volumes. The purpose in this chapter is to speak to those implementation issues which specifically concern process education as an innovation.

Before considering specific aspects of implementation procedures it is important to examine the meaning of the term, some basic philosophical and methodological considerations as well as a conceptualization of how those relatively stable, change-resisting bureaucratic social institutions, the schools, may be changed through multiple temporary social systems.

An Operational Definition for Implementation

Implementation as generally used simply means changing the practice of some social institution to incorporate some new knowledge, product, procedure, value, etc., toward improved service to its clients. In the words of Chin and Benne (1969, p. 33) implementation can be defined as "planned change" toward the "conscious utilization and application of knowledge as an instrument or tool for modifying patterns and institutions of practice."

In this chapter implementation of process education is defined as changing existing school practice toward those value positions and derivative pupil and teacher role expectations stated in Table 6 and away from those opposed value positions and role expectations stated in Table 5 (see Chapter 3). Furthermore, it is assumed that the change implemented in institutional value positions and role expectations toward the practice of process education can be observed and measured in the behavior patterns exhibited by pupils and teachers over periods of days, weeks, and years. This can be done in part by the existing observational instrument, *Indicators of Quality,* and the 40 signs of good teaching developed by Vincent *et al.* and discussed in Chapter 3. It is also possible to identify and develop other procedures to determine consistent behavior patterns and their convergence toward or deviation from the stated role expectations for process education.

Differing Philosophies Underlying Change Strategies

In reviewing procedures for effecting change in human systems, Robert Chin and Kenneth D. Benne developed three general categories of change strategies. They label these the empirical-rational, the normative-reeducative, and the power-coercive. Each represents a different philosophical position, is based upon differing assumptions, and is supportive of different tactics for changing social systems. An important question concerns whether or not one of these generic categories is particularly congruent with the values and ideals of process education. If so, one would expect the tactics suggested and endorsed by the philosophical position to consist of implementation means in accord with goals or ends of process education. Let us now examine each of the three generic categories to determine their general assumptions, tactics, characteristics, limits, and congruence with the goals of process education.

Empirical-Rational Strategies

Empirical-rational strategies assume that men are first and foremost rational. Men are also assumed to be motivated primarily by their self-interest. The implementation of a new practice, product, or knowledge is assumed to occur, provided (1) the innovation can be rationally justified to the group whose practice is to be changed and (2) the benefit of the innovation to the group can be demonstrated. The source of power in empirical-rational strategies is knowledge or "know-how" and the individuals who have and can demonstrate the utility of that knowledge. Barriers to change in the form of values, beliefs, attitudes, personality need-dispositions, and organizational climates which conflict with the goals and means of the innovation are ignored in empirical-rational strategies. Such interpersonal and institutional strife is seen as being no obstacle, provided that both the rationality and utility of the innovation can be demonstrated to the individuals involved.

Examples of rational-empirical strategies are common in agricultural settings where the innovation is, for instance, a new hybrid corn for livestock feed that can be demonstrated to be higher in both protein content and in crop yield per acre. Empirical-rational strategies appear to work well when the innovation is basically a "thing" or a specific and well defined technique where performance measures are easily recognizable, visible, and concrete (such as the increased nutritive value of the corn, the increased bushels per acre in yield, and the resulting increased dollars in profit to the farmer-livestock producer).

Chin and Benne point out (1969, p. 36) that empirical-rational strategies do not generally work well unless there is a public readiness for accepting the innovation. That is, the values, attitudes, and belief patterns of the group which is to receive the innovation must be supportive and not opposed to the change. Thus the agricultural innovations of the United States which can be demonstrated to be just as rational and valuable to other nations are often slow to be implemented by those other nations, not simply because of a less well developed technology and lack of resources but because of traditional socio-cultural values and norms which prevent changing from old to new practices. Resources and technology are not sufficient to create change in human systems when prevailing ethos and values prohibit the change.

Empirical-rational strategies do not seem particularly well suited to implement the practice of process education. This becomes clear from Chapter 3, where it is shown that prevailing educational practices, as expressed in the institutional role expectations of schools for pupils and teachers, are generally opposed to the goals and values of process education. The many points of conflict discussed are apt to act as barriers to change toward the implementation of new roles and procedures appropriate to process education. Empirical-rational strategies ignore these barriers to change.

However, empirical-rational strategies have been widely used in educational innovation in recent years. Where the goals of the innovation have been anticipated and supported by public sentiment this approach has worked well. For example, following the orbiting of Sputnik on October 4, 1957, by the U.S.S.R., a powerful sentiment was created in the U.S. for emphasis upon science education. This sentiment resulted in a readiness for expenditures for curriculum development and teacher education at both the federal and local levels. Empirical-rational strategies were designed, proposed, and heavily funded for the development of massive curriculum projects, as well as preservice and inservice teacher education programs sponsored largely by the National Science Foundation. It is doubtful that these innovative changes in the practice of curriculum development and teacher education could have occurred without the necessary public readiness, no matter how rational and useful the outcomes could have been demonstrated to be.

More recently empirical-rational strategies have been applied to attempt to implement into school practice the many curricula and educational products developed in the sixties under the impetus of a United States population spooked by Sputnik. As Chin and Benne (1969, p. 40) point out, federally supported research and development centers and regional laboratories have frequently used empirical-rational strategies. They usually select a carefully developed and well researched curriculum or instructional product and seek to install it into actual school settings.

Attention is usually directed toward the question of whether or not the innovation will accomplish certain changes in measured pupil performance once it is installed. Chin and Benne point out that questions of *how* to get the educational innovation properly installed and used are usually ignored. Evaluative measures and procedures other than psychometric and concept mastery tests for pupils are usually lacking. Under such an evaluative procedure when, as frequently happens, the innovation fails to be widely disseminated and implemented, little is known about why the failure occurred. Likewise, when the innovation is successfully implemented, little is known about the reasons for success.

Generally it would seem the empirical-rational approach to change in education can be expected to work when that which is to be implemented is a more or less concrete product or set of techniques which does not call for a drastic change in the prevailing value orientation of the school or the institutional role expectations of the teacher and the pupil. An example would be the implementation of an automated or individualized learning sequence in a school where the new learning program simply assumes the authoritative transfer of the usual content, knowledge, and values to the pupil in the place of the similar and typical function of the textbook and teacher. More simply, the less innovative the innovation, the more likely it will be successfully implemented by empirical-rational means. But even relatively "non-innovative" educational innovations are not apt to be widely disseminated and installed by empirical-rational strategies. As pointed out earlier, such strategies assume that establishing the merit, utility, and worth of the innovation insures its implementation. From his review of many empirical findings, Miles (1967d, p. 635) concludes, "Educational innovations are almost never installed on their merits." He suggests the critical factors are characteristics of the individuals and groups which comprise the client system which is to be changed and the change agency which is to bring about the change.

As attempts have been and are being made to use the massive amounts of new technical knowledge and programs recently developed in education in schools, the problem has shifted to (Chin & Benne, 1969, p. 33):

> . . .dealing with the resistances, anxieties, threats to morale, conflicts, disrupted interpersonal communications and so on, which prospective changes in patterns of practice evoke in the people affected by change.

Thus implementation of even relatively "non-innovative" innovations increasingly demands a knowledge of how change occurs in individual and institutional behavior in social systems. The old "thing technology" used widely in the sixties to develop many new instructional and curricular programs is inadequate to implement the very products it generated. A new "people technology" which recognizes the complexity of human social systems and their barriers to change and which develops knowledge of how to overcome those barriers is needed to open the classroom door to those curricular and instructional innovations of the sixties. Without it they will continue to be "blunted on the classroom door."

Normative-Reeducative Strategies

Under the normative-reeducative philosophy man is assumed to be an active seeker in quest of experience and satisfaction of needs, not a passive acceptor of the rationality and knowledgeable authority of others. The motivation for change is not assumed to be simply self-interest but the powerful need to seek new experience, and make meaning from that experience. Intelligence, problem-solving, and meaning making are considered not only as individual but as social phenomena. Man is assumed to be rational, but his rationality is recognized as hindered and biased by values, beliefs, and expectations of the social systems to which he belongs. These form socio-cultural norms which limit and direct both the rationality and behavior patterns of individuals and groups. Individuals internalize the normative socio-cultural values and expectations as habits and attitudes which are commitments of affective regard independent of rationality. Consequently (Chin & Benne, 1969, p. 43):

> Changes in patterns of action or practice are, therefore, changes, not alone in the rational informational equipment of men, but at the personal level, in habits and values as well and, at the socio-cultural level, changes are alterations in normative structures and in institutionalized roles and relationships, as well as in cognitive and perceptual orientations.

The close correspondence between the values and assumptions of process education as presented in Chapter 2 and those of normative-reeducative strategies is striking. Furthermore, the attention of normative-reeducative strategies to the interaction of culture, institutions, and individuals in social systems is consistent with the framework provided by the Getzels model discussed in Chapter 3. The normative-reeducative approach deals directly with the topic of implementing change in practice through attention to institutional role expectations and individual habits and attitudes or need-dispositions.

The locus of power in the normative-reeducative approach to change is *not* in knowledge or persons knowledgeable about things and specific "thing" oriented technology. Rather it is in a combination of the special experience of the social group which is to be changed, knowledge about "people" oriented technology, and the knowledgeable person skilled in human relations and group dynamics. The group itself and the human relations specialist are expected to select technical methods, procedures, materials, and other expert knowledge resources and personnel which are relevant to the solution of particular problems involved in the particular process of change in which the client group is engaged.

Several common elements in normative-reeducative strategies are identified by Chin and Benne (1969, pp. 44-45). These can be summarized as: (1) the involvement of the client or client system in working out the program of change is emphasized; (2) the client and the change agent develop a dialogic relationship about each other and the way each perceives the problem; (3) the problem confronting the client is not assumed to be one which can be solved by technical knowledge alone, but this is not ruled out; (4) the change agent must collaborate with the client to define and solve the problem; (5) relevant methods, concepts, and knowledge of the behavioral sciences are selected by the change agent and client and used selectively to attack the problem.

Havelock (1969, Chapter 11, p. 14), notes that normative-reeducative strategies have not been particularly common as means for the wide scale implementation of educational innovations.[15] Perhaps this is because as usually practiced this type of strategy is best suited to small scale efforts to change the behavior patterns of a classroom rather than a larger social system such as a school district. A good example of normative-reeducative strategies for implementation of change in educational practice is the procedures developed by Ronald Lippitt and Robert Fox and their colleagues. Their procedures are designed to change the classroom norms of the pupil peer group and the teacher toward self-initiated, cooperative, and inquiry learning activity. (These have been previously discussed in Chapter 2.) Such procedures seem to be ideally suited for changing institutional role expectations and individual attitudes and habits and, as such, are central to the needs of process education in its attempt to change pupil and teacher roles.

15. Havelock refers to this category of strategies as the "problem-solver perspective."

One of the chief problems with normative-reeducative strategies is that until recently there has been relatively little effort devoted to the development of knowledge about change through "people" technology compared to change through "thing" technology (Chin & Benne, 1969). Other problems noted by Havelock (1969, Chapter 11, pp. 14-15) concern the failure to attend to valuable outside resources and knowledge, the questionable capacity of the typical client group or user system to innovate and change themselves, and the provincial nature of the innovative activity which results in isolated settings but does not rapidly and easily spread on a large scale to many settings. While it would seem that the philosophy of normative-reeducative strategies is most appropriate to the task of implementing the practice of process education, attention must be directed to overcoming the limitations of this approach.

Power-Coercive Strategies

The basic assumption underlying power-coercive strategies is that both groups and individuals must be forced to change their behavior patterns in compliance with the change sought by some powerful authority. Change is by forcible decree, either by legitimate or illegitimate power. Political and economic sanctions are used to force individuals and groups to change their behavior patterns and practices according to the plans, direction, and leadership of those with greater power. Frequently added to the political and economic sanctions are tactics of intimidation through the use of fear, shame, and guilt. The attempt is to coerce the individual and the group to comply with mandated change.

Power-coercive tactics are very noticeable in the attempts of political parties and special interest groups to change practice in many aspects of municipal and federal government. They are also noticeable and common tactics in the struggle within and between corporate organizations as they vie for access to production resources, consumer markets, and increased profits. Chin and

Benne point out that the philosophy of the power-coercive change strategy is well and widely entrenched in our society. It is a common strategy used by those in legitimate control of the various social systems in society including educational systems and schools (Chin & Benne, 1969, p. 53). Power-coercive strategies function well within a bureaucratic social system where there is a clear "chain of command." From Chapter 3 it is evident that schools are indeed such places, and it is not surprising to find that the approach to innovation in education is frequently one of mandate by authority.

Even though they may be a reality in the operation of change strategies in social systems, power-coercive approaches have two great failings (Chin & Benne, 1969, pp. 55-57). First, it is assumed that changes mandated by authority and power will result in changed practice. Second, it is assumed that only those individuals and groups in lower positions of authority, power, and status need to be changed, can be changed, and cannot themselves implement change. Both of these are poor assumptions.

As an example of the failing of the first assumption, consider the large amount of legislation which requires equal employment opportunity, open housing, and other civil rights. It is frequently assumed that once such changes are decreed by law they will be implemented into practice, yet this is seldom the case. The change process is only partially begun when legislation has been completed. What remains is the more major task of changing existing norms and the reeducation of the population to the new practices. Without attention to this normative-reeducative approach the legislatively decreed change is not apt to occur in practice. As another example, consider the school superintendent who decides to utilize the instructional strategy of team teaching. He may demand that team teaching become the mode of operation. He can use his power to change building and classroom schedules, assign teachers in multiples to particular groups of pupils, and insure that what goes on in the school has the appearance of team teaching.

However, as many recent articles about differentiated staffing and team teaching observe, all this activity will not insure that the members of the team will behave much differently than they usually do. To implement the *practice* of team teaching, the superintendent's decree and power-coercive manipulations are inadequate. Additional efforts aimed at changing the norms of the teachers' reference groups are required. New habits, attitudes, and skills must be developed. Again the normative-reeducative approach is required to insure that the new practice will actually be carried out.

The second failing of the power-coercive philosophy concerns the notion that only those individuals and groups in lower positions of power and authority can be or need to be changed by those in higher positions. In the first place it is possible for individuals and groups having low or moderate status and power to effect change in the practices of both their leaders and their peers (Havelock, 1970). This change process by subordinates can be, but is not restricted to, the formation of a powerful counter group such as a union which also employs power-coercive tactics. Subordinates can also employ normative-reeducative and empirical-rational approaches to change their leaders' perceptions, habits, attitudes, and practices. Admittedly, it is more difficult to implement change in the practice of an organization from the "bottom up" than in the reverse direction, but it is possible. Havelock (1970, pp. 22-27, 33-36) provides two good examples of this form of implementation of change in school practice by subordinate members of the social system. In one case study the change agent is a 13-year-old girl who was instrumental in the implementation of a black studies program in a white suburban school. In the second case study the change agent was a teacher who successfully implemented a family life, emotional health, and sex education curriculum in a junior high school.

Perhaps an even more serious issue in the failure of the power-coercive philosophy is the assumption that only those individuals and groups in lower power and status positions need to be changed! Acceptance of this position is simply acknowledgement of the dictum, "Might is right and authority is true and good." It was shown in Chapter 3 that it is precisely this view which underlies the traditional approach to educational practice and which is opposed to process education. Paradoxically, in many social systems it is the high power-status members who are often most resistant to, but in most need of, change. It may be recalled from Chapter 3 that pupils, who have the lowest power and status in the school hierarchy, are more emergent and receptive to changing values and needs of society than are established teachers and administrators, who tend to resist change in favor of tradition. This is not uncharacteristic of leaders in many social systems and in the larger educational social systems especially. By ignoring the need for change in the practices of leaders in educational social systems in favor of changing only the habits, attitudes, and practices of subordinate members, power-coercive strategies may actually inhibit rather than promote the implementation of innovations in education. Frequently pupils, their parents, and teachers are more aware of the need to change existing educational practices—and are more willing to do so—than are their educational leaders such as principals, superintendents, school board members, and state education department officials. As Chin and Benne indicate (1969, pp. 56-57), it is imperative that normative-reeducative strategies be directed not only at teachers but also specifically at power elites in order that they may lead as more committed, informed, and competent individuals, improving the practices of their educational systems in the light of expanding knowledge and changing values.

The values and philosophy underlying power-coercive change strategies as well as the tactics employed are in direct opposition with the values and goals of process education as presented in Chapters 2 and 3. The means of such strategies contradict the goals sought by process education. In addition, power-coercive strategies seem to be particularly ill-suited to develop stable institutional changes in values and role expectations through the internalization of personal habits, attitudes, and skills in individual personality need-dispositions. Yet the implementation of process education depends centrally upon producing rather stable changes in institutions and individuals.

Practical Considerations

Despite these contradictions in philosophy, means, and goals of process education and power-coercive strategies, it must be recognized that the educational system is predominantly a bureaucracy consisting of many groups and individuals with vested interests. Some of these will be extremely resistant and immune to normative-reeducative strategies designed to change current practices. This is understandable, since many of the proposed changes would lessen their power and status rather than increase it. Therefore, entry strategies designed to let change agencies into schools to begin normative-reeducative programs for implementation of process education may have to be essentially power-coercive in nature and directed at the power groups and gatekeeps who would rather promote their own positions and self-interests in the big business of education than improve the quality and relevance of learning and instruction. If such individuals and agencies cannot be forced to change their views and practices, implementation of normative-reeducative training programs for process education may require that ways be found to eliminate or circumvent their power and influence. This type of thinking and tactic is coming increasingly to the forefront as relationships among political power, cultural values, and school practice are being recognized by educators and laymen alike who are concerned with improving educational practice (Gesler, 1970; Karns, 1970; Kubiak, 1970; Loving, 1970; Mann, 1970; Massialas, 1970; Turner, 1970).

It is pointed out by Benne, Bennis, and Chin (1969, p. 30), that the helping or service professions, including teachers, physicians, and social workers, among others, have become oriented "deliberately to induce and coach changes in the future behaviors and relationships of their various 'client' populations." They remark that:

> Human interventions designed to shape and modify the institutionalized behaviors of men are now familiar features of our social landscapes.

Furthermore, they note that changes in human social systems which these professional groups strive to implement are not motivated primarily by ideology but by the practical need to adapt social systems to the demands of the modern world. This is precisely the rationale which has been developed in Chapters 2 and 3 for changing current school practice in the direction of process education. The justification for changes in school practice toward process education are the reality conditions of the modern world—not ideological considerations.

The ideal way to achieve such change is through normative-reeducative strategies, since the means of such approaches are congruent with the goals of process education. The goal for social systems is the same as for individuals. Both should become self-initiated, adaptive problem-solvers and meaning makers. Neither empirical-rational nor power-coercive strategies aspire to these critical goals. Yet in the practical approach to implementing the practice of process education, the change agent or agency undoubtedly needs to use both of these strategies, when appropriate, to deal with particular power groups. However, such tactics should not constitute the overwhelming nature of his contact with the client system. By and large the strategies used should be normative-reeducative, since only these are capable of effecting the types of change in institutional values and roles which are required. Havelock (1969, Chapter 8, pp. 48-51) and Miles (1967d, pp. 638-639) have independently concluded from theoretical and empirical considerations that the ease of implementation of an innovation is inversely related to the degree to which it deviates from traditional practice. Thus, the educational innovation easiest to implement into practice is one which calls simply for a substitution of an existing textbook series with a new set of curriculum materials which do not appreciably alter the content of instruction and traditional pupil and teacher roles. Innovations requiring somewhat more alteration in existing practice are more difficult to implement. Programs requiring the elimination of old behaviors and attitudes are harder yet to implement. And finally, as Miles (1967d, p. 639) notes, innovations requiring changes in value orientations of the accepting group are most difficult of all to implement. Power-coercive and empirical-rational strategies work best for implementing those relatively "non-innovative" innovations at the lower end of the scale. The implementation of innovations which call for changes in institutional values and role expectations requires normative-reeducative strategies.

Temporary Systems as Means to Change

After reading the section in Chapter 3 dealing with the bureaucratic nature of schools and the educational system, one might despair of being able to implement change in educational practice toward the practice of process education. Schools are indeed bureaucracies and they are apt to remain so. As bureaucracies they tend to abide by tradition and resist change. This is both functional and nonfunctional. As schools rely upon tradition, they provide the essential service of insuring the transfer of basic knowledge and values which are needed to prevent chaos and preserve a climate of cultural order and stability, even in a very rapidly changing world. This is the positive side of the bureaucratic nature of the schools. But to the degree that schools resist change, in accordance with emerging societal and cultural values, needs, and conditions, they help perpetuate outmoded ways of thinking, feeling, and responding to a changing world. This is the negative and nonfunctional aspect of a bureaucratically organized educational system.

The problem is not how to "liberate" schools from being bureaucracies. It is rather how to help them become more responsive to change. Even though they resist change, bureaucratic social institutions can change, do change, and must change if they are to continue to serve a changing society. Change toward improved practice or innovation appears to be more difficult and slower in the educational social system and schools than in agricultural, industrial, and medical social systems and their counterpart institutions (Miles, 1967d, p. 634). Obviously if schools are to become more rather than less functional, they must change. The thesis of this entire book is, of course, that to become more functional, schools must change in the direction of the value positions and pupil and teacher role expectations stated in Chapter 3. How can this be done? How can relatively stable, bureaucratically organized institutions like schools be assisted to be more responsive to needed change? The appropriate methodological answer seems to be: *through multiple temporary social systems.* Very powerful and logical arguments have been made for moving existing bureaucratic social institutions toward the goal of incorporating and utilizing multiple temporary social systems as a means to adaptive change (Bennis, 1969; Bennis & Slater, 1968). This is a condition required by "the temporary society" in which we live.

An excellent conceptualization of the nature, characteristics, and advantages of temporary social systems as a method to effect change in more permanent social systems has been presented by Matthew Miles (1967c). In the next few pages the key concepts underlying his conceptualization which relate to implementing the practice of process education will be examined.

Definitions

A temporary system is defined by Havelock (1970, Appendix A, p. 10) as "any of a number of non-permanent designs which are employed to introduce an innovation to participants." An innovation may be defined simply as "change toward improved practice." The design is a social system of some sort which has the general characteristics of the social system represented by the Getzels model (see Chapter 3, Figure 1), with one important exception. The temporary social system is highly flexible on the nomothetic dimension. Institutional roles and expectations, rather than being soundly established, are emergent. More simply, temporary social systems are new. They have no tradition. They do not exist long enough to become rigidly bureaucratized. If they do become rigidly bureaucratized, they are no longer temporary social systems.

Basic Assumptions

The basic assumption underlying the methodology of change through temporary systems is that multiple social systems exist simultaneously and that they influence one another and the individuals who inhabit them. Thus, as was pointed out in Chapter 3, the educational social system or school is influenced and changed by other social systems which are simultaneously inhabited by the institutional role incumbents of schools. A specific illustration was provided which showed how one particular set of temporary social systems (pupil and teacher peer groups) influenced the permanent social system, the school, to alter institutional expectations for teachers and pupils with respect to male hair and female skirt lengths. Other examples of more goal-directed temporary systems which may deliberately change institutional role expectations and individual behavior patterns in permanent systems are inservice workshops, conferences, *ad hoc* committees, and task forces.

A second and very important assumption founded on

empirical evidence is that temporary systems can be reeducative. They can effect lasting changes in the perceptions, attitudes, and behaviors of individuals and in institutional value orientations, goals, and role expectations.

Another important assumption is that temporary systems are prime mechanisms for creating change, because they can bypass many of the anti-change forces in permanent systems. In permanent social systems most human energy is directed toward the operation and maintenance of the existing social functions and relationships. Little energy is devoted to reflective thinking, diagnosis of problems, and planning. Management of the social system is characterized by enforcing old rules and procedures. Adaption to new problems and conditions through new approaches is resisted and avoided in favor of old procedures. Thus, change is inhibited. In the temporary system, however, nearly all energy can be devoted to the solution of problems through diagnosis, planning, and deliberate implementation of newer and more appropriate practices and procedures.

Characteristics of Temporary Systems

Temporary systems have a number of properties which make them effective means to changing individual roles, perception, and behavior patterns. Miles (1967c) has categorized these properties as "input," "process," and "output" characteristics. Input characteristics tend to describe the general properties of temporary systems. Process characteristics describe their method of operation. Output characteristics describe the products of temporary systems. These characteristics, which have been stated by Miles, are summarized below.

First, unlike permanent systems, all members of the temporary system expect the system to terminate at some predetermined time or when some particular product or activity has been completed.

Second, there is a clear mission to be achieved. Unlike

permanent systems, which usually have multiple and confounded goals, the goals of temporary systems are singular, clear, and achievable. This tends to produce greater task orientation, persistency, and efficiency in the members of temporary systems.

Third, the membership of the temporary system tends to be explicitly defined and maintained. For example, it is very clear who is and who is not a member of a committee or task force. Furthermore, addition or withdrawal of members from such a temporary system is unlikely. Rather a particular group of people are brought together to accomplish a specified task in a specified time. Group membership is well defined and stable over the period of activity.

Fourth, members of temporary systems are frequently isolated from other members of the permanent social systems to which they belong. Sometimes the isolation is both physical and social, as when a group of managers in a firm retires to a mountain lodge for two weeks to hammer out a new production policy and schedule. At other times the isolation is more social and less physical or physical for only short intervals within the permanent social system. An example of this latter case might be an *ad hoc* committee established to solve some particular problem over a period of weeks. The committee is physically isolated for perhaps only a few hours a week. Yet the membership is restricted and unchanging, and there is a degree of social isolation of the committee from the permanent institutional goals, concerns, roles, and tasks. This isolation—physical, social or both—serves to produce what Miles calls a "cultural island" which provides a freedom and protection not possible within permanent systems. Specifically, the isolation tends to make it possible for the group and its individuals to put aside old and well established roles, expectations, and ideas of the permanent system. Therefore in the temporary system, new norms, new roles, and changed practices and procedures can easily develop. Creativity and innovation can flourish. Another important function of the isolation of the temporary system from permanent systems is that the penalties for making an error are reduced. If the group fails in the temporary system, individuals will not lose their jobs or be destroyed in their professions. The worst that can happen is that the special project will be terminated or the committee findings and recommendations will be rejected. Individual members may return to their normal roles and responsibilities in the permanent systems to which they belong, even if the mission is aborted. On the other hand, what can and often does happen is that the special project's or the committee's findings will be incorporated into the ongoing program and practice of one or more permanent systems. This, of course, is an effective means for implementing change or innovative practices into permanent systems.

A fifth basic property of temporary systems concerns their size and distribution. Effective temporary systems tend to be small and their members tend to be in frequent and repeated contact with each other. Miles suggests that maximum effective size for temporary systems is a "few hundred" members and that these must be organized into smaller subsystems. He points out that larger temporary systems tend to become bureaucratized and serve compensatory and maintenance functions rather than to induce change toward improved practice.

The operation of temporary systems is characterized by very efficient use of time; the development of clearly stated and mutually agreed-upon goals and procedures for attaining those goals; the development of new group norms, new roles for individuals, and new social relationships among group members; and the emergence of an efficient communication and power structure essential to decision-making.

Temporary systems tend to accomplish a great deal more productive work in a much shorter period of time than do permanent systems. In the beginning, activity is directed toward the definition of group goals, the building of social relationships, and the emergence of the group's communication and power structure. Consequently, productivity is initially low. However, as the group establishes its ground rules and goals, task orientation and productivity increase to very high levels with maximum output toward the end of the temporary system's existence. The great degree of productivity and task orientation seems to be a function of the personal commitment of individual members to group goals and procedures which they have helped to establish and the assumption of new roles and social interactions which leads to a strong positive group climate or *esprit de corps.*

Miles notes a series of norms which usually develop in temporary systems and which support the positive group climate and high productivity. These include what he labels as *equalitarianism, authenticity, inquiry, hypotheticallity, newism,* and *effortfulness* (Miles, 1967c, pp. 473-476). The *equalitarian* norm presses for equal status relationships among members of the temporary system, despite real or imagined differences in power and status in their roles in the permanent systems to which they belong. *Authenticity* is a norm which establishes a high level of interpersonal regard among members calling for both a sincerity of expression of one's own ideas and feelings and an increased awareness and responsiveness to those of others. *Inquiry* is a norm which supports an increased motivation and commitment of the group to utilize problem-solving techniques to solve problems rather than rely upon traditional, authoritative, or dogmatic approaches. *Hypotheticallity* is a norm concerned with a willingness to experiment, pose multiple hypotheses, defer judgment, and collect factual data to evaluate alternative solutions to problems. *Newism* is a norm which presses for innovation, change, and newness for its own sake. It is supportive of brainstorming and idea generation activities. The sixth and last common temporary system norm that Miles notes is *effortfulness.* This norm demands serious, hard, and dedicated work from members of the group and is usually strongly enforced by the group.

Temporary systems tend to provide peak experiences for

both the motivation, dedication, and activity of the members and the productivity of the group. As such, temporary systems can have lasting and useful effects upon both individuals and the permanent social systems to which those individuals belong.

Temporary systems produce a number of important outcomes. These include relatively permanent changes in the attitudes, knowledge, and behavior patterns of individuals, lasting changes in relationships and communication among members of permanent systems, changes in individual role perceptions and definitions and institutional role expectations, and compelling personal and institutional decisions to act in new ways to implement new programs and procedures. Temporary systems also produce new materials and products. The curriculum development projects of the sixties which involved many individuals from various permanent social systems, including universities, public schools, publishing houses, private and government foundations, and state education departments, were really temporary systems. They resulted in many new curriculum and instructional materials as well as all of the outcomes mentioned above. They brought about changes in the attitudes, behaviors, perceptions, and roles of many individuals and some schools and educational agencies. The reason, as asserted in Chapter 1, that these products have not been more properly or fully realized is that different temporary systems are needed for their general dissemination and implementation. These have been lacking.

The list of accomplishments for temporary systems in effecting change in permanent social systems sounds too good to be true. But numerous empirical findings and observations support these facts. Collectively, Miles (1967c, 1967d) and Havelock (1969) cite scores of studies which support the assumption that temporary social systems can be and frequently are able to perform normative reeducative functions required to change institutional role expectations, individual attitudes, perceptions, and capabilities, and resultant behavior pattern outcomes of social systems such as schools.

The observations of Miles and Havelock concerning the effectiveness of temporary systems in changing individual and institutional behavior patterns and perceptions are independently supported by the efforts and research of numerous scholars and change agents affiliated with the Creative Problem-Solving Institute sponsored annually by the Creative Education Foundation in Buffalo, New York. The group creative problem-solving techniques developed by Sidney Parnes and his colleagues have all the properties of temporary systems. Many studies and much experience, especially in business and industry, have shown that relatively short-term creative problem-solving sessions often have a lasting impact upon the behavior of members and subsequently upon the permanent social systems to which they belong (Parnes, 1967).

Problems of Temporary Systems

Despite their many advantages in introducing innovative practices into permanent social systems, temporary systems can and do sometimes fail to have lasting impact. There are a number of reasons for this which have been stated by Miles (1967c, pp. 480-484). Sometimes temporary systems fail to clearly delimit their task sufficiently and engage in too broad a range of activity. Goals are sometimes unrealistic, aspirations too high. Sometimes the members of temporary systems lack skills needed for the technical and/or human relations aspects of the task. That is, both "thing oriented" and "people oriented" skills and know-how may be lacking. If, however, the temporary system overcomes these problems and functions very effectively it can sometimes reeducate its members to a degree that they become alienated from their permanent system or systems. The goals, ideals, values, norms, roles, attitudes, and perceptions developed by the temporary system may be in such great conflict with the permanent system that members returning to their permanent position may undergo increased role conflict or become so alienated they are forced to drop out. This is the experience of many an excited teacher who having become involved in a temporary system concerned with developing innovative curriculum and instructional materials finds he is subsequently "ruined" for teaching in his old position. He can no longer assume the role that is required of him.

The problem of temporary systems producing people or hard products too radical for use in contemporary permanent social systems is closely related to another very serious problem. This is the problem of *linkage* between temporary and permanent social systems.

Linkage Between Temporary and Permanent Systems

In its simplest and most general sense, linkage is a concept which refers to connecting the activities and products of temporary systems to utilization functions by permanent systems. Linkage is necessary in order that the activities, products, and the personal and social changes developed by temporary systems may be incorporated into permanent systems toward improved practice. Linkage depends upon a continual two-way flow of information between the temporary systems which create the innovations and the permanent systems which first need, and second utilize, the innovations. This is essentially the concept of linkage developed both by Miles (1967c) and Havelock (1969). Innovation originates in temporary systems, but implementation of innovations occurs in permanent systems. Linkage is essential to insure the transfer of new knowledge, ideas, products, goals, beliefs, roles, and attitudes from the womb of temporary social systems to the harsh reality and unprotected environments of permanent social systems. Temporary systems are the incubators for innovations. Permanent systems are the laboratory where innovations mature or die as they are applied, tested, accepted, modified or rejected. Attention to linkage insures that the innovations of temporary systems are developed in accordance with the general needs of permanent systems and will be given a fair trial.

Linkage Problems in Implementing Educational Innovations

The numerous curriculum development projects of the sixties were temporary systems. They exhibited most of the characteristics of temporary systems which have been previously discussed. For the most part they were designed and funded to produce educational products and technology which were generally recognized to be needed to produce a scientifically literate population skilled in problem-solving, analytic thinking, and other conceptual and affective tools of the scientist. They have produced many new products in the form of curricular and instructional materials, new educational technologies, as well as new attitudes, beliefs, and perceptions about the roles of pupils and teachers and the design of materials, curriculum, and instruction. In short, they have been the creators of many types and varieties of educational innovations. As pointed out in Chapter 1, generally the innovations from these projects have not been widely implemented into practice. The numerous innovations of these temporary systems have initially had little effect upon changing current practice. There has been a failure in linkage between the temporary product development systems and the permanent user systems.

In the curriculum reform movement of the sixties effective linkage was established between basic research, applied research, and the developers of instructional products. As a result many quality educational innovations were developed. The failure in linkage has been in the realm of dissemination and utilization of these products. There has been inadequate linkage between the temporary development systems and the permanent user systems, the schools. In recent years, awareness of this problem has caused the United States Office of Education, the National Science Foundation, and other agencies and foundations to direct more and more of their funds toward developing means to implement the existing educational products and technology produced by the temporary development systems which they earlier funded. The task of implementing new knowledge, products, and technology in education is not now assumed to be simple and routine, as it was only a few years ago. It remains and is now recognized as a difficult task, especially when, as in the case of process education, the educational innovation calls for implementing new institutional value orientations and role expectations for pupils and teachers.

Scope of Temporary Systems

Temporary systems are usually conceptualized in a narrow way. Examples of temporary systems which are usually given include short-term workshops, conferences of short duration, committees, and task forces. It is true that these are temporary systems, but other sizable and longer duration temporary systems also exist. Included among these are groups brought together for periods of several months, or perhaps even a year or two, to develop or disseminate particular educational products, materials, or services. In reality most such larger temporary systems consist of multiples of smaller and interrelated temporary subsystems. Furthermore, in the more effective ones, the multiple temporary subsystems are comprised of individuals drawn from many different roles in the permanent systems in which the educational innovation is to be implemented. Such a structure facilitates linkage between the producers and users of innovations, as is shown in many empirical studies (Havelock, 1969).

Temporary Systems Within Classrooms

If one wishes to implement the practice of process education, one can and must ultimately choose to work directly in the classroom with pupils and teachers to change their perceptions, attitudes, and behavior patterns to be consistent with the value positions and role expectations stated for process education in Chapter 3. Many existing perceptions, attitudes, and behavior patterns of pupils and teachers which derive from the prevailing institutional value positions and role expectations can and must also be unlearned or extinguished. The philosophical underpinnings of such a strategy are by definition normative-reeducative. Pupils and teachers are being reeducated to new roles and unlearning old.

Temporary systems comprised of pupils, teachers, and some additional change agents or consultants skilled in both human relations techniques and the acquisition of technical knowledge and resources can produce very significant and lasting changes in the learning behavior and roles of teachers and pupils toward the goals of process education. Both the best operational models and empirical evidence for the success of such group problem-solving, normative-reeducative change strategies are found in the previously referenced works of Lippitt, Fox, Schmuck, Chesler, Luszki, Miles, and their associates.[16] As was shown earlier in this chapter, normative-reeducative group problem-solving approaches of this type are essential to change pupil and teacher behavior patterns toward the role expectations for process education. However, used alone with particular groups of teachers and pupils in particular schools, such temporary systems are inadequate. They cannot alone implement the practice of process education in any large scale or systematic way. Such procedures are effective in implementing lasting and needed change in pupil and teacher behavior, but only in a provincial way and not on a grand scale. Such limited-scope change strategies tend to effectively promote change in pupil and teacher roles in the desired direction in given and limited social systems such as a few classrooms or a school, but do little to modify other important social relationships within the larger educational social system.

Havelock (1969, Chapter 11, p. 14) notes three shortcomings to the usual group problem-solving approaches as a model for implementing change into current educational practice. He says of such a model that:

16. These strategies and their utility for changing pupil and teacher roles in the direction of process education were discussed in Chapter 3.

> . . .first, it puts excessive strain on the user; second, it minimizes the role of outside resources; and third, it does not provide an effective model for mass diffusion and utilization.

The scope of such temporary systems is too narrow. Membership is frequently limited to pupils, teachers, a few consultants and perhaps an administrator or two. Other individuals from other influential institutions within the larger educational system are usually excluded from the normative-reeducative activity. Yet, their power and influence is not excluded. Hence, any change in pupil and teacher roles is apt to be localized and not easily spread. Furthermore, it is likely that the changed educational practice which results from such programs can exist only insofar as powerful individuals from state education departments, boards of education, universities, teacher colleges, industrial, labor, and community groups either do not know about the significance of the change or do not feel threatened by it. In the case of implementing the practice of process education, or any other innovation calling for value orientations and pupil and teacher roles different from the traditional, the significance of the change is great. Many powerful individuals in the larger educational system are certain to feel threatened by such changes and oppose the innovation, if they too are not involved in normative-reeducative programs. This failure to attend to normative-reeducative functions in the larger educational social system results in a linkage failure, which at best inhibits wide scale adoption of new practices and procedures and at worst causes them to be officially denounced.

Extended Temporary Systems Within the Broad Educational Enterprise

The scope of the larger educational system in the United States within which schooling takes place is very broad. In the introductory chapter to *Innovation in Education* Miles (1967b) discusses the extent of the greater educational system and calls to attention the need to deal with many of the subsystem components in order to change educational practice within the classroom. Miles's schematic of the American educational system is reproduced in Figure 3.

There is a need for temporary systems concerned with the implementation of process education, or any other educational innovation, to involve members from many, if not all, of the agencies which comprise the total educational system. This has been recognized and in recent years change agencies concerned with implementing educational innovations have constructed elaborate networks involving private and public foundations, colleges and universities, state education departments, Title III agencies, regional educational laboratories, research and development centers, public and private schools, curriculum and instructional materials developers, and commercial producers and vendors. Much of the work of the Eastern Regional Institute for Education in the installation of selected process curricula has been accomplished within such extensive temporary systems involving individuals from many of the member agencies which comprise the larger educational system.[17] Such extensive systems are required for the wide scale dissemination of an educational innovation. This is their chief advantage, and for this reason they have been widely used in recent years (Havelock, 1969, Chapter 11, pp. 5-7). As Havelock notes, the major spokesmen for the establishment of such extensive temporary systems have been Henry M. Brickell, David Clark, and Egon Guba (Brickell, 1961, 1964a, 1964b, 1967a, 1967b, 1967c; Clark, 1967; Clark & Guba, 1967).

17. The reader interested in the models, strategies, and tactics used to establish the curriculum installation and dissemination networks of the Institute will find it informative to refer to the following reports and proposals: Cole, 1970b; Cole, Andreas, and Archer, 1969; Cole and Herlihy, 1971; Herlihy, Cole, and Herlihy, 1971; Herlihy, Andreas, and Archer, 1969; Mahan, 1970a; Herlihy and Wallace, 1970.

Figure 3

The American Educational System[18]

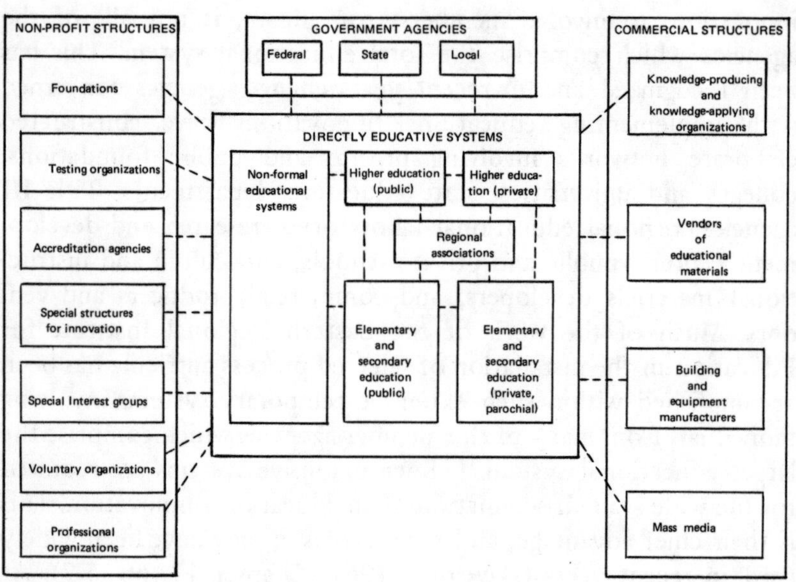

18. Reprinted with the permission of the publisher from Miles, Matthew B. *Innovation in education.* New York: Teachers College Press, 1964, p. 33.

A frequent problem with such extensive dissemination networks is that they often give the appearance of being able to effect more change in actual classroom practice than actually occurs. Such extensive temporary systems may theoretically operate in any one or some combination of the empirical-rational, power-coercive, or normative-reeducative modes. By and large, however, they have tended to operate in the empirical-rational and power-coercive modes and ignore vital normative-reeducative functions. It is assumed that if the temporary system is set up to include key individuals from important educational agencies within the larger educational system, the innovation can be implemented by pressure on local school boards, principals, and teachers (Clark, 1967; Brickell, 1967a). It is also assumed that the demonstration of the advantages of the educational innovation to the various individuals from the agencies involved as well as to the practitioners who are to use the new educational product will result in acceptance by these persons. The major shortcomings of this approach are the same as those which have been discussed earlier in this chapter under the limitations of empirical-rational and power-coercive strategies. In summary, the limitations are that such strategies tend to decree rather than actually implement change; they tend to ignore and thus be defeated by numerous non-rational barriers to change; they tend to be concerned with "pushing" products which may not be needed by or in the best interest of the user; and they are generally successful *only* when the innovation to be implemented is relatively non-innovative and reeducation is not required. Havelock (1969, Chapter 11, p. 7) categorizes such large scale attempts to disseminate educational innovations as the "research, development, and diffusion perspective" and identifies their chief limitations as being "...over-rational, over-idealized, excessively research oriented, and inadequately user oriented..." Perhaps a few personal observations will make the shortcomings of such approaches even more apparent.

Upon several occasions within the last few years I have been privileged to be in a position to observe several change agencies attempting to implement new educational programs in elementary schools. Typically much attention is devoted to developing an extensive series of relationships and collaborative agreements among the change agency, the program developers and vendors, state and district school officials, and local school administrators. Teachers and teacher groups are not usually involved in this stage.

The establishment of such a network of relationships seems to be a quite reasonable and necessary arrangement to implement new educational programs. However, what is shocking is the lack of attention which is usually paid to the nature and substance of the innovation itself, the changes it will require in pupil and teacher roles and the normative-reeducative training programs which will be required. The key individuals in the various agencies involved who make the critical decisions concerning program implementation in the schools are typically very uninformed about the innovation itself and have little comprehension of the type of teacher education and project management which will be required for successful implementation. Local principals and teachers who are recruited for involvement in the project are typically inadequately informed about the nature of the program to be implemented. The prevailing viewpoint among the collaborating leaders seems to be that once they as a power structure decide that the new program will be implemented, it will be indeed! Questions of how to get the program properly implemented and utilized are either ignored or dealt with at a very superficial level. Consequently, most teacher education workshops prior to and during the installation of the program consist of two types of activity.

First, teachers are taught the actual instructional management procedures necessary for using the particular program which is being installed. They learn how and when to use particular materials and equipment, how to report pupil progress, and how to inventory materials and equipment. Second, feeble attempts are made to provide teachers with the conceptual and attitudinal insights and skills which will enable them to see the broader purpose of the particular innovation and use it more adaptively and creatively. This later objective is usually lost in the shuffle while the former predominates. In addition, the approach to the second objective is usually extremely naive. I have upon many occasions visited workshops for teachers where program developers and scholarly experts were delivering lectures on cognitive psychology, child development, curriculum theory, behavioral objectives, instructional product development and related matters. Such activities are billed as part of the theoretical education of the teachers directed toward improving classroom performance, but as Lippitt and Havelock (1968), Smith, *et al.* (1969), and Schmuck (1968) point out, this is nonsense. Schmuck's studies are particularly relevant to this problem. They have shown that lectures and discussions about such topics may indeed change the teacher's views and performance in future discussions and on pencil and paper tests but do *not* change his behavior in the classroom (Schmuck, 1970, p. 733). The necessary normative-reeducative functions cannot be achieved only by talking at or with teachers, or simply showing them how to use the technology associated with a particular educational innovation. Needless to say, such approaches often lead to situations where teachers and pupils go through the motions of implementing someone else's educational innovation without feeling the necessary and proper commitment to make it their innovation. What they actually do in the classroom, the way they feel about themselves, learning, knowledge, and the school and their roles may not change. If this is so, reeducation has not occurred.

A Dilemma

It is apparent that the normative-reeducative strategies common to the limited temporary system approaches represented in the work of Lippitt, Fox, Schmuck and their colleagues are essential to the implementation of process education. It is also apparent that temporary systems of similar scope and organization as those represented in the work of Brickell, Clark, and Guba are essential to the wide scale implementation of process education. The inattention of the former strategy to the building of a network of temporary subsystems which can support and maintain normative-reeducative efforts in teacher and pupil roles at the local classroom level must be corrected. Also, the very serious flaw of inattention of the latter approach to essential normative-reeducative functions must be corrected. The normative-reeducative strategies for educational innovation have attended thoroughly to the "how" of implementation as a process of change in the user. The empirical-rational or research, development, and diffusion strategists have attended thoroughly to the building of extensive social systems to implement educational innovations. A new approach is needed which is concerned with both the process of change in all the members of the temporary system and establishment of extended social systems in order to widely implement changed practice at many levels in the larger educational system. Havelock's linkage model combines both of these functions and as such may be an answer to the dilemma.

A General Model for Implementing Process Education

Havelock has developed a very comprehensive master model for the dissemination and utilization of new knowledge arising from innovations in any field of human endeavor. The term "knowledge" is used very broadly in the Havelock model. It encompasses the innovative products of creative individuals and groups which include new theories, ideas, beliefs, feelings, values, technologies, skills, procedures, and things. Of course, new educational technologies, products, materials, and procedures represent knowledge which, having originated from research and development activities, can be disseminated to and utilized by those users of such products which include schools, teachers, and pupils. Process education is a generic name for a particular type and variety of such educational innovations. It may be disseminated to schools, teachers, and pupils for utilization by specific procedures derived from Havelock's general model. Specific curricular and instructional products which have been developed to promote the value orientations and roles central to process education do exist and the knowledge they contain can be used to change current educational practice in the direction of those values and roles through procedures derived from Havelock's model.

Origins of the Havelock Model

The general model developed by Havelock is extremely well founded in theory and research. In his exhaustive review of the literature on change strategies, Havelock (1969, Chapter 11) has organized empirical approaches to the implementation of innovations into three categories. These include what he calls the research, development, and diffusion perspective (RD & D), the social-interaction perspective (S-I), and the problem-solver perspective (P-S). It is clear that the RD & D perspective is based on the general philosophy of the empirical-rational approach. RD & D approaches have the same underlying assumptions, advantages, and disadvantages as the tactics which have been previously discussed under empirical-rational strategies. The P-S perspective is clearly based on the philosophy of the normative-reeducative approach, and likewise it has the same assumptions, advantages, and disadvantages as normative-reeducative strategies. The social-interactive perspective as discussed by Havelock is not really a change strategy at all in the sense that it is designed to implement change.

It is, instead, designed to describe change and is largely based on descriptive sociology and anthropology. Consequently, it is not congruent with any of the three basic change philosophies discussed earlier. The empirical work done under the S-I approach does, however, add information gathering and diagnostic techniques which may be used within empirical-rational, power-coercive, or normative-reeducative based change strategies. Havelock notes no clear empirical approach to change which corresponds to the power-coercive philosophy. However, he recognizes (Havelock, 1969, 1970) that power-coercive tactics may be and are used within both RD & D and P-S perspectives. The ultimate model derived by Havelock is a combination of the RD & D and P-S perspectives which incorporates the best features of the normative-reeducative and empirical-rational philosophies, and recognizes the importance of power in establishing major systems and normative-reeducative functions within those systems needed for implementing educational innovations.

Basic Concepts Underlying the Model

The basic and most important characteristic of the Havelock model is the conceptualization of knowledge dissemination as both a system for information flow among groups and agencies and as a process of information transfer among individuals who link those agencies which comprise the system. These two basic functions are described quite clearly in a paper by Lippitt and Havelock (1968). In the first part of the paper Lippitt describes the process of transfer of knowledge among the individuals within the subsystems which comprise the total system. In the second part of the paper Havelock describes the external characteristics of systems within which the knowledge transfer process described by Lippitt needs to occur, if the innovation is to be widely implemented into practice. Consequently, the model has an external structure characteristic of typical research, development and diffusion change strategies. However, unlike these similar-appearing approaches, it has as both its core objective and internal mode of operation the normative-reeducative "group process" approach to changing individual attitudes, perceptions, cognitions, and performance.

The Knowledge Transfer Process

Havelock (1969, Chapter 1, p. 10) characterizes the process aspects of the model in a series of questions. These are, essentially, *who* transfers *what* knowledge to *whom* by what *channel* (means, media) to *what effect* for *what* purpose. The knowledge transfer process aspects of the model are further categorized as indicated in Figure 4.

The *who* part of the model is conceptualized as a resource system which may consist of theoreticians, basic and applied researchers, and developers who are the creators of the new knowledge. The resource system may also include agencies or individuals skilled in gathering such resources together for purposes of applying the knowledge in the user system, and such individuals are definitely part of the transfer process. Examples of resource systems in education are curriculum development projects and agencies who involve scholars, theoreticians, behavioral scientists, experienced teachers, and pupils in the application of basic and applied research to produce new programs designed to improve some area of learning such as reading, mathematics or scientific inquiry.

The *whom* part of the model is conceptualized as the user system, the agencies, and individuals who implement into practice the new knowledge which has been developed. Examples of user systems in education are school districts, classrooms, teachers, and pupils who put into practice the educational innovations devel-

Figure 4

Basic Concepts of Havelock's Knowledge Transfer Process[19]

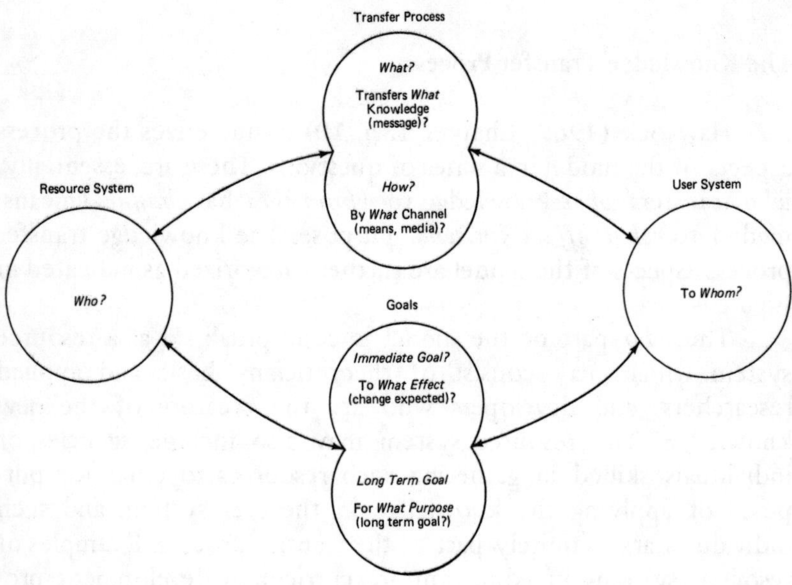

19. The basic components and relationships of the Havelock model are presented in great detail and in numerous schematics in his *Planning for innovation through dissemination and utilization of knowledge* (Havelock, 1969). The above schematic and accompanying explanation in this text represent this author's attempt to condense the Havelock knowledge transfer process to a conceptualization of its basic properties.

oped by educational resource systems. Other users might be teacher colleges and universities who use new training programs and procedures for teachers. A third user system might be a commercial vendor who mass produces an innovative educational program or training package for wide scale dissemination.

The transfer process or dissemination of the new knowledge is conceptualized as a *message* which is transferred from the resource system to the user system by some means. The transfer process also serves to send messages from the user system to the resource system about its needs for new knowledge and innovations which can be identified or developed by the resource system to meet those needs. Messages are conceptualized as a wide variety of knowledges. They originate as outputs from both resource and client systems. Typical messages from resource systems concern new basic knowledge and techniques for applying that knowledge to improve practice. Examples of resource system messages in education might be basic research which produces new knowledge about the conditions governing inquiry learning, applied research which develops techniques and materials to facilitate inquiry learning, and curriculum development efforts which produce new programs for actual use in inquiry development in schools. Examples of typical messages originating from user systems would be evidence that inquiry training programs are needed and wanted by schools and teachers, and that prototype inquiry development programs developed by resource systems need certain alterations to make them more manageable, effective, and adaptable.

The channel for transfer of knowledge concerns the media and means of communication. This can be, and often is, individuals who serve a linkage function. They tell and show both the resource and user systems things each must know about the other. The medium of transmission may also be in the form of an exemplary curriculum vehicle which demonstrates how to implement new educational theory, technology, or practice. Other media may be books or audiovisual presentations which contain similar information. These are common means or channels by which resource systems transfer messages to user systems. Memos, reports, discussions with change agents, consultants, and questionnaires originated or completed by members of the user system are means commonly used to transfer messages from the user system back to the resource system. In actual operation, the means employed to transfer messages between resources and user systems involves a wide variety of these devices.

The "to *what effect*" and "for *what purpose*" aspects of the Havelock model are goals which are established by both the resource system and the client. The "to *what effect*" question may be considered to represent more immediate changes in the behavior of individuals in user or resource systems. For example, a resource system may wish to implement a new curriculum to produce behavior changes in the question-asking strategies of pupils and teachers. This would be the "to *what effect*" short term goal. The longer goal implied in "for *what purpose*" might be to improve the inquiry behavior of pupils and teachers. Likewise, schools as user systems might have as immediate goals improving the reading skills of pupils and the competency of teachers for instructing those reading skills. They may communicate this need to resource systems with the short term expectation ("to *what effect*") that additional reading materials for pupils and training programs for teachers will be developed. The long term goal would, however, not be the development of more materials but the general improvement of teacher competence in teaching reading and fluent self-initiated reading activity among pupils.

It should be pointed out that the model Havelock has developed does not prescribe to *what* effect and for *what* purpose innovative knowledge in education will be disseminated. Rather it speaks in great detail as to *who* can transfer *what* types of knowledge to *whom* by what *channel* or means. That is, the model, although founded largely on values which underlie the normative-reeducative and empirical-rational philosophies, is not explicitly directed toward promoting particular educational philosophies or values. The implementation procedures derived from the general model can be used to promote the dissemination of existing curricular and instructional materials and practices either congruent or opposed to the value positions and role expectations for process education. The Havelock model provides great insight about the means to implement educational innovations but does not state what type of innovations should be implemented for what purpose.

The Knowledge Dissemination System

The knowledge transfer process of the Havelock model represented in Figure 4 describes the internal operation and activity of knowledge flow within the system. However, it does not define the extent and organizational membership of the system in which the knowledge transfer process occurs. In the Havelock model the knowledge dissemination system is conceptualized similar to the typical research, development, and diffusion manner. An example of the system conceptualization is given in Figure 5. It shows the general variety and number of organizations which might be involved in an extended temporary system concerned with the development, dissemination, and utilization of a particular educational innovation which could be a product, such as a new mathematics curriculum for the primary grades.

Knowledge Dissemination and Utilization as Process Within a System

In the Havelock model the member organizations within an extended system, such as the one presented in Figure 5, are linked by the knowledge transfer process shown in Figure 4. Subsystems

Figure 5

A Representative Knowledge Dissemination System

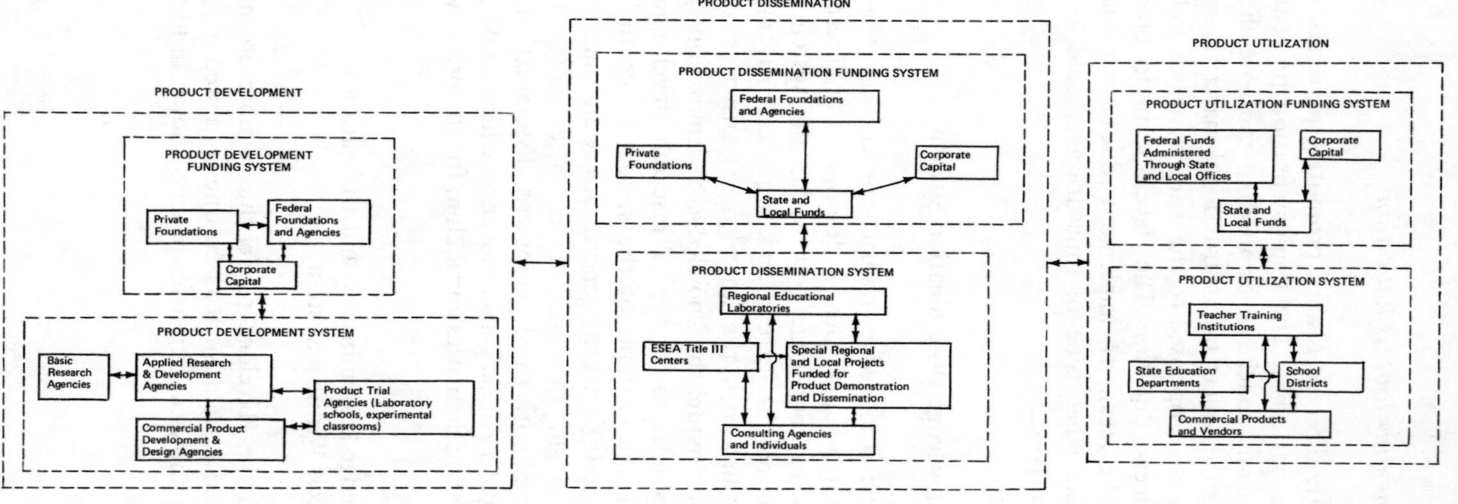

within and between the member organizations are also linked by the same process, as are any two individuals whose roles call for them to communicate between the user system at any point in the flow of knowledge. Havelock has diagramed this system-process relationship in a schematic which is reproduced in Figure 6. His diagram of the knowledge transfer process shown under the magnifying glass is the same process represented in Figure 4. It performs linking functions at the interpersonal, sub-organization, and organizational levels within the extended temporary system.

Important Properties of the Model

A most important property of the model is that its transfer process provides linkage between resource and user systems in extended temporary social systems. The resource system in such an extended system could include theorists, scholars, and basic and applied researchers, all from universities, as well as funding agencies and curriculum development projects. The user system in the extended social system might include teacher colleges, state education departments, commercial producers and vendors of materials, and school districts and classrooms. The means for transfer of knowledge in such a system could be regional laboratories, Title III centers, or other interagency agencies. The questions and concerns raised by the model define important features which must be attended to in building relationships among the numerous agencies in the extended temporary system or what frequently is referred to as the dissemination and diffusion network.

Such a complex extended temporary system is, however, made up of many subsystems, all of which have resource persons, user persons, messages to transfer, procedures to use for message transfer, and long and short term goals to be attained. Therefore, the Havelock model applies not only at the macro extended

Figure 6

Havelock's Conceptualization of Knowledge Transfer Within Knowledge Dissemination and Utilization Systems[20]

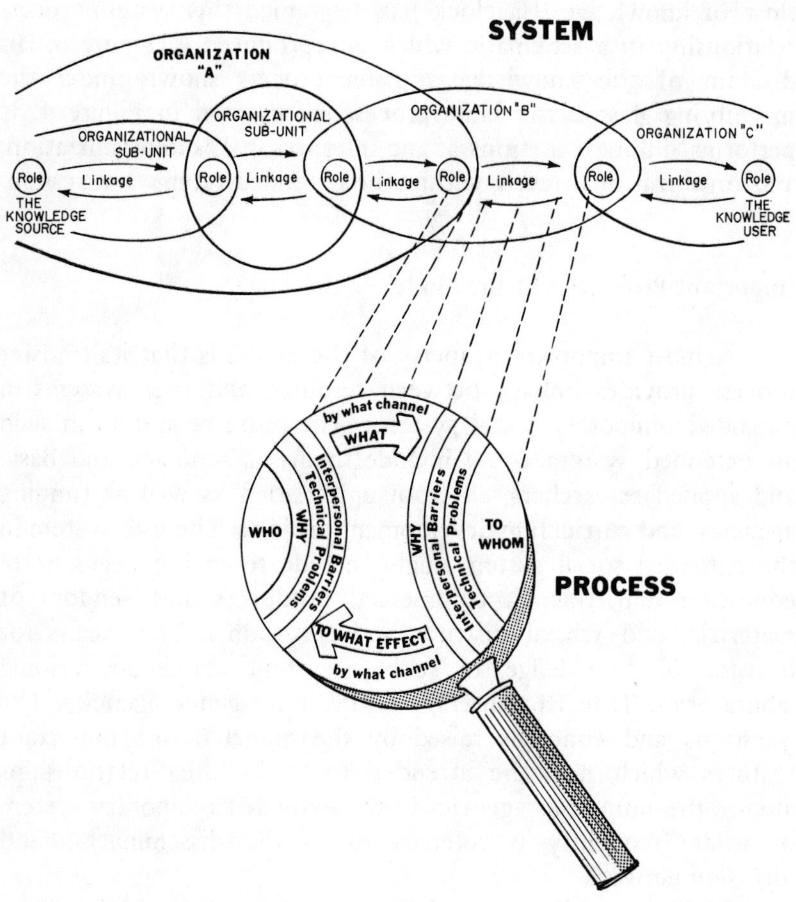

20. From Havelock, Ronald G. *Planning for innovation through dissemination and utilization of knowledge.* Ann Arbor, Michigan: Institute for Social Research, University of Michigan, 1969, Chapter 1, p. 13.

system level, but at the intermediate subsystem level as well. Thus within each of the agencies in the extended system described above—whether they be user systems, resource systems, or change agencies—there are individuals or groups which represent sub-resource systems and sub-user systems. There are also individuals who have linking roles between major agencies in the extended system and between subsystems within the member agencies of the extended social system. The Havelock model also applies to relationships among such sub-groups. One chapter of Havelock's report is devoted to the use of the model to describe the interaction of two-person subsystems where one is the resource (consultant) and the other is the user (teacher or client).

The model can also be construed in an individual psychological framework. A given individual can be considered to have within himself needs comparable to a "user system." He also has, in the form of his experience, knowledge, and skills, resources to meet those needs. Both short term and long term goals exist for him and he has procedures for transferring his knowledge, experience, and skills to obtain goals consistent with his needs. Another chapter in the Havelock report uses the model in this manner to explore the problems in overcoming resistance to change at an individual or personal level.

As Havelock (1969) notes in his introductory chapter, his knowledge and dissemination model may be applied to implement changed behavior in extended social systems, organizations within extended social systems, interpersonal relationships between persons in linking roles within and between organizations, and individuals themselves. This most important property of the model makes it very adaptable and useful.

Two other critical properties of the model concern reciprocity between resource and client systems and the opportunity for entry from any position in the model by user, resource, or change agent personnel. This may be seen from the schematic presented in Figure 4. Both the resource system and the user system can transmit messages to one another by means *they* choose for goals *they* desire. Information and knowledge flows through the system both ways. Furthermore, a change or innovation may be initiated by the user system which seeks a more appropriate practice to achieve a particular goal, or the resource system which seeks to apply basic knowledge to improve practice, or by a change agent who seeks to improve practice through linking resource systems and user systems. This important property is called to attention and discussed by Lippitt in an earlier paper (Lippitt & Havelock, 1968).

Appropriateness of the Havelock Model for Implementing Process Education

With its focus on the problem-solver perspective, the Havelock model is definitely normative-reeducative in its underlying philosophy. Consequently, its means for implementing change into educational practice are consistent with end goals of process education. This is important, since the groups involved in the change strategies will themselves be involved in what is essentially a process education approach to problem-solving and learning about how to change their current behavior and practice toward the value orientations and pupil and teacher role expectations stated in Chapter 3. Principals, teachers, college professors, and preservice students can learn much about process education and its goals from the behavior and tactics of change agents attempting to implement innovative educational programs and practices.

The normative-reeducative predisposition of the Havelock model also makes it very appropriate for implementing "innovative" innovations. The implementation of process education requires changing value orientations and institutional role expectations of schools. At the individual level attitudes, perceptions, understandings, and performances of many individuals within the educational system must be changed. As was noted earlier, power-coercive and empirical-rational strategies are not effective in implementing these types of major changes in individuals, institutions, and social systems. Rather, these strategies work well only for relatively "non-innovative" innovations.

The points of conflict which were discussed in Chapter 3 as inhibitory to the implementation of process education are recognized in the Havelock model. Specific principles and procedures are developed by Havelock to overcome these barriers to change.

The model also overcomes the disadvantage of the usual provincial nature of simple normative-reeducative strategies. It does so by organizing and coordinating normative-reeducative activities within the framework of a knowledge dissemination and utilization system. Such systems are not uncommon, but they usually lack attention as to *how* the behavior of individuals and groups will be or can be changed and *how* resistance to change can be overcome at the organizational and individual level. Consequently, they tend to decree change and establish a system within which change could occur, but fail to reeducate for change. The Havelock model provides for both the system to disseminate innovations and the normative-reeducation activities needed to implement them.

The extended systems conceptualized in the Havelock model are really multiple temporary systems combined with permanent social systems. What results is a more or less temporary extended system which cuts across many components of the larger educational social system for the purpose of achieving some set of well-defined goals within a given time. The advantages of temporary systems relative to explicit goal definition, task orientation, efficiency, and productivity have been discussed previously. All of these advantages can be realized by the multiple temporary systems within the extended system of the Havelock model.

The most appropriate aspect of the Havelock model for implementing the practice of process education derives from its extensive base in empiricism. The experience from thousands of attempts to implement changes in roles, attitudes, perceptions, and behaviors of individuals in social systems is examined. From this many principles are developed which can be used to develop detailed procedures for implementing changes in institutions, groups, and individuals of the types required for process education to be practiced. In the report, *Planning for Innovation Through Dissemination and Utilization of Knowledge* (Havelock, 1969), entire chapters are devoted to reviewing procedures and developing principles for changing individual, small group, and organizational behavior. In *A Guide to Innovation in Education* (Havelock, 1970), these principles are used to develop an extremely detailed but flexible set of procedures which are effectively a manual for resource systems personnel, change agents, or user systems interested in implementing educational innovations. These procedures, which are derived from the model, seem especially appropriate to the task of implementing process education through existing process curricula and their affiliated instructional methodology. Such programs represent important and major sources of knowledge about the practice of process education. The Havelock model and procedures provide detailed guidelines to disseminate and implement that knowledge on a wide scale.

Applying the Models, Principles, and Procedures

It is beyond the scope of this chapter to examine in detail the application of principles and procedures from the Havelock model to the implementation of process education through specific curriculum vehicles and networks of educational agencies. This is the proper function of proposals and detailed program development documents. However, a brief example of how the model and its procedures may be applied is provided. The example is based on a project designed and implemented at the Institute under the author's leadership (Cole, Andreas, & Archer, 1969; Cole & Herlihy, 1971; Herlihy, Cole, & Herlihy, 1971).

The project concerned the education of professors from teacher colleges, teachers from teacher college laboratory schools, preservice teachers from the colleges, and inservice teachers from surrounding schools along with their elementary school pupils. The general objectives of the project were to reeducate the teachers of teachers (professors), teachers, and pupils involved in new learning roles appropriate to analytic thinking, inquiry, and self-directed learning skills, all of which are basic to process education. It was anticipated that the extended temporary system set up to perform this task could: 1) accommodate the necessary normative-reeducative functions for the various groups by focusing on the generalizable theory, methodology, and teacher-pupil roles within a given curriculum vehicle; 2) be used to implement the curriculum vehicle and its related theory, methodology, and pupil-teacher roles into practice in selected elementary schools; 3) be used in subsequent years to implement additional changes in the attitudes, perceptions, cognitions, and performances of all individuals involved through installation of additional exemplary curricular and instructional materials; 4) consequently, change the normative expectations of teacher education institutions and elementary schools to be more consistent with the value orientations and role expectations for process education; 5) change the objectives, methods, and content of instruction in both preservice teacher education college courses and elementary school classrooms.

Teams from teacher colleges consisting of a professor and a campus laboratory elementary school teacher were instructed in the basic methodology and theory of a particular exemplary process curriculum.[21] They also actually taught the program to elementary school pupils as part of their training experience. Each team then returned to its home base at a teacher college where it performed several functions. First, the team planned a year-long inservice training program for teachers from local schools which would actually be installing the innovative process curriculum. Second, each team planned a one-semester college course for preservice teachers enrolled in the college. Both inservice and preservice teachers were to be grounded in the basic theory and methodology underlying the process curriculum. In addition, preservice teachers as well as inservice teachers were to have direct experience in applying the theory and utilizing the materials, techniques, and procedures of the curriculum. The participating inservice teachers accomplished this in their own elementary classrooms. The preservice teachers were to experience actually working with pupils with the new curriculum in the campus laboratory school classrooms or in the local classrooms of participating inservice teacher trainees. A third function of the campus based professor, campus laboratory school teacher team was to act as a consultant team to teachers from local schools involved in installing the curriculum. The campus team provided information and assistance to the local schools and teachers installing the new program. In addition, the campus team relayed needs, requests, desires, problems, and information arising from the use of the program in local schools back to the central project staff.

The basic knowledge dissemination system for the project is shown in Figure 7. The portion to the left of the vertical double line shows the origin of the curriculum. The portion to the right of

21. The curriculum vehicle used was the upper elementary social science *Man: A Course of Study* program developed by Education Development Center under the leadership of Jerome Bruner and Peter Dow and now produced by Curriculum Development Associates, 1211 Connecticut Avenue, N.W., Washington, D.C.

Figure 7

An Extended Temporary System for the Implementation of Process Education via Curriculum/Instructional Vehicles[22]

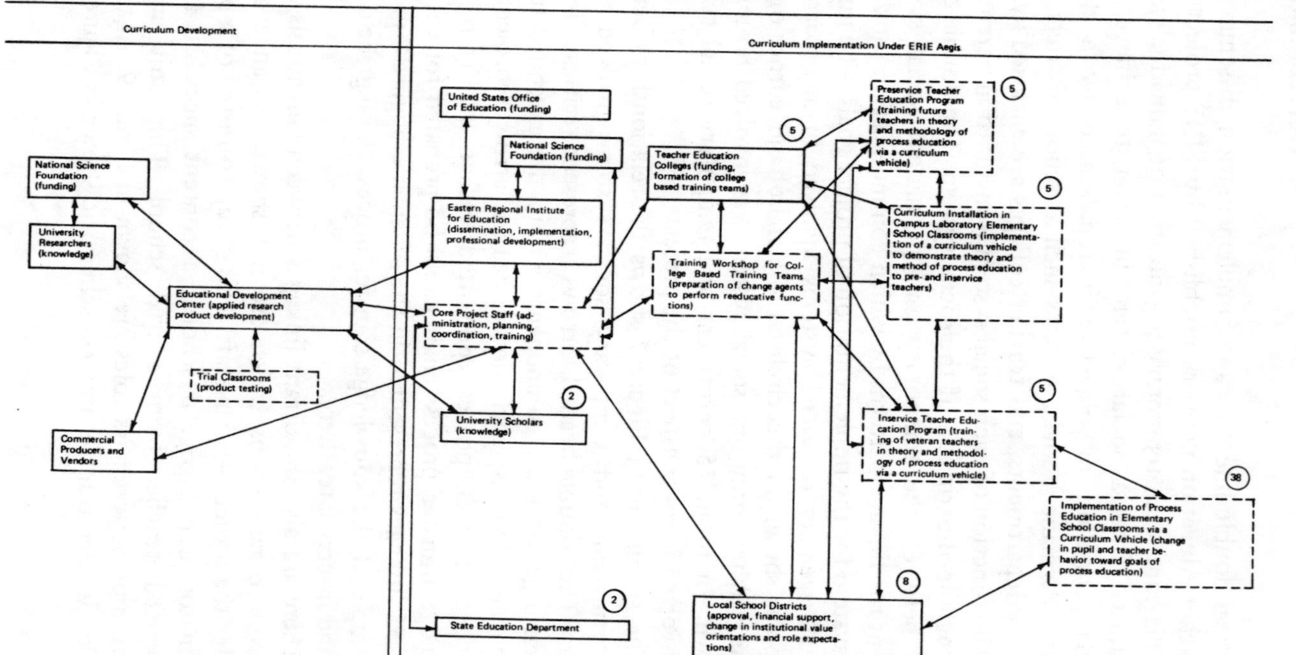

22. Temporary systems are bounded in dotted lines and permanent systems in solid lines. The double-headed arrows represent linkage points where the knowledge transfer process occurs. The system shown was established for the dissemination and utilization of a particular innovative process curriculum. However, the system could be used to implement other innovations (or knowledge resources) developed by other agencies.

the vertical double line shows the implementation, dissemination, and teacher education network established by ERIE project staff. In the diagram, each temporary organization of individuals which is organized into a social system in order to achieve some particular function or objective is represented by a dotted rectangle. Permanent social systems such as school districts, state education departments, and teacher colleges are enclosed by solid lines. The function of each social system is included in parentheses following the description of the social system. The double-ended arrows between the temporary and permanent social systems represent the linkage patterns by which communication took place in the system for the implementation of project goals. The number of actual agencies or social systems involved in any particular function is shown in the circle at the right-hand corner of each enclosure. Where only one social system was involved no number is shown. In total, 75 permanent and temporary social systems were involved in some aspect of the project.

The schematic in Figure 7 shows the relationships between each permanent and temporary social system involved in the project. The double-headed arrows represent critical linkages between organizational components within the extended temporary system. That is, each double-headed arrow represents the knowledge transfer process presented earlier in Figure 4. A knowledge transfer process chart could be prepared for each one of the 33 linkages represented in the schematic. Figure 8 provides an example of the knowledge transfer process linking the campus team and inservice teachers.

There are also important linkages between individuals within the major organizations which are not shown. As an example, consider the project system staff. This group consisted of a project coordinator, a pedagogical scholar, a content specialist, and an experienced teacher from a trial school. This unit and the relationships between its roles are shown in Figure 9. Again, the same knowledge transfer process schematic shown in Figure 4 can

Figure 8

An Example of the Knowledge Transfer Process Between Member Organizations of an Extended Temporary System[23]

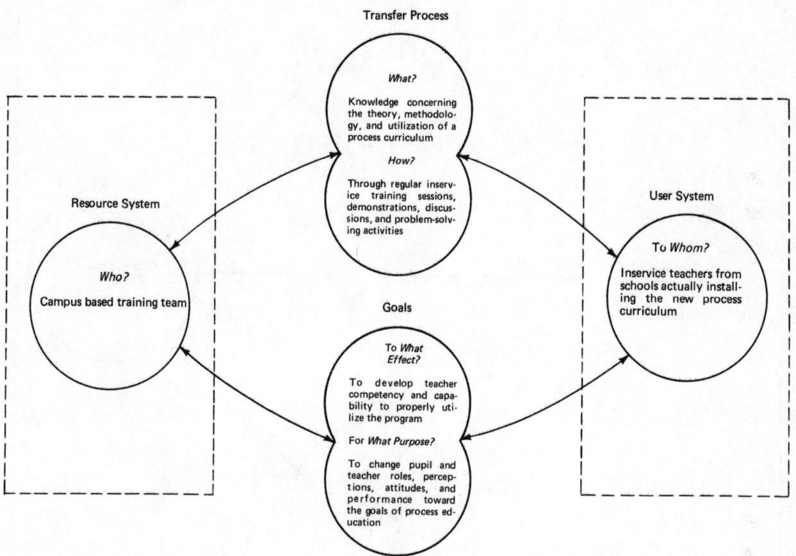

23. The knowledge transfer process shown here is one of several which constitute the linkage between two of the subsystems shown in the extended temporary system in Figure 7. One or more schematics similar to this particular one could be prepared for each of the double arrows which link the member organizations in Figure 7.

Figure 9

Relationships Among Members of the Project Subsystem Displayed in Figure 7[24]

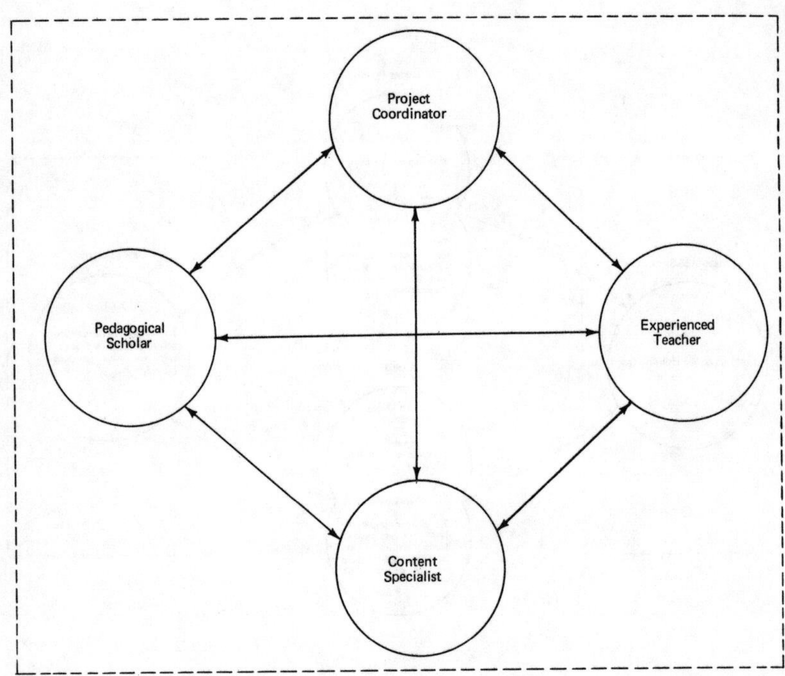

24. Each double-headed arrow represents a knowledge transfer process between the members of the project staff. One particular knowledge transfer process between the experienced teacher and the other members of the system is represented in Figure 10.

be applied to each of the linkages between roles within this subsystem. Figure 10 shows one such linkage relationship within this subsystem. Similar schematics could be prepared for each of the other arrows or linkage points in Figures 7 and 10. For instance, Table 8 shows, in more detail, the specification of the knowledge transfer process for another subsystem in this project. This relationship is between the campus school teacher who was a member of the teacher education team at each college site and the preservice teachers who were students enrolled in courses at the colleges.

The Havelock model is useful in specifying all the linkages between and within member organizations and individuals in an extended temporary system. It can specify *who* transfers *what message* to *whom* by *what channel* to *what effect* and for *what purpose.* Attention to such details within such an extended system may be cumbersome, but it is important to insure the system serves its normative-reeducative functions and meets its long term objectives.

Havelock provides specific guidelines, checklists, and procedures which can be used to establish both the broad parameters of a knowledge dissemination system and the details of normative -reeducative functions within and between components of that system. Specifically he provides seven general factors which relate to the efficiency of knowledge dissemination and utilization. These are placed in a matrix and intersect the major elements of the knowledge transfer process. This matrix is reproduced in Table 9. It provides a series of checklists which can be used to diagnose the strengths and weaknesses of particular resource persons and systems, user persons and systems, innovations to be implemented, and means or tactics for doing so (Havelock, 1969, Chapter 11, pp. 22-41). The application of such a set of procedures prior to setting up an extended temporary system is certain to: 1) give a better understanding of the feasibility of the particular project planned; 2) identify points of conflict and problems which

Figure 10

An Example of the Knowledge Transfer Process Within a Temporary Subsystem[25]

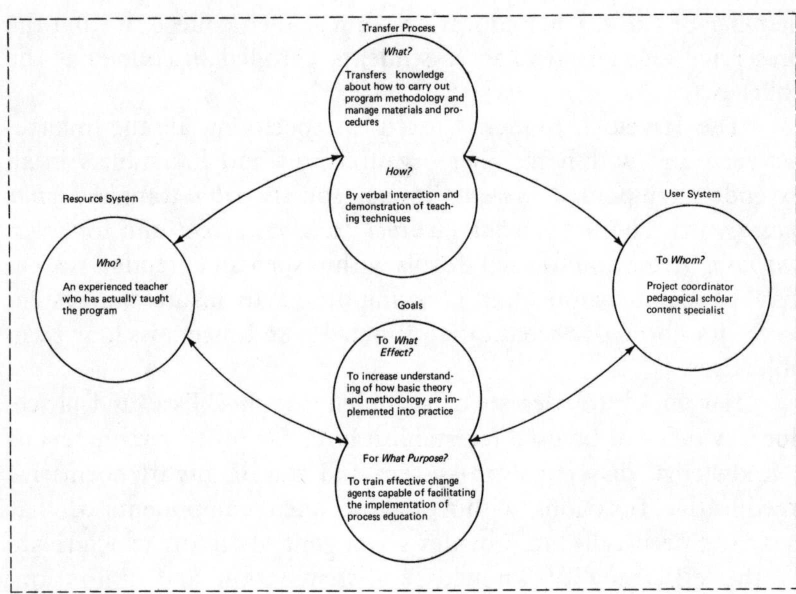

25. The knowledge transfer process shown is one of several which constitute the linkages between members of the temporary project subsystem displayed in Figures 7 and 9. Similar relationships can be established for intra-subsystem linkages within each of the member organizations shown in the extended temporary system in Figure 7.

Table 8

Detailed Example of the Knowledge Transfer Process Within a Temporary Subsystem

Knowledge Resource

The campus school teacher (member of the campus team)

Knowledge User

Preservice teachers in methods courses at the college

Knowledge to be Transferred from Resource to User

Practical experience in using a process oriented social science curriculum to instruct elementary school pupils. The knowledge to be transferred concerns how to use the teacher guides; group pupils for learning activities; arrange and manage materials and equipment necessary to particular lessons; stimulate and guide pupil discussion and independent learning activity; relate the curriculum content to current events in the social and physical world of the pupil, as well as to reading, language arts, and other areas of the school curriculum.

Method, Channel, and Means for Knowledge Transfer

Active participation of preservice teachers in the elementary classroom of the campus school teacher. Means for participation include observation of the classroom activity, assisting the teacher in instructing groups of pupils in portions of lessons and activities, direct teaching and interaction with pupils using the process curriculum, assisting the teacher in planning and preparation for pupil learning activity, and helping evaluate pupil progress.

Anticipated Immediate Effect of the Knowledge Transfer Process

Preservice teachers who are skilled in the practical aspects of proper utilization of the new curriculum and its methodology.

Long Term Goal Sought by the Knowledge Transfer Process

Preservice teachers who go on to become full-time professional teachers who (1) are excited and committed to the practice of education via the process approach of the curriculum; (2) seek to implement this or related process curricula and methods into their own classroom teaching; (3) will interact with other educators and individuals and communicate information about the value of process education.

Table 9

Intersection of Dissemination and Utilization Factors with Basic Elements of the Havelock Knowledge Transfer Process[26]

How General Factors Relate to:

GENERAL D&U FACTORS	RESOURCE PERSONS & SYSTEMS --- SENDERS-DISSEMINATORS (Who)	USER PERSONS & SYSTEMS --- CONSUMERS-CLIENTS (To Whom)	MESSAGE --- KNOWLEDGE INNOVATION (What)	MEDIUM --- CHANNEL-STRATEGY-TACTICS (How)
1. LINKAGE	Collaboration, 2-way interaction with user and other resources. Simulation of user's problem-solving process.	Collaboration, 2-way interaction with other users and resources. Simulation of resource system's R&D process.	Relevance to user. Adequacy of derivation and congruence with scientific knowledge.	Allows direct contact. Two-way interaction.
2. STRUCTURE	Systematic planning of D&U efforts. Division of labor and coordination.	Systematic planning and execution of problem-solving efforts. --- Integrated social organization of receiver system.	Coherence. Systematic preparation (design, test, package).	Systematic strategy. Timing to fit user's problem-solving cycle.
3. OPENNESS	Willingness to help. Readiness to be influenced by user feedback and by new scientific knowledge. Flexibility and accessibility.	Willingness to be helped, desire to change, to see potential of outside resources. Active seeking and willingness to adapt outside resources.	Adaptability, divisibility, demonstrability of the innovation.	Flexible strategies. Best medium allows informal communications between sender and receiver about the innovation.
4. CAPACITY	Ability to summon and invest diverse resources --- Skill and experience in the helping-resource person role. Power, Capital.	Ability to assemble and invest internal resources. Self-confidence, intelligence. Amount of available time, energy, capital. Skill, sophistication.	Innovations which result from heavy investment and sophisticated design and development will diffuse more effectively.	Capacity of medium to carry maximum information. Accessibility to maximum number of users in minimum time.
5. REWARD	Reward for investment in D&U activities in terms of dollars, recognition, knowledge, self-esteem.	Past experience of reward for utilization effort. Return on effort invested in dollars, time, capacity, growth, well-being.	Relative advantage, profitability. Time and labor saving potential. Life-liberty-happiness benefit potential.	Medium which can convey feedback (+ and - reinforcement). Most effective medium has best reward history for sender and receiver.
6. PROXIMITY	Closeness and ready access to diverse resources and to users.	Closeness and ready access to resources, other users. Cosmopoliteness. Psychological proximity: similarity to and identification with other users, resources.	Relatedness and congruity with user and user needs. Similarity and congruence with past innovations which the user has adopted. Familiarity to user.	Easily accessible medium, familiar to the user.
7. SYNERGY	The number and diversity of resource persons and change agents who gain access to the user. Continuity, persistence, and synchronization of effort.	The number and diversity of different users reached will accelerate the diffusion to social system as a whole.	Redundancy of message. The number and variety of forms in which the message appears and the continuity among forms.	The number and diversity, continuity and persistence of different media used to transmit the message.

26. From Havelock, Ronald G. *Planning for innovation through dissemination and utilization of knowledge.* Ann Arbor, Michigan: Institute for Social Research, University of Michigan, 1969, Chapter 11, p. 22.

otherwise might be ignored and perhaps prevent successful implementation; 3) result in specific delineation of roles and procedures designed to serve needed normative-reeducative functions for the various groups and individuals involved.

The Havelock model, principles, and procedures can also be applied during the operation of an extended temporary system concerned with the implementation of some particular process curriculum or other innovation. The degree to which implementation of changed roles and practice toward the goals of the innovation has actually occurred can also be assessed by the checklists provided.

A More Specific Derivative Model

The extended temporary system depicted in Figure 7 and described above is in reality a model itself. It provides means to gradually implement the practice of process education into schools, teacher colleges, state education departments, and other member organizations of the larger educational system.

The system shown was initially used for the dissemination and utilization of a particular innovative process curriculum. The intention was to use the curricular innovation to move educational practice in the various educational agencies involved more in the direction of value orientations and pupil and teacher roles appropriate to process education. However, the system can be used to disseminate other educational innovations produced by other development agencies into the same user system. That is, the system on the right-hand side of the double vertical line in Figure 7 can remain somewhat constant over a period of years, while the particular development agencies and their innovations represented on the left-hand side of the line can be varied. In successive years, the right-hand portion of the system shown in Figure 7 could be used to implement a wide variety and number of innovative educational practices and procedures originating from different development agencies into the user systems on the left. If the educational innovations selected are particularly exemplary of certain aspects of process education, the cumulative effect of such an activity could result in great changes in the various member organizations of the user system toward the practice of process education. Such an approach has the advantage of trying to implement major changes in educational practice over a long period of time with multiple temporary systems such as conferences, workshops, and special projects, and through the use of multiple resource systems and persons.

Another option might be to produce other temporary systems within the overall extended system established in the first year. That is, the temporary project system, the workshops, and inservice programs might involve completely different resource persons as well as completely different trainees in subsequent years, but still persons from the same permanent member organizations. Still a third option would be for the innovation development system depicted on the left of Figure 7 to establish multiple innovation and diffusion systems for its particular innovation or series of innovations. Again, either of these two approaches might further the cause of process education, *provided* that the innovations being developed and implemented were appropriate to the task of changing pupil and teacher roles to be consistent with the basic value positions underlying process education. These latter two options cannot, however, be expected to be as effective as the first option. The primary problem is that the latter two approaches lack continuity of training for a particular group of individuals over extended periods of time. As pointed out earlier, implementing change as drastic as required by process education will undoubtedly require intensive efforts with particular individuals and agencies over extended periods of time. The third option has the additional disadvantage of being too ingrown and biased. It also tends to ignore the existence of resources in the form of other types and varieties of educational innovations equally or perhaps more appropriate to implementing the practice of process education.

In any case, the problem that remains in applying such a model to the implementation of process education, no matter which option is used, is the development, identification, and selection of educational innovations which can act as appropriate vehicles to serve normative-reeducative functions. It has previously been assumed, on the basis of much study, that there already exist many excellent curriculum and instructional vehicles appropriate to the facilitation of process education. How can existing curriculum and instructional vehicles be selected which can be used to implement the practice of process education? This question, which was first suggested in Chapter 1, is the topic of Chapter 5.

Conclusion

This chapter has examined three general change strategies which have different philosophical underpinnings. Empirical-rational strategies have been found to be attentive to setting up extensive networks, or social systems, for the dissemination and utilization of new knowledge. However, they have been found to be lacking in attention to the barriers which exist to implementing new practices within social systems. Rational-empirical strategies are effective in disseminating new knowledge only when the client system is eager for that new knowledge and only when no major changes are called for in institutional value orientations, role expectations, and individual perceptions, attitudes, and habits. Changes in value orientations, role expectations, attitudes, habits, and perceptions require reeducating the individuals and institutions in social systems to new normative standards and behavior patterns.

Implementation of process education requires changing value orientation, attitudes, perceptions, and roles. Barriers which prevent the implementing of process education arise from the many points of conflict between process education and conventional educational practice which have been discussed in Chapter 3. The failure of empirical-rational strategies to attend to normative-reeducative functions designed to overcome individual and institutional barriers to new value orientations, roles, perceptions, attitudes, and habits makes them inappropriate to the implementation of process education. Rather, empirical-rational strategies are appropriate for relatively "non-innovative" innovations where underlying roles and values are not changed.

Normative-reeducative strategies are philosophically appropriate to implementing the practice of process education. They are aimed at overcoming social-psychological barriers to change. They are known empirically to be effective in changing the value orientations and role expectations of social groups as well as the attitudes, perceptions, and behavior of individual group members. The common and practical failing of such strategies is that they are usually very provincial. They usually center around only a few very small groups, and are not suited to the wide scale dissemination and utilization of new knowledge and practice within extended social systems. When normative-reeducative strategies are used in education, typically only the behavior of a few teachers and pupils is changed. Other individuals from other agencies within the extended educational system whose support is needed to maintain the change in teacher and pupil behavior are often uninformed and non-supportive of the new practices. Their behavior has not been changed. Therefore, whatever changes in classroom behavior patterns which occur are likely to be both very local and very short-lived. Any permanent and major change in classroom practice must be supported and facilitated by local and state administrators, teacher educators, curriculum developers, educational materials producers, and other influential individuals in the educational system. Consequently, typical small scale normative-reeducative strategies are inappropriate to the wide scale implementation of process education. While they are ideally suited to the necessary normative-reeducative functions required to implement the role changes called for by process education, they are not suited to insuring that the change induced is either locally maintained or disseminated on a large scale.

Power-coercive strategies are very common in educational systems. They operate by authoritative decrees that change is to occur. They fail simply because decreeing that some new practice shall be implemented does not develop either the commitment or the knowledge necessary for the practitioner to carry out the command. Consequently, power-coercive strategies tend to produce new legislation, rules, and regulations, but little in the way of changed behavior patterns in individuals and institutions. Furthermore, the behavior changes which do result from such authoritative decrees are often more defensive *against* the proposed change than adaptive toward it.

The strategy most appropriate for implementing process education incorporates the best features of the normative-reeducative change process within the empirical-rational system framework.

Schools and educational agencies are bureaucratic institutions, and this situation is not likely to change. When the bureaucratic nature of schools prevents them from adapting to a changing society, they become dysfunctional. The goal is not to "liberate" the schools, but to make them much more receptive and responsive to needed change. A means to this objective is to establish multiple temporary systems which include individuals from many agencies in the larger educational system. The task within the temporary systems is the reeducation of specific groups of teachers, administrators, and other educators toward specific and immediate objectives concerned with changing some aspects of current educational practice in the direction of the value orientations and role expectations for process education. The behavior, perceptions, attitudes, and roles of individuals who are members of permanent educational systems can be changed through their experiences in multiple temporary systems. In time, the nature of permanent systems themselves can become more and more temporary by virtue of the repeated and simultaneous involvement of their individual members in many normative-reeducative workshops, projects, task forces, and training sessions. Multiple temporary systems offer the means to produce great changes in individual and institutional patterns of behavior. In other words, temporary systems operating outside existing institutions with their bureaucratic limitations, but consisting of individuals from those same bureaucracies, can cause those permanent institutions to become more responsive to needed change.

The temporary systems used to implement process education or any other innovation have two important aspects. The first, or "system," aspect concerns the extent and membership of the system. The second, or "process," aspect concerns the normative-reeducative activity within and between component members of the system.

The "system" aspect of temporary systems can be represented in diagrams such as Figure 7 which shows an extended social system comprised of member agencies and individuals. The entire extended social system has certain objectives to attain, limited resources, and a finite period of time in which the objectives are to be achieved. This is also true for each of the components or the subsystems within the extended temporary system.

The second, or "process," aspect of extended temporary systems is concerned with the transmission of information between individuals and agencies through linkages. Linkages are the means to the communication between the members of the extended temporary system which allow normative-reeducative activity to occur. The question appropriate for *every* linkage point—both within and between member agencies and individuals in the extended temporary system—is, "*Who* transmits *what information,* by *what means,* to *whom,* to *what immediate effect,* and for *what long term goal?*"

The critical information for process education concerns particular value orientations and pupil and teacher role expectations which have been presented in Chapter 3. Specific information appropriate to the practice of process education as the immediate objectives for an extended temporary system can be selected from Table 6 in Chapter 3. Existing curricular and instructional vehicles can be selected which contain the specific information which is to be transmitted. Those vehicles can be used to develop a commitment to process education and to demonstrate how some specific aspects of process education can be implemented into classroom practice. Extensive networks of the type depicted in Figure 7 can be established. The curriculum and instructional vehicles selected can become the focus of a series of normative-reeducative activities for the many temporary subsystems within the larger extended temporary system. The immediate goal of such a network might be the facilitation of only a few changes in pupil and teacher roles in relation to the utilization of a particular curriculum and instructional vehicle. The normative-reeducative activity in such an extended temporary system would involve not only pupils and teachers but those persons throughout the larger educational system whose support is critical to implementing and maintaining major changes in classroom practice. The long term goal should be to both transfer these role changes to other teaching-learning activities outside the specific curriculum and instructional vehicle and to develop additional pupil and teacher roles essential to process education through other vehicles and other temporary systems. Procedures for selecting and using curriculum and instructional vehicles to obtain these immediate and long term goals are described in the next chapter.

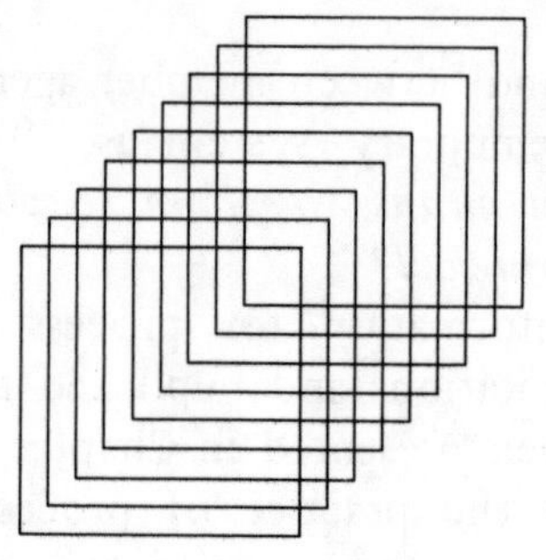

CHAPTER 5

GUIDELINES FOR SELECTING AND USING CURRICULUM AND INSTRUCTIONAL VEHICLES

In the previous chapters it has been suggested that the practice of process education can be facilitated through the use of existing exemplary curriculum and instructional vehicles. Many of these vehicles have been developed with value orientations similar to those stated for process education. This chapter is concerned with means for the selection of such curriculum and instructional vehicles in order that the practice of process education can be implemented through time.

Properties of Curriculum and Instructional Vehicles

Before considering how curriculum and instructional vehicles can be selected as being appropriate to implementing the practice of process education, it is important to consider the general properties of those vehicles. Curriculum and instructional vehicles are not simply existing curriculum programs or materials. Rather they include a variety of materials and strategies, different types of messages, and fundamental structural elements.

Curriculum and Instructional Vehicles as Messages

There are many types and varieties of educational materials and programs which can be used to facilitate pupil and teacher roles central to process education. These have been previously and will continue to be referred to as curriculum and instructional vehicles, or simply as vehicles. They may also be considered to be "messages" which contain information about new educational practices which can be disseminated to and used by members of the educational system. To the extent that existing curriculum and instructional vehicles convey "messages" about the theory, the application of the theory, and the actual practice of process education, they can be used to normative-reeducative ends. That is, they can be used not simply as programs in their own right but as means to create new awareness, perceptions, value orientations, competencies, and behavior patterns more in keeping with the practice of process education.

Types of Messages Conveyed by Curriculum and Instructional Vehicles

Havelock (1969, Chapter 2, p. 38) notes several general types of "messages" which result from resource systems and their activities. Three particular types of messages are represented by particular curriculum and instructional vehicles which now exist. Some vehicles contain all three types of messages. Others contain only one type of message.

The first and most fundamental type of messages (Type I) are those which are concerned with communicating basic knowledge in the form of philosophies, theories, laws, classification schemata or other conceptual organizations of observed phenomena. In education, good examples of such fundamental messages are Robert Gagné's *The Conditions of Learning* (1965a), Jerome

Bruner's *Toward a Theory of Instruction* (1968), E. Paul Torrance's *Rewarding Creative Behavior* (1965) and Rubin's *Life Skills in School and Society* (1969a). The positions stated for education in these and similar books represent basic philosophies and theories derived from extensive study of empirical phenomena. The knowledge presented in such works is based upon an assessment of the educational needs of modern society. The recommendations made are based upon what has been learned about preparing individuals to function effectively in the modern world. Chapters 1, 2, and 3 of this book have considered much of this basic knowledge about the nature of society, the individual, and education and woven it into a rationale which calls for process education, which is a particular philosophic approach to education based upon certain justifications, assumptions, value positions, and expectations for pupil and teacher behavior.

A second general type of message (Type II) deals with essentially the same information contained in basic philosophies, theories, and conceptual organizations, but in a form concerned with the application of this knowledge toward changing and improving performance in some area of human endeavor. Messages of this type contain information about how basic knowledge in the form of theories and principles can be applied to some particular activity. There are numerous examples in education. The basic empirically derived knowledge which is set forth in Gagné's *The Conditions of Learning* has been translated into numerous documents concerned with curriculum and instructional design and organization (Gagné, 1963, 1965a, 1965b, 1966, 1968a, 1968b; Livermore, 1964). The basic philosophy and approach to education described by Bruner in *Toward a Theory of Instruction* has likewise been translated into documents for teachers and other educators concerned with applying that theory (Bruner & Dow, 1967; Dow, 1968). Similarly, Torrance has translated his empirical findings concerning the facilitation and measurement of creative behavior described in *Rewarding Creative*

Behavior (1965) to *Encouraging Creativity in the Classroom* (1970). The latter book explains to teachers how much of the basic and empirically derived knowledge contained in the former book can be applied in the practical classroom situation.

A third type of message (Type III) is one which is designed explicitly for the practitioner. It usually requires little, if any, translation of theory into practical procedures by the practitioner. This type of message commonly exists in the form of a service or product which has been developed and tested toward achieving particular objectives in practice. Again, examples of such message types are common in education. Examples may be found among the numerous curriculum innovations developed in the sixties. Many of these programs have been based upon extensive and well explicated theory and empirical research (message Type I) which has been used to establish the broad goals, design, and organization of instructional procedures and learning materials (message Type II) for the actual development of instructional products and techniques (message Type III). Examples of such programs were discussed briefly in Chapter 1. They include the AAAS Commission *Science–A Process Approach*, based on the theoretical and empirical work of Gagné; the *Man: A Course of Study* social science curriculum based on Bruner's theories and philosophical observations; and the Ginn and Company Reading 360 and Imagi/Craft series based upon the work of Torrance.

Not all educational materials have a basis in message Types I and II. Many, if not most, educational materials are based upon little or no theoretical and empirical considerations, but rather upon tradition. Basic knowledge in the form of epistemological, pedagogical, and learning theory and research is usually not a consideration in the development of such materials. Basic rationales for such programs do not exist. Typically the procedure used to certify such educational materials appropriate for use in schools are testimonials by scholarly "experts" and teachers who have used the programs. Such programs and their developers are concerned with presenting the usual content via the usual means and media. The goal is to produce not new and improved innovative programs but materials which will be readily acceptable under prevailing institutional conditions and role expectations. The assumptions and basic philosophical orientations underlying such programs are typically not explicated in any meaningful way. However, they frequently tend to be opposed to process education. The value orientations and teacher and pupil role expectations likewise are often more opposed to than congruent with the goals of process education. Such curriculum and instructional vehicles have little relevance as means for the facilitation of process education. They tend to reinforce traditional educational practice and patterns rather than change them in the direction of the value positions and role expectations for process education.

This is not to say that all curriculum and instructional vehicles appropriate to the practice of process education must be based upon Type I and Type II messages. They need not be. However, the position taken here is that educational products and practices with a good basis in theory and research underlying process education can serve as more effective vehicles for facilitating and generalizing the practice of process education throughout the larger educational system. This is true at all levels within the larger educational system. Theoretically and empirically based curriculum and instructional vehicles can be used to change the behavior of pupils and teachers, college professors who train teachers, and curriculum developers who design and organize learning materials. Educational products and practices without adequate roots in the knowledge base of message Types I and II are deficient in the information which they can transmit toward general improvement of educational practice. They cannot easily be used for normative-reeducative functions of the many individuals within the extended temporary systems described in Chapter 4. They lack the power of more carefully conceptualized and developed educational innovations such as *Man: A Course of*

Study, Science—A Process Approach, the *Ginn Reading 360 Series,* the *Productive Thinking Program, Materials and Activities for Teachers and Children,* and many other existing curriculum vehicles well suited to the task of effecting change in educational practice toward process education.[27]

Varieties of Curriculum and Instructional Vehicles

The vehicles which may be used to promote the practice of process education are very diverse in their content, organization, and design. Some represent elaborate and comprehensive manipulative and instructional materials which have been carefully organized into a series of activities or lessons forming an extended learning sequence for pupils. Other vehicles consist of no materials at all for pupils but teacher education strategies and materials designed to enable teachers to select, modify, and construct learning sequences toward achieving pupil competence in specified processes or skills. Still other vehicles exist in the form of particularly well designed lessons, activities, and materials in the form of short duration packages or units which are designed to be incorporated at various points within the ongoing school curriculum. Vehicles having these characteristics exist across many content areas and grade levels. The discussion that follows is based upon the study of only those vehicles appropriate for use within elementary schools.

Extensive Curriculum Material Sequences

A number of extensive and comprehensive curriculum vehicles appropriate to implementing the practice of process education

27. These and some other vehicles for promoting process education are described in *Encounters in thinking: A compendium of curricula for process education* (Seferian & Cole, 1970).

exist. Often they represent the products of major curriculum development efforts which have been funded over a period of from five to ten years. Typically such extensive vehicles have been well rooted in basic theory, basic and applied research, and have undergone trial utilization in prototype versions. The terminal behavior goals are usually clearly stated for such extensive curriculum and instructional vehicles. More specific short term instructional objectives are usually stated either explicitly or imbedded in the narrative of teacher guides and manuals for particular lessons and activities. Detailed daily and weekly lesson plans are typically provided for teachers. The materials, content, and activity for the program are usually well specified and packaged within subcomponents of the overall program. In addition to providing specific information on how to conduct particular lessons and activities, teacher guides and manuals usually make many suggestions about types of teaching-learning strategies to be employed, the role to be played by the pupil and teacher, and the extension or generalization of the learning experiences contained in the program to relevant aspects of the pupils' experience and interests. Additional reading materials and activities for teachers are often provided by such programs with the intention of making them more knowledgeable and competent in the purpose and philosophy of the program, its content, organization, and pedagogical procedures.

Good examples of this type of program include *Man: A Course of Study,* a one-year upper elementary social science curriculum; *Science—A Process Approach,* a seven-year kindergarten through sixth grade science curriculum; the *Minnesota Mathematics and Science Teaching Project Materials,* a three-year primary school science and mathematics curriculum; and the *Science Curriculum Improvement Study,* a non-graded kindergarten through grade eight science curriculum consisting of six levels. Such programs represent very complete and extensive instructional products which have been constructed as largely self-contained packages and which have been designed toward the attainment of specific short and long term learning goals.

Teacher Education Strategies

Other appropriate vehicles for facilitating the practice of process education provide little or nothing in the way of materials and organized learning sequences for pupils. Rather, they are teacher education programs designed to instruct the teacher in the construction and use of learning activities designed to achieve certain long and short term objectives. Programs of this type are in reality a series of guidelines and techniques designed to help the teacher to gather and select materials, develop topics, and design learning activities for pupils appropriate for developing particular attitudes, habits, and skills of feeling and thinking. The content of the learning activity is usually that which is normally found within the school curriculum. That is, the teacher designs learning activities for pupils within the areas of science, social science, reading, and mathematics. A good example of this type of program is the *National Schools Project* developed by Frank E. Williams.

The goal of the *National Schools Project* materials is to facilitate productive thinking in elementary school children. The program is based upon a productive thinking model derived from the theoretical and empirical work of Guilford, Torrance, Bloom, and Piaget, among others. The model enumerates eight intellectual processes (fluency, flexibility, originality, elaboration, risk taking, preference for complexity, curiosity, and imagination) and 17 teaching strategies which cut across all traditional elementary school content. The model has been used as the basis of a teacher education program. Teachers are taught to select, modify, and design learning materials and activities within particular content areas of the school curriculum toward developing pupil competence in the specified skills. The model has also been used to categorize a large number of existing educational materials such as films, books, booklets, and records within the 8 process categories and 17 teaching strategies and across the content areas of the typical elementary school curriculum. Teachers engaged in the project have also produced a large number of "ideas" which are specific instances of how a given teaching strategy may be used to promote a particular process or skill within a given content area (Williams, 1968a, 1970). The *National Schools Project* program serves a normative-reeducative function for teachers relative to the selection and design of materials and activities appropriate to developing divergent and productive thinking skills in pupils.

Another example of an existing set of teacher education strategies as vehicles appropriate to the implementation of process education is found in the SRA series titled *Teacher Resource Booklets on Classroom Social Relations and Learning.* Included in this series are: *Role-Playing Methods in the Classroom* (Chesler & Fox, 1966); *Diagnosing Classroom Learning Environments* (Fox, Luszki, & Schmuck, 1966); *The Teacher's Role in Social Science Investigation* (Lippitt, Fox, & Schaible, 1969); and *Problem-Solving to Improve Classroom Learning* (Schmuck, Chesler, & Lippitt, 1966). As noted in earlier chapters, these books contain the elements of an inservice teacher education program which has the goal of helping the teacher and pupils determine the existing norms for the learning activity within the classroom in order to improve motivations and efficiency of learning, and establish more functional pupil and teacher learning roles. These strategies are designed to serve a normative-reeducative function for teachers and pupils relative to the establishment of classroom interpersonal relationships and climates needed to support learning and inquiry activity.

Short Duration Instructional Packages

Another variety of curriculum and instructional vehicles appropriate to the practice of process education includes carefully designed and packaged learning materials and activities which may or may not be based upon theoretical and empirical knowledge. These types of vehicles are usually very discrete packages or sets of learning materials and activities. Typically they are used for a duration of only a few minutes, hours, or weeks. They are not part of a larger overall carefully organized instructional sequence. Rather, they typically consist of particular manipulative devices and materials, such as records, films, filmstrips, games, or group activities. They are designed to be used not as major components within the school curriculum but as subcomponents which may be selected and articulated by pupils and teachers into the content and sequence of the usual curriculum areas.

There are numerous examples of this type of short duration curriculum and instructional products. The Torrance and Cunnington Imagi/Craft series, consisting of phonograph records and creative thinking exercises, is one example. Particular sets of materials are designed to be used as the focus of individual lessons lasting from 20 to 40 minutes. "Sounds and Images" is one such activity designed to stimulate imaginative and creative thinking on the part of pupils about a number of usual and unusual sounds presented on a record. Other records in the series dramatize great moments of discovery in the lives of widely recognized creative thinkers and inventors. These materials do not comprise an integrated and major instructional package of learning activities. Rather, they provide a number of carefully developed, short duration instructional packages that may be incorporated at numerous times and places within the normal curriculum or program of instruction in elementary schools.

Another example of short duration curriculum and instructional vehicles is the Elementary Science Study (ESS) units developed by Education Development Center. ESS units are self-contained packages of materials designed to provide motivating and informative experiences for pupils and teachers. The materials do not constitute a course of study nor is any one component deliberately related to any other. Rather, the units are designed for flexible utilization in any sequence and in relation to many topics and activities which are common to elementary school science. The emphasis for the units is not on obtaining particular instructional objectives but upon having the pupils and teachers engage in exploratory behavior and inquiry activity. The intent of the units is to foster favorable attitudes and increased commitment of pupils to engage in discovery learning through direct manipulation of materials and variables. A particular unit may be used by a number of pupils for a period of one to a few weeks, depending upon the activity and the pupils' interests. Teachers' guides are provided for the units, but consistent with the philosophy of the program they are non-prescriptive and open-ended. Rather than explain in detail how to use the units, the guides suggest a number of procedures and activities and encourage the teacher to experiment to find additional uses for the units consistent with pupil interests and needs.

Still another example of excellent short term instructional packages appropriate to implementing the practice of process education are the units developed by the Children's Museum. The more well known and most exemplary of these were developed under the direction of Frederick Kresse and are called the *Materials and Activities for Teachers and Children* (MATCH) units. These units are self-contained packages of materials and media, each one being designed for use in a series of intensive learning activities occurring daily over a period of two to three weeks in elementary school classrooms. The units are intended to be incorporated as short term topics of study within the larger on-going curriculum. MATCH units are rich in materials and activities which transmit much information and develop a wide variety of intellectual, emotional, and social interactive skills central to process education. Furthermore, they do so largely by non-verbal means through the use of carefully designed and sequenced experiences with a large number of fascinating materials and objects. Within each MATCH unit a teacher's guide provides direction for managing materials and directing the sequence of learning activities for the two- to three-week period in accordance with pupil and teacher needs and preferences, and for establishing proper teacher and pupil learning roles and relationships. The teaching-learning strategies used and pupil and teacher role behaviors called for are particularly congruent with the value positions and role expectations of process education stated in Chapter 3 (Kresse, 1968).

Non-Uniform Nature of Curriculum and Instructional Vehicles

In Chapter 1 there is a brief account of how the Institute staff searched for, identified, and selected existing curriculum and instructional vehicles for use in implementing the practice of process education. A more detailed account of this procedure may be found in another document (Cole & Seferian, 1970). The search activity identified curriculum and instructional vehicles which included all the varieties indicated above. It soon became clear that a given variety of curriculum and instructional materials—whether they were an extensive set of curriculum materials, teacher education strategies, or short duration packages of some instructional products—might be very appropriate to the practice of process education. It was learned that each of these varieties of curriculum and instructional vehicles sometimes is, and sometimes is not, based upon educational theory and basic and applied research. Each also may, or may not, provide a direct translation of that educational theory and research into specific practices and procedures to be used in the classroom. That is, in the language of the previous section, curriculum and instructional vehicles of all varieties may contain varying amounts of information characteristic of Type I, II, or III messages.

The vehicles which appear to be most appropriate for use in implementing process education tend to be those which, regardless of their variety, have information characteristic of all three types of messages to communicate to members of the larger educational system. Examples of the varieties and message type characteristics of such vehicles appropriate to implementing process education are shown in Table 10.

The search conducted at the Institute showed that most curriculum and instructional vehicles have little or no theoretical and research basis. They are typically a collection of content arranged in some sequence in one or more textbooks. They are designed primarily for use within the norms of existing pupil-teacher classroom behavior which include silent reading by pupils; oral reading by pupils in class; teacher led and dominated classroom discussion concerning the content presented in the textbooks; teacher directed question and answer sessions; and pupil activities such as answering questions which occur at the end of chapters in the textbooks, or completion of reports or "projects" related to the content of the textbook but perhaps based upon outside reading and references. The bulk of existing commercially developed and prepared educational materials have these characteristics. They are sorely lacking in a Type I knowledge base. Rather, they represent sequences of content to be used in the traditional instructional fashion. When programs of this type are examined in the framework of Table 10, it becomes apparent that they have little or no Type I and II messages to communicate. Furthermore, the Type III messages communicated are frequently teaching and learning strategies opposed to the value positions and teacher and pupil role expectations stated for process education in Chapter 3.

The varieties of curriculum and instructional vehicles and the different types of messages they contain make the problem of selecting particular vehicles for the implementation of process education a complex task. There is no uniform set of structural

Table 10

Examples of Three Varieties of Existing Curriculum and Instructional Vehicles and the Messages They Contain

Variety of Vehicle	Example of Vehicle	Message Contained in the Vehicle: Type I	Type II	Type III
Extensive Curriculum Materials Sequence	*Science—A Process Approach*	Gagne's theoretical and empirical conditions of learning and related conceptualization of learning hierarchies which undergird problem-solving behavior.	Techniques of curriculum design which translate Gagne's theoretical and empirical conceptualizations into effective learning sequences designed to enhance analytic thinking and problem-solving skills.	Procedures, materials, and practices for use in classrooms to both diagnose and facilitate pupil subordinate behavioral capabilities required for achieving specified analytic thinking and problem-solving skills.
Extensive Curriculum Materials Sequence	*Man: A Course of Study*	Bruner's theoretical and philosophical conceptualizations of learning as structured inquiry or knowledge building activity by which the content of the disciplines is created and by which the individual makes meaning. Related concepts of unifying conceptual themes as the framework for spiral curricula.	Techniques of curriculum design which incorporate new and incomplete knowledge from the frontiers of scientific disciplines into learning experiences and activities for children organized in a spiral fashion around elegant and unifying conceptual themes.	Procedures, materials, and practices for use in classrooms to facilitate pupil inquiry and knowledge building activity from 1) examination of incomplete data, hypotheses, inquiry strategies, and theories of scientists currently engaged in extending the boundaries of knowledge, 2) engaging in their own knowledge building activities within areas of interest and experience.
Teacher Education Strategy	*National Schools Project*	The theoretical and empirical conceptualizations of Guilford and Torrance concerning the importance of divergent and productive thinking to adaptive behavior.	Techniques for instructional designs which relate the essential theoretical and empirical aspects of divergent and productive thinking to a wide variety of teaching-learning strategies and curriculum content.	Specific classroom strategies, techniques, and procedures for selecting, modifying, or designing materials and teaching-learning strategies toward facilitation of specified divergent thinking skills or processes in pupil behavior within and across the content of the typical elementary school curriculum.
Teacher Education Strategy	The SRA Series of *Teacher Resource Booklets on Classroom Social Relations and Learning*	The theoretical and empirical considerations of Lewin, Lippitt, Fox, and other social psychologists concerning the social conditions and requirements for effective learning, inquiry, and problem-solving.	Techniques for curriculum and instructional designs which incorporate the theory and research of social psychology for improving classroom normative expectations, roles, and climates to facilitate individual and group learning, inquiry, and problem-solving behavior.	Specific classroom strategies, techniques, and materials for diagnosing and modifying existing classroom normative expectations for teacher and pupil roles toward improved individual and group learning, inquiry, and problem-solving.
Short Duration Instructional Package	*Sounds and Images*	Theoretical and empirical conceptualizations of Torrance concerning fluency and flexibility as critical aspects of creative thinking.	Techniques for translating theoretical and empirical conceptualizations of fluency and flexibility into instructional designs for both the diagnosis and facilitation of these characteristics.	Instructional materials and procedures for use in classrooms for diagnosing and facilitating fluent and flexible thinking in pupils.
Short Duration Instructional Package	The MATCH Unit Titled *The City*	Theoretical, philosophical, and empirical considerations compiled by Kresse which show the critical importance of real materials and manipulative activity as non-verbal mediators of learning and inquiry activity.	Techniques for the design of instructional and curriculum packages which utilize a wide array of highly motivating concrete objects and materials 1) as the focus for pupil inquiry and learning activity, and 2) which serve as the primary medium of communication of knowledge to pupils rather than usual verbal media.	A package of instructional materials and procedures for use in classrooms and by which information is transmitted to pupils as they engage in largely self-directed non-verbal inquiry activity.

characteristics which appropriate vehicles exhibit. Some very appropriate vehicles may be simply teacher education materials for fostering particular teaching-learning strategies but they contain no materials for direct use with pupils. Other appropriate vehicles may consist only of instructional materials for pupils with no accompanying teacher education materials for developing proper teaching-learning strategies. Still other appropriate vehicles may consist of diagnostic procedures and strategies for effecting change in pupil and teacher roles within the classroom.

Fundamental Elements of Curriculum and Instructional Vehicles

Although there is no uniform set of structural characteristics exhibited by the variety of curriculum and instructional vehicles available and potentially useful for implementing process education, there are certain common elements which exist in all vehicles. These include the objectives or goals for the learning activity, the content and materials of the learning experience, and the teaching-learning strategies by which learning is to occur. Collectively, these three elements, as they are prescribed by the underlying theory, as they are applied in the design of curriculum and instructional materials, and as they are executed in practice in the classroom, reveal whether or not the messages contained in a particular vehicle are appropriate to process education.

Objectives for the Learning Activity

No matter what the variety of the curriculum and instructional vehicle, some terminal expectation or goal for the ultimate consumer, the pupil, is usually stated. These objectives may or may not be behaviorally stated. Even when behaviorally specific, they tend to be broad, rather than narrow, objectives. For example, a terminal and behaviorally stated but broad objective for the *National Schools Project* is to "increase the ideational fluency and flexibility of pupils." The objective is behaviorally specific in the sense that it refers specifically to the ability to generate a large number and variety of ideas, solutions, interpretations, perceptions, etc., as a response to any of a large number of situations. It is broad in the sense that the particular situations in which the fluent and flexible responses are to be exhibited are not specified. It should also be noted that although this particular vehicle is the variety referred to above as "teacher education strategies," it nevertheless has as its terminal objectives changes in pupil behavior. This is characteristic of all curriculum and instructional vehicles, whatever their variety. They ultimately seek to effect change in pupil behavior and, consequently, they usually state long term or terminal objectives for the learning activity of the pupil. Similar terminal goals are also frequently stated for the learning activity of the teacher.

Content and Materials of the Learning Experience

Whatever the variety of the curriculum and instructional vehicle, it either provides or influences the selection of content and materials within which the learning activity occurs. In the case of extensive curriculum materials sequences and short duration instructional packages, the content and materials of the learning experience are usually well specified and included as a major part of the program. In the case of teacher education strategy vehicles, the content and materials for the learning experience are not usually provided. Rather, guidelines, suggestions, and advice are provided for the teacher in order to develop his competence in selecting and designing appropriate content and materials as the basis of the learning experience for pupils. Thus, in the teacher education strategy approach of the *National Schools Project,* teachers are assisted in the selection of content and materials for learning experiences appropriate to developing specified divergent and productive thinking skills. In the other teacher education strategy approach listed in Table 10, teachers are assisted in selecting behavioral specimens drawn from the daily social interaction among pupils as the content and material to be used in developing social interactive and cooperative learning skills. Each of the three varieties of curriculum and instructional vehicles shown in Table 10 provides or suggests specific content and materials within which the learning activity occurs.

Teaching-Learning Strategies

Curriculum and instructional vehicles of all varieties in some way speak to the teaching-learning strategies which are to be used to accomplish the learning. The teaching-learning strategies collectively define the role expectation for the pupils and teachers in the learning activity. In many curriculum and instructional vehicles, extensive directions are provided in teacher guidebooks which explain the teaching-learning strategies and pupil and teacher roles to be used with the vehicle. The *Man: A Course of Study, Science—A Process Approach, Materials and Activities for Teachers and Children,* and *Science Curriculum Improvement Study* programs are excellent examples of vehicles which provide great attention and direction to this topic. Virtually every lesson in each of these programs has an extensive series of suggestions, recommendations, and classroom management procedures which define the teaching-learning strategy to be used within the context of the specific learning activity. Furthermore, inservice teacher education activities and materials which are frequently used with these programs are centrally concerned with developing teacher familiarity and competence in appropriate, but typically non-traditional, teaching-learning strategies.

Other curriculum and instructional vehicles of the teacher education strategy variety are even more centrally concerned with teaching-learning strategies. Thus, we see in the *National Schools Project* program a major objective of developing teacher competence in using 17 different teaching-learning strategies, many of which are relatively atypical to the usual teacher and pupil classroom roles. In the SRA *Teacher Resource Booklets on Classroom Social Relations and Learning* the objective is to develop particular teaching-learning strategies which, while quite atypical to the usual classroom, are known empirically to be supportive of self-motivated and directed individual and group inquiry and problem-solving. The teaching-learning strategies called for require that new learning roles be assumed by both pupils and teachers. Vehicles of the teacher education variety seek to change pupil and teacher roles toward improving the pupil learning activity and meeting terminal objectives for pupil performance.

Selecting Curriculum and Instructional Vehicles Appropriate to Process Education

So far it has been shown that curriculum and instructional vehicles contain three basic types of messages. Type I messages concern the philosophy, theory, and basic research which underlie the rationale for the vehicle. Type II messages concern techniques for applying the underlying philosophy, theory, and research to the actual design and organization of curriculum and instructional materials and activities. Type III messages concern how the basic philosophy, theory, and research are actually translated into teaching-learning practices within the classroom.

Curriculum and instructional vehicles may also be categorized as belonging to one of three varieties. These include extensive curriculum material sequences, teacher education strategies, and short duration instructional packages.

In addition, curriculum and instructional vehicles have three fundamental elements. These are the goals or objectives for the learning activity, the content and materials of the learning experience, and the teaching-learning strategies by which the learning activity is to occur.

These are properties which are common to all curriculum and instructional vehicles. Obviously, some of these vehicles are appropriate to implementing the practice of process education, while others are inappropriate. The problem is how to select, from among the many existing vehicles which can be identified, those most useful in implementing the practice of process education.

Procedures for the identification and collection of existing curriculum and instructional vehicles are not considered in this chapter. The reader interested in such procedures is advised to refer to *A Guide to Innovation in Education* (Havelock, 1970). This book contains an extensive set of procedures for the search, identification, and selection of existing curriculum and instructional vehicles according to change agent or user needs. In addition, Havelock provides a very comprehensive appendix which lists the major sources capable of providing information about educational innovations and curriculum and instructional vehicles. "Analysis of Process Curricula" (Cole & Seferian, 1970) provides an additional, but less extensive, description of procedures and information sources used by the Institute to search and select curriculum and instructional vehicles appropriate to process education.

Critical Questions for Selecting Curriculum and Instructional Vehicles

There are three critical questions whose answers determine whether or not existing curriculum and instructional vehicles are appropriate for implementing the practice of process education. These include:

1. Are the types of messages contained in the vehicle supportive or opposed to the value positions and

derivative pupil and teacher role expectations stated for process education in Chapter 3?

2. Are the objectives for learning, the content and materials of the learning experience, and the teaching-learning strategies inherent in or prescribed by the vehicle supportive or opposed to the value positions and derivative pupil and teacher role expectations for process education stated in Chapter 3?

3. Are the messages contained in the vehicle appropriate to user needs and implementation objectives?

There are two reference frameworks from which to approach these questions. The first referent is the value positions and derivative teacher and pupil role expectations stated for process education in Chapter 3. The second referent is the model of the extended temporary social system described in Chapter 4 as a means to implement change into educational practice. Attention to the first referent provides information about the congruence of the curriculum and instructional vehicle with the philosophy and goals of process education. Attention to the second referent provides information about the utility of the vehicle for changing, in specified ways, the behavior of many member organizations and their individuals within extended temporary knowledge dissemination and utilization systems. The first two questions require attention to the value positions and derivative role expectations stated for process education. The last question requires attention to the implementation model described in Chapter 4.

Selecting Vehicles Congruent with the Philosophy and Goals of Process Education

Information which determines whether or not a curriculum and instructional vehicle is appropriate to the value positions and derivative role expectations for process education is contained in the messages of the vehicle. The fundamental elements of the vehicle, which include the objectives for learning, the content and materials of the learning experience, and the teaching-learning strategies by which the learning activity occurs, are the major but nonexclusive sources of information about the messages contained in the vehicle. Other sources of information about the messages contained in the vehicle include supporting documents which explain the rationale of the vehicle and provide evaluative data and research concerning the effectiveness of the vehicle in causing particular changes in attitudes, perceptions, and performance and how the vehicle was designed and tested. Still other sources of information are the individuals who conceptualized and designed the vehicle, change agents and consultants who have assisted teachers and pupils in using the vehicle, and the teachers and pupils who have actually used the vehicle in the classroom. All of these information sources can provide data which determine the types of messages the vehicle contains, the quality of those messages, and the congruence of the messages with the philosophy and goals of process education. The procedures for conducting such an analysis of a curriculum and instructional vehicle are shown in Tables 11, 12, and 13. They consist of gathering information about the Type I, II, and III messages contained in the vehicle relative to the four value positions and derivative pupil and teacher role expectations for process education which have been previously stated in Tables 4, 5, and 6 of Chapter 3. The questions to be answered are: "What do the vehicle's messages communicate about *knowledge, learning,* the *learner,* and the *school?*" and "Are the messages about these topics congruent with or opposed to the value positions and derivative pupil and teacher role expectations stated for process education?" Table 11 provides a procedure for analyzing the Type I message content of the vehicle and deciding if the messages are congruent with the value orientations of process education. Table 12 provides a similar procedure for analyzing the Type II messages of the vehicles and

Table 11

Assessing Curriculum and Instructional Vehicles for Process Education on the Basis of Their Underlying Value Positions

Message Type	Data Sources	Means of Obtaining Data	Questions to Be Answered	Judgments Based on Four Value Dimensions[28]			
				Knowledge	Learning	Learner	School
I	Terminal goals or objectives for the learning activity. Supporting documents which provide the theoretical, philosophical, and empirical basis for the vehicle. Individuals involved in conceptualizing and designing the vehicle.	Study of terminal objectives and supporting documentation. Conferences with the conceptualizers and designers of the vehicle.	Do Type I messages exist relative to the function of:	___Yes ___No	___Yes ___No	___Yes ___No	___Yes ___No
			What are the specific sources or references for the Type I message relative to:	List Sources:	List Sources:	List Sources:	List Sources:
			What is the nature of the Type I message stated relative to:	Summarize message:	Summarize message:	Summarize message:	Summarize message:
			What is the value position of the Type I messages stated relative to process education?	___(-) absolute and true / *Knowledge* is: \ ___(+) tentative and arbitrary	___(-) unnatural and difficult / *Learning* is: \ ___(+) natural and enjoyable	___(-) a humble and passive recipient of knowledge / The *Learner* is: \ ___(+) an aggressive and active seeker of knowledge and experience	___(-) the authoritative transmitter of established values and knowledge / The *School* is: \ ___(+) the setting for emergence of values and knowledge through inquiry

28. To be meaningful, this portion of the table must be interpreted within the structure of Tables 4, 5, and 6 in Chapter 3, which describe in detail the four value dimensions.

Table 12

Assessing Curriculum and Instructional Vehicles for Process Education on the Basis of Their Pupil and Teacher Role Expectations

Message Type	Data Sources	Means of Obtaining Data	Questions to Be Answered	Procedures for Answering Questions	Judgment
II	Instructional objectives, content, and materials included or recommended for the learning experience and its evaluation. Teacher guides and inservice education materials which specify or recommend particular teaching-learning strategies and roles for the learning activity and instructional arrangements and procedures. Designers, developers, and testers of the vehicle. Evaluate data and reports on the trial utilization and effect of the vehicle.	Collection and study of all the instructional objectives, materials, and content provided or recommended for pupils and for teachers, all evaluative data reports on trial utilization of the vehicle. Study of the instructional objectives, learning activities and sequences, and pupil or teacher diagnostic devices and procedures recommended or provided. Conference with the designers, testers, and trial users of the vehicle.	Do the techniques of curriculum and instructional design translate basic philosophy, theory, and empirical knowledge which underlie the terminal objectives into practical procedures for progressing toward those goals?	Comparison of the vehicle's fundamental elements with the Type I messages stated for the vehicle in its supporting documentation and the value positions underlying process education. Table 6 in Chapter 3 can serve as a checklist for the latter part of this procedure while Table 11 above is useful for the former comparison.	The vehicle is (inappropriate, appropriate) to the task of illustrating how the basic value positions and derivative pupil and teacher role expectations for process education can be applied in practice.
			Do the objectives for the learning activity, the content and materials of the learning experience, and the teaching-learning strategies called for facilitate pupil and teacher role expectations central to process education?	Examine objectives, content and materials, and teacher-learning strategies provided or suggested against the individual pupil and teacher role expectations derivative from the four value positions for process education. Table 6 in Chapter 3 can serve as a checklist upon which each element of the vehicle is examined.	The vehicle (is not, is) consistent with the value positions underlying process education and facilitative of the derivative pupil and teacher role expectations.

Table 13

Assessing Curriculum and Instructional Vehicles for Process Education on the Basis of Their Operational Behavior Patterns

Message Type	Data Sources	Means for Obtaining Data	Questions to Be Answered	Procedures for Answering Questions	Judgment
III	Trial, laboratory, and demonstration schools where teachers and pupils are actually using the vehicle in a classroom setting.	Visiting and observing the vehicle in operation in classroom settings. Systematic observation of pupil and teacher behavior patterns where the vehicle is being used on instruments similar to *Indicators of Quality.* Reports and studies which describe the characteristic pupil and teacher behavior patterns which result from using the vehicle.	Are the behavior patterns exhibited by pupils and teachers actually using the vehicle consistent with the role expectations for process education?	Comparison of data collected on pupil and teacher behavior patterns with each pupil and teacher role expectation for process education. Table 6 in Chapter 3 can serve as both the basis for observational devices to gather the data and as a checklist to judge the effectiveness of the vehicle in promoting desired roles.	In actual operation the vehicle (does, does not) promote pupil and teacher behavior patterns consistent with role expectations for process education.
			To what extent is the philosophy, theory, and rationale for process education which underlies the vehicle translated into operational practice within the classroom situation?	Comparison of behavior patterns exhibited by pupils and teachers using the vehicle with the contents of Table 11 completed for the vehicle and with the value positions stated for process education in Chapter 3.	In actual operation the vehicle (does, does not) translate basic philosophy and theory underlying process education into particular operational procedures, techniques and materials for use in the classroom.

judging their appropriateness to process education. Table 13 repeats the basic procedure relative to Type III messages contained in the vehicle.

The Tables and the procedures they contain define inclusion and exclusion rules for the selection of curriculum and instructional vehicles appropriate to implementing process education. Complete analysis of a vehicle involves collecting and studying all information which can be obtained about the underlying philosophy, goals, and theory used to guide the development of the vehicle. In addition, all the actual materials associated with the vehicle need to be gathered and studied. These include all pupil learning objectives, materials, and tests, all teacher education materials and guidebooks, and any other supplementary materials and information which may exist in connection with the vehicle. Finally, the vehicle needs to be examined and studied in actual operation to determine if it does indeed effect desired changes in teacher and pupil behavior patterns, and the type and degree of change which does occur. Data of this type are sometimes, but frequently are not, available from pilot studies or trial utilizations of the vehicle. If such data are not available, arrangements should be made to undertake limited pilot studies to learn more about the operational characteristics of the vehicle. Failure to do so prior to selecting a particular vehicle as the focus of an extended temporary system designed to effect change in many member organizations of the educational system is very risky. When at all possible, vehicles selected as the means for change should contain worthy and critical messages in line with both the goals of process education and the objectives for the implementation strategy. A vehicle should also be known to be effective in communicating specific messages in order that when the vehicle is installed, changes in individual and institutional behavior patterns occur in the desired direction.

The magnitude of the task of collecting and organizing the information needed to reach a decision about the appropriateness of a curriculum and instructional vehicle to implement some desired change in educational practice depends upon the variety of the vehicle. First-hand experience at the Institute has shown that it is an enormous task to collect and study all the supporting documents and materials affiliated with extended curriculum materials sequences such as the *Science–A Process Approach, Minnesota Mathematics and Science Teaching,* and *Man: A Course of Study* programs. The amount of information in such programs is immense. A given individual may spend months becoming thoroughly familiar with the huge array of materials and procedures involved.

Short duration instructional packages are much easier to analyze. They simply contain much less information at all levels. Therefore, it is much easier to obtain and study all the documents, reports, and materials which provide the information about the messages contained in the package and its effectiveness in communicating these messages.

Vehicles of the teacher education variety are also usually quite difficult to analyze. Typically, their procedures are not as well packaged and they depend upon the utilization of a wide array of content and materials drawn from many sources for the learning experience. It is frequently much more difficult to identify the limits and component elements of teacher education strategy vehicles than to identify extended sequences of curriculum materials and short duration instructional packages. In the language of Chapter 4, the latter two varieties of vehicles tend to be "thing technologies," while teacher education strategies are "people technologies," not based primarily on materials or things but upon processes and procedures. However, many such programs are known empirically to be effective vehicles for effecting normative-reeducative changes in human social systems.

The advantage of the selection procedures outlined in Tables 11, 12, and 13 is that highly useful vehicles are not rejected simply because they are not "thing oriented." Most existing criteria which have been used for the selection of curriculum and instructional vehicles have been excessively "thing oriented" and have been insensitive to selecting very appropriate and effective teacher education strategy vehicles. Typical curriculum analysis criteria such as those of Abt (1970), although useful at various stages of the process, are very inadequate for the larger task of selecting curriculum and instructional vehicles appropriate to implementing process education or any other change in practice in the educational system. As has been shown, curriculum and instructional vehicles are considerably broader than sets of materials which can be judged appropriate or inappropriate on dimensions of attractiveness of format, print size, and reading levels. For many curriculum and instructional vehicles, these and similar criteria are inappropriate and irrelevant.

Selecting Vehicles Appropriate to User Needs and Implementation Objectives

As was pointed out in Chapter 4, educational innovations develop from the activity of temporary systems, but their implementation occurs in permanent systems. The critical problem is one of building linkage relationships between the resource systems which have developed the innovations and the user systems who have need for the innovation. Failure to establish appropriate linkage relationships prevents implementation of new and improved ideas, patterns, and practices in permanent social systems.

The curriculum and instructional vehicles which have been referred to in this and other chapters are messages. They contain innovative information or knowledge which can be used to improve conventional practice within many levels of the larger educational system. Vehicles which contain messages particularly appropriate to implementing changed practice in education consistent with the value positions and role expectations of process education can be selected by the procedures described in the preceding section. Once a pool of vehicles containing messages appropriate for implementing process education has been established, a task which remains is to select from that pool those particular vehicles most appropriate to the needs of particular schools and educational agencies and most congruent with specific implementation objectives of the change agent.

Building Linkage Relationships

The task of building the necessary linkage relationships has been considered in Chapter 4. In brief review, necessary linkage relationships between resource and user systems can be achieved through the construction of extended temporary social systems designed to implement particular changes in the attitudes, perceptions, and practices of member individuals and organizations. Once the implementation objectives for an extended temporary system have been stated, it is possible to prepare charts such as Figures 7 and 9 in Chapter 4. These charts are based upon the Havelock conceptualization of the knowledge dissemination and utilization process within extended social systems (see Figures 3 and 5 in Chapter 4). They define *who* is to transfer *what* message or knowledge by what *means* to *whom* for *what immediate effect* for *what long term purpose.* When such charts have been prepared for the key linkage roles between and within the member organizations of the extended temporary system, the operational objectives and procedures of the system are specified. It becomes clear that particular messages need to be communicated by particular groups and individuals to other groups and individuals.

As Havelock (1970) has pointed out, it is critical that the linkage relationships be developed with the collaboration of individuals from the member organizations to be involved in the extended temporary system. This insures that the implementation objectives will be more congruent with both the user's needs and the change agent's goals. Such cooperative planning determines the extent of the temporary system and the primary roles and responsibilities of resource and client personnel within the system.

Determining User Needs

The problems of determining user needs is primarily one of answering the questions, "What messages does the user (teacher, teacher educator, pupil, principal, etc.) need to improve some aspect of his practice?" and "What new knowledge or information does the user seek in order to improve his practice?"

Most client systems in the form of school districts, teachers, and other groups or organizations in the larger educational system have needs to change and improve aspects of their practice. Sometimes the effects of the problem are evident to the individuals involved, but they are unaware of how to solve the problem. At other times, serious problems exist but are unrecognized. The function of the change agent or agency is to examine the client member organizations within a potential extended temporary social system for the purpose of noting practices which should be improved, needs which may exist, and problems which need to be clarified and resolved. The change agent needs to help the various users in the potential extended temporary social system become more aware of the need to change from outmoded conventional practices in favor of those known to be useful, adaptive, and more relevant to present conditions. In the case of process education this involves helping principals, teachers, teacher educators, and other members of educational organizations to become more aware of the need to become attuned to the value positions of process education and to strive to develop the derivative pupil and teacher role expectations. However, developing awareness of the need is not sufficient. There are many educators who are aware of the need to change educational practice toward the goals of process education. However, many of these individuals do not understand how to go about such a task.

Existing barriers in the form of institutional roles, organization, and practice which inhibit the necessary changes are often not apparent to those inside the institutions.

The change agent can act as a catalyst for change. He can help educational agencies become more aware of their need to introduce new knowledge and practices. He can assist them in more clearly recognizing and formulating their problems. He can assist them in designing or identifying solutions to the problems. And he can help them apply particular information and knowledge which exist in curriculum and instructional vehicles to the solution of problems, the meeting of needs, and the improvement of general educational practice. Havelock (1970) outlines detailed sets of procedures which can be used by change agents and the members of educational institutions to determine user needs for change and to cooperatively establish procedures to implement those changes. The basic steps in the procedure are shown in Figure 11. The three functions of the change agent in the activity are shown in Figure 12. One entire chapter in *A Guide to Innovation in Education* is devoted to how this diagnostic activity can be effectively carried out.

Determining Specific Implementation Objectives

Here the basic task is for the change agent to clearly specify the particular messages which are to be communicated to the member organizations and their individuals in the extended temporary system. Prior to this activity the general changes which the change agent seeks to implement as outcomes in the user systems must have been stated. In addition, many specific and derivative behavior changes in the target populations to be changed must have been developed and stated. In the case of process education, these prerequisite general outcomes and specific derivative behavior changes have been stated in Chapter 3. The former are represented by the four value positions for process education. The latter are represented in the derivative pupil and

Figure 11

Basic Steps in Implementing Change in Educational Institutions[29]

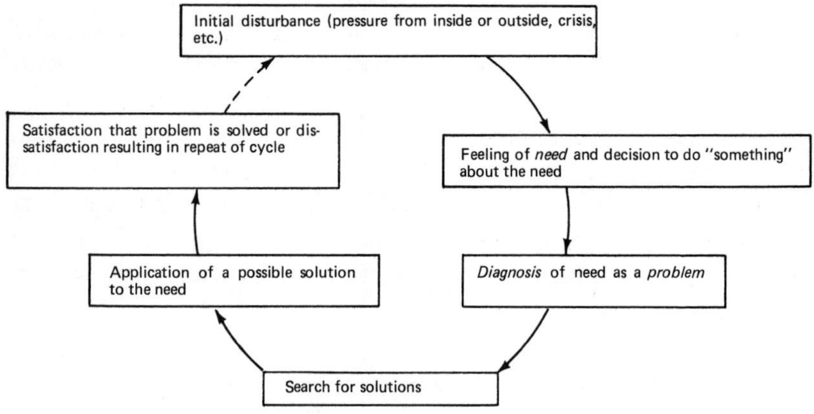

29. Reprinted with permission from Havelock, Ronald G. *A guide to innovation in education.* Ann Arbor, Michigan: Institute for Social Research, University of Michigan, 1970, p. 5.

Figure 12

Functions of the Change Agent[30]

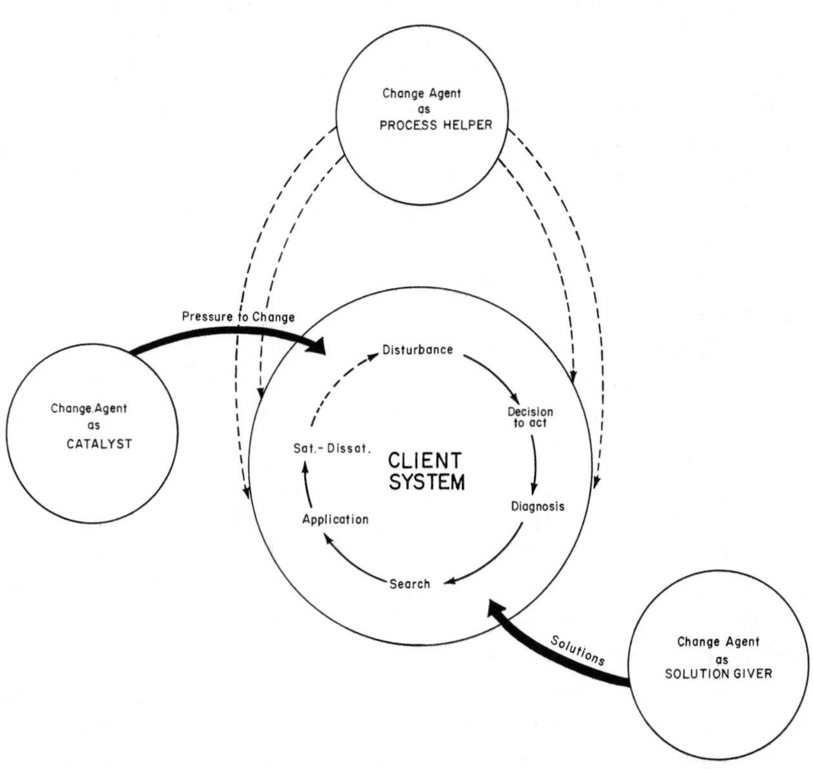

30. Reprinted with permission from Havelock, Ronald G. *A guide to innovation in education.* Ann Arbor, Michigan: Institute for Social Research, University of Michigan, 1970, p. 6.

teacher institutional role expectations.

It is not possible in any one temporary social system to implement all the desired outcomes for process education into practice in schools and other educational agencies. Some subset of outcomes from within the broad value positions and detailed role expectations must be selected as the specific objectives to be achieved in any given project or network of schools and educational agencies and resources. The task becomes one of selecting some finite, and perhaps relatively few, expected changes in pupil and teacher roles which become immediate objectives. Those particular role expectations selected should also be ones which are congruent with the recognized needs and desires of the client systems involved. That is, the change agent interested in implementing the practice of process education needs to select from among the multiple role expectations stated for pupils and teachers in Chapter 4 those for which an awareness of the need already exists or can be developed in the schools and educational agencies involved.

In summary, the selection of particular implementation objectives is from within the broad and quite inclusive set of value positions and role expectations for process education. However, those particular role expectations selected as outcomes for the client members in given extended temporary social systems must reflect the change agent's assessment of the needs of the various user member organizations in the system. In addition, the implementation objectives must be supported by curriculum and instructional vehicles which the change agent has identified as containing the messages appropriate to implementing the changed individual and institutional behavior patterns selected as the immediate objectives.

Selecting Particular Vehicles as Messages

Once the general goals for implementation have been stated, extensive lists of institutional pupil and teacher role expectations have been generated, the needs of particular user systems diagnosed, the necessary linkage relationships established for temporary social systems, and a pool of existing curriculum and instructional vehicles containing messages appropriate to the goals of process education identified, particular vehicles can be selected.

The information obtained from the analysis of many curriculum and instructional vehicles through the procedures described earlier in this chapter in Tables 11, 12, and 13 can be reviewed against user needs and specific implementation objectives selected for a given project or temporary system. Charts similar to these Tables and Table 10 can be prepared which summarize the type and message content of individual curriculum and instructional vehicles of all three common varieties. Change agents and individuals from the member user systems in the extended temporary system can, on the basis of these data, collaboratively select those particular vehicles which contain messages most appropriate to the specific needs and objectives. A large file of existing curriculum and instructional vehicles analyzed on the basis of the procedures described in Tables 11, 12, and 13 would be an invaluable resource to individuals or agencies interested in implementing process education.

Using Selected Curriculum and Instructional Vehicles to Implement Process Education

There are a number of practical procedures which can be used to change educational practice in the direction of the value positions and pupil and teacher role expectations for process education. These procedures are based upon the foregoing considerations of this and previous chapters. They represent operational steps for building multiple extended temporary systems designed to effect needed changes in educational practice through the knowledge resources associated with existing curriculum and instructional vehicles. The procedures also represent the means to engage in a large scale normative-reeducative activity involving the retraining of many individuals within member organizations of the larger educational system.

Taking Stock of Existing Resources

Existing curriculum and instructional vehicles appropriate to the practice of process education should be identified. Their objectives, organization, content, and procedures should be studied. Research and evaluation concerning the use of these vehicles should be collected and reviewed. Ideally, the vehicles should be observed in actual operation in classroom situations.

Installing Selected Curriculum and Instructional Vehicles in Multiple School Settings

Curriculum and instructional vehicles identified and subsequently judged as having potential for implementing process education as well as having congruence with user needs should be installed in multiple school settings. The important condition to be achieved is establishing several groups of schools where a number of different vehicles are in use. Initially, it might be wise to install each vehicle in different school settings. In later years, it might be advisable to install multiple vehicles in the same school settings. For instance, in the first year, three vehicles such as the *Science Curriculum Improvement Study,* the *Materials and Activities for Teachers and Children*, and the *Productive Thinking Program* might each be installed in three separate school networks or extended temporary systems. In a second and third year, each school network could add first one, and then the second, vehicle until each was using all three. Some of the cadre for second and third year installation and support activities could be comprised of teachers and school staff familiar with the vehicle from the first year's activity. After the first year, each school network could contribute staff and experience to a reciprocal training effort having mutual advantage to all parties involved. All three networks could cut across school districts in order that the reciprocal training procedures could be conducted within or across districts. The need for outside consultant assistance would be decreased by this plan of operation.

The installation of selected vehicles should not be viewed as an end in itself. The vehicles should *not* be considered primarily as things to be taught or curricula to be adopted. Rather, they should be viewed as the focal points around which the following activities can occur.

Increasing the Benefit/Cost Ratio of Selected Vehicles

In conjunction with the developers of the vehicle, teachers and school districts involved, the commercial producers of the materials, and other agencies in the extended temporary system, ways can and should be developed to lower the cost of the vehicles and to increase their effectiveness. One example of a procedure designed to increase the benefit/cost ratio for expensive new innovative programs could include arranging for local teacher education colleges and universities to conduct necessary inservice training. Courses taken under such an arrangement could become part of the approved program of study for the professional education of teachers. Such an arrangement could result in more relevant higher education for the preparation of teachers, while at the same time reducing the need for costly additional inservice training of teachers at local expense. Another example of reducing the cost of such vehicles would be the design of school- and district-wide management systems for the more efficient use of the large number of films and instructional materials frequently associated with such vehicles. Some materials for appropriate educational innovations could even be developed, produced, and distributed within a school district by teachers and students under a vocational education or some other program. A benefit of such a plan could be the development of a relevant and up-to-date vocational education program for the local schools involved in the production. Another benefit could be the reduction of the cost of the finished package prepared by the commercial producer of the program. One option the commercial producer might offer for schools could be a cheaper "build some of the materials yourself" package. Such an arrangement might also produce a more flexible curriculum package better suited for adaptation to local educational needs. At least one school district presently operates such a production program to the mutual benefit of the local student producers and consumers.

Preparing a Cadre of Change Agents

A cadre of well trained teacher educators, teachers experienced in using innovative curriculum and instructional vehicles, and consultants needed to work with teachers, school districts, teacher colleges, community groups, and other agencies involved in education can be developed through the multiple extended temporary systems. This cadre can be instrumental in the further and continual dissemination and utilization of new knowledge in educational theory and practice.

The cadre should include not only college professors and inservice education staffs of school districts but instructional specialists, coordinators, administrators, and teacher leaders from local schools as well. The existing curriculum and instructional vehicles selected for installation in school settings can be a focal point for the training activity of such a cadre. Care must be taken to prepare these individuals to serve as facilitators of the practice of process education generally and not simply as experts in the use of a given curriculum or instructional innovation. This could possibly be achieved by insuring that the individuals being trained have the opportunity to work both in numerous study sessions and in actual classroom settings with a variety of existing vehicles in order to become very familiar with the differential objectives, techniques, and procedures which can be used to promote the practice of process education. Some phase of their training should provide them opportunity to examine existing curriculum and instructional vehicles for the purpose of exercising their judgment in selecting approaches promising to process education. Another phase of training should involve their working with pupils and teachers within some portion of the common existing curriculum of a school for the purpose of helping that particular segment of educational practice to become more oriented in the direction of the value positions and the role expectations for process education. The task would specifically involve assisting teachers and pupils in specifying skills to be achieved (process objectives), and selecting content, learning materials, and teaching-learning strategies appropriate to the development of those skills. Specifying roles for pupils and teachers appropriate to learning would be another task. The experience of consultants, teachers, and pupils with particular exemplary curriculum and instructional vehicles which had previously been installed in schools in such networks should provide more than ample opportunity to capitalize upon the transfer of the practice of process education to other areas of the typical school curriculum. The existence of multiple school networks or extended temporary systems, each working with different instructional vehicles, as suggested above, also provides adequate opportunity for a broadly based training program for a cadre of change agents.

The existence of such a broadly trained and competent cadre of personnel would help insure that the available resources in the form of many excellent existing curriculum and instructional innovations devoted to skill development would be properly and adequately used to promote the practice of process education. Furthermore, such a staff would be capable of assisting teachers and pupils to extend the practice of process education first encountered through a vehicle like *Man: A Course of Study*, *Science—A Process Approach*, or *Materials and Activities for Teachers and Children* to other areas of the school curriculum.

Developing Preservice Teacher Education Programs

The trained cadre of teacher educators and consultants and the multiple school settings, where vehicles appropriate to process education have been installed, can and should be utilized for the preservice preparation of future teachers enrolled at colleges and universities. It is widely recognized that most teacher education courses at institutions of higher education are inadequate. The cadre of personnel discussed above includes college professors, as well as instructional specialists, coordinators, administrators, and teachers from local schools. This group could and should be involved in the formal preparation of preservice teachers. The schools where the actual installation of new vehicles is underway can serve as multiple clinical settings where the trained cadre can work with preservice teachers toward developing understanding, commitment, and competence for the practice of a more appropriate education devoted to the development of a wide array of skills and pupil and teacher roles underlying process education. Most preservice teachers and their professors accept the position that education devoted to the development of skills of learning, thinking, expressing, problem-solving, and creating is more appropriate than conventional education devoted largely to acquisition of knowledge and information. The problem is that, frequently, neither they nor their professors know how to implement actual educational practice consistent with these goals or how to establish the necessary learning roles. It is often assumed that rhetoric about goals of education directed to prospective and current teachers will be translated into means to achieve those goals. This is not likely. It is too difficult a task to occur so easily. With the assistance of a cadre of appropriately trained teacher educators and consultants, and with school settings actually using curriculum and instructional vehicles designed purposely for the development of important skills and the roles appropriate to using those skills, the means to achieve the goals of process education can be readily learned and practiced by future teachers.

Developing Inservice Teacher Education Programs

The trained cadre and the multiple school settings where curriculum and instructional vehicles appropriate for implementing process education have been installed can and should be used for the training of inservice teachers. Inservice teachers need to learn more about the means for practicing process education. As new vehicles are installed in their schools, teachers will need much additional training. Ideally, their training should parallel that of the cadre of teacher educators and consultants. That is, teachers should have the opportunity to learn much about a particular exemplary curriculum or instructional vehicle and its proper utilization in order to obtain specific objectives of skill development and pupil and teacher learning roles. However, care must again be taken to insure that teachers are broadly trained and experienced in many curriculum materials, instructional procedures and methods which can be used to promote the practice of process education. The teachers must be aware that the goal for them to achieve is competence in selecting, designing, and using instructional materials and practices toward the goals of process education generally. They are not simply to become experts in the use of a given curriculum or instructional system. One phase of inservice teacher training concerned with the proper utilization of a given vehicle, such as *Man: A Course of Study,* should *always* deal with how skills and techniques learned through this experience can be transferred to general instructional practice within the context of the broader school curriculum. Great attention should be paid to assisting teachers and pupils to identify and to more consistently assume the learning roles appropriate for the practice of process education. The inservice education program should also provide opportunity for teachers and their pupils to use their newly acquired competencies and experiences gained from their work with particular vehicles in the business of training other preservice and inservice teachers. Undoubtedly, much of the inservice education of teachers could be planned and implemented in direct conjunction with the preservice education of future teachers.

Studying the Effects of Particular Vehicles Upon Pupil and Teacher Behavior

Basic assumptions underlying process education generally, as well as particular curriculum and instructional vehicles appropriate to the practice of process education, can be empirically tested. Some of the specific questions which can and should be tested are: Do pupils achieve competence in the skills which are the objectives of these instructional programs? Specifically, do the skills of inferring, observing, and predicting emphasized in *Science–A Process Approach* increase both the propensity of the child to use such skills and his competency in doing so outside the context of the lessons in that program? One can ask essentially the same question about many of the other skills emphasized in other programs. These include skills of affective and cognitive fluency and flexibility emphasized by the *National Schools Project*; human relation skills dealt with by the *SRA Social Science Laboratory Units*; or the skills of analytically relating differential behavior patterns of individuals and cultures to differences in underlying values and value systems, which are the concern of *Man: A Course of Study*. Other important questions which can be answered empirically deal with motivation for learning, the amount of information and knowledge learned and retained, the rate and extent of increase of skill development, and changes in the learning roles of teachers and pupils. Specifically, do particular curriculum and instructional vehicles devoted to the facilitation of skills increase motivation toward and competence for self-initiated learning? Do pupils educated under such programs acquire as much or more knowledge and information as pupils instructed in the more conventional manner? Do the skills emphasized by particular vehicles exhibit transfer for pupils and teachers when working with similar tasks in other areas of the school curriculum? For example, do children and teachers experienced in the AAAS *Science–A Process Approach* activities concerned with skills of inference and hypothesis formation exhibit competence in using those same skills in the *House of Ancient Greece* MATCH unit developed by the Children's Museum? In using such programs, do teachers become generally less directive? Do teachers make frequent and good use of the special talents, experience, and knowledge of their pupils toward achieving stated program goals? In short, do pupil and teacher behavior patterns change in the direction of the value positions and derivative role expectations for process education which have been stated in Chapter 3?

Still other important questions relate to the interaction between pupils, teachers, and particular curriculum and instructional vehicles. Some of these are: What are the distinguishing characteristics of teachers who best achieve developing the competencies of pupils in certain areas of skills? Which teachers, procedures, and materials are most motivating to which pupils? What are the optimum conditions for the development of competency in particular areas of skills for particular types of pupils? What vehicles, materials, and conditions are most conducive to developing specified learning roles appropriate to process education?

Many of these are difficult and complex questions and will not be easily answered. However, all of these questions are subject to resolution by empirical procedures centered around the observation and study of existing instructional vehicles in use in actual schools. If process education is to be more fully empirically justified as a feasible approach to general education, these questions must be answered more completely than they have been in past educational research and evaluation.

Summary

This chapter has been concerned with developing general guidelines for selecting and using curriculum and instructional vehicles for promoting the values, roles, and behavior patterns central to process education. In selecting curriculum and instructional programs as vehicles for reeducative functions, it is important to consider their message content, varieties, and general structural properties.

Curriculum and instructional vehicles may be considered to contain three types of messages. Type I messages concern basic knowledge in the form of philosophies, theories, laws, or other conceptual organizations; they arise out of scholarly activity and research. Type II messages contain information about how the basic knowledge contained in Type I messages can be applied to some area of human endeavor. Type III messages are translations of theory and research into services or products for use by the practitioner.

There are three varieties of curriculum and instructional vehicles. Some programs can be characterized as extensive sequences of materials and activities for pupils. Others consist primarily of teacher education materials and strategies designed to enable the teacher to select, design and construct learning activities and materials for pupils. A third variety consists of short duration, carefully designed and packaged sets of learning materials and activities for use by pupils. Examples of each vehicle variety are discussed in the chapter. Regardless of their message content and variety, curriculum and instructional vehicles in use exhibit three fundamental structural elements. These include the objectives for the learning activity, the content and materials of the learning experience, and the teaching-learning strategies employed.

When selecting particular curriculum and instructional vehicles to be used to implement process education there are two reference frameworks from which to make decisions. First, the contents of the three message types of curriculum and instructional vehicles, as well as their operational objectives, materials, and teaching-learning strategies can be studied and compared to the value positions and derivative role expectations stated for pupils and teachers in Chapter 3. From such an analysis one can decide if a particular program is generally facilitative or inhibitory of process education. A second reference framework for decision-making is provided by the model in Chapter 4 concerned with establishing temporary systems for the dissemination of new knowledge. Through such procedures the needs of schools can be diagnosed. Linkage relationships, essential to using selected curriculum and instructional vehicles as knowledge sources for reeducative activity through multiple temporary systems, can be established.

The last section of this chapter makes a number of practical suggestions for using selected programs to implement process education. It is suggested that further effort should be devoted to the identification and study of programs with potential for process education. Once identified and logically analyzed, selected programs should be installed in multiple school settings through multiple temporary systems. The installation and study of curriculum and instructional vehicles in multiple settings can provide both data and means for increasing the benefits from well designed, but expensive, new programs.

The multiple settings for the installation of selected exemplary programs can and should be designed to serve preservice and inservice teacher education functions. The programs installed can also serve as vehicles for the preparation of a cadre of change agents competent in the use of selected process curricula and instructional programs for promoting teacher and administrator commitment and competence in the roles and behavior patterns critical to process education. The end goal for such inservice activity should not be viewed as the installation of a particular curriculum but the development of teacher commitment to and competence in the practices of more effective instruction and learning.

Finally, it is pointed out that the assumptions which underlie process education and process curricula can be empirically tested to a much greater degree than they have been so far. A number of questions are raised which should be answered more completely than they have been in past educational research and evaluation in order to more fully empirically validate process education as a feasible approach to general education.

REFERENCES

Abt, C.C. An evaluation model: How to compare curriculum materials. *Nation's Schools,* 1970, 86 (1): 21-28.

Allen, D.W. & Hawkes, G.W. Reconstruction of teacher education and professional growth programs, or how the third little pig escaped the wolf. *Phi Delta Kappan,* 1970, 52 (1): 4-12.

AAAS (American Association for the Advancement of Science Commission on Science Education). *An evaluation model and its application.* (2nd ed.) Washington, D.C.: American Association for the Advancement of Science, 1968. (a)

AAAS (American Association for the Advancement of Science Commission on Science Education). *Science–A process approach.* Commentary for teachers. (3rd experimental ed.) Washington, D.C.: American Association for the Advancement of Science, Miscellaneous publication 68-7, 1968. (b)

American college dictionary, The. New York: Random House, 1964.

Amidon, E.J. & Flanders, N.A. *The role of the teacher in the classroom. A manual for understanding and improving teacher classroom behavior.* (Rev. ed.) Minneapolis, Minn.: Association for Productive Thinking, 1967.

Amidon, E.J. & Hough, J.B. (Eds.) *Interaction analysis: Theory, research, and application.* Reading, Mass.: Addison-Wesley, 1967.

Anderson, H.H. On the meaning of creativity. In F.E. Williams (Ed.), *Creativity at home and in the school.* St. Paul, Minn.: Macalester Creativity Project, 1968. Pp. 33-53.

Anderson, R.C. & Ausubel, D.P. *Readings in the psychology of cognition.* New York: Holt, Rinehart & Winston, 1966.

Andreas, B.G. *Psychological science and the educational enterprise.* New York: John Wiley & Sons, 1968.

Andreas, B.G. Improving process education: A comprehensive plan. In *Research into process curricula.* Syracuse, N.Y.: Eastern Regional Institute for Education, 1970. Pp. 1-14.

Andrulis, R.S. Variables affecting installation. In *Research into process curricula.* Syracuse, N.Y.: Eastern Regional Institute for Education, 1970. Pp. 165-193.

Beatty, W.H. Emotion: The missing link in education. In W.H. Beatty (Ed.), *Improving educational assessment: An inventory of measures of affective behavior.* Washington, D.C.: Association for Supervision and Curriculum Development Commission on Assessment of Educational Outcomes, 1969. Pp. 74-88.

Benne, K.D., Bennis, W.G., & Chin, R. Planned change in America. In W.G. Bennis, K.D. Benne, & R. Chin (Eds.), *The planning of change.* New York: Holt, Rinehart & Winston, 1969. Pp. 28-32.

Bennis, W.G. *Changing organizations.* New York: McGraw-Hill, 1966.

Bennis, W.G. The temporary society. *Journal of Creative Behavior,* 1969, 3 (4): 223-241.

Bennis, W.G. Organic populism: A conversation with T. George Harris. *Psychology Today,* 1970, 3 (9): 48-54, 68-71.

Bennis, W.G., Benne, K.D., & Chin, R. *The planning of change.* New York: Holt, Rinehart & Winston, 1969.

Bennis, W.G. & Slater, P.E. *The temporary society.* New York: Harper & Row, 1968.

Berlyne, D.E. *Conflict, arousal, and curiosity.* New York: McGraw-Hill, 1960.

Berlyne, D.E. Motivational problems raised by exploratory and epistemic behavior. In S. Koch (Ed.), *Psychology: A study of a science.* Vol. 5. New York: McGraw-Hill, 1963. Pp. 284-364.

Berlyne, D.E. *Structure and direction in thinking.* New York: John Wiley & Sons, 1965.

Berlyne, D.E. Notes on intrinsic motivation and intrinsic reward in relation to instruction. In J. Bruner (Ed.), *Learning about learning: A conference report.* Washington, D.C.: U.S. Government Printing Office, 1966. Catalog No. FS5.212:12019. Pp. 105-110.

Bettelheim, B. Autonomy and inner freedom: Skills of emotional management. In L.J. Rubin (Ed.), *Life skills in school and society. Yearbook 1969.* Washington, D.C.: Association for Supervision and Curriculum Development, 1969. Pp. 73-94.

Blackburn, R.T. *Interrelations: The biological and physical sciences.* Chicago: Scott, Foresman & Co., 1966.

Bloom, B.S., Engelhart, M.D., Furst, E.J., Hill, W.H., & Krathwohl, D.R. *Taxonomy of educational objectives, handbook I: Cognitive domain.* New York: David McKay, 1956.

Bower, E.M. Mental health in education. *Review of Educational Research,* 1968, 38 (5): 447-459.

Brandwein, P.F. Skills of compassion and competence. In L.J. Rubin (Ed.), *Life skills in school and society. Yearbook 1969.* Washington, D.C.: Association for Supervision and Curriculum Development, 1969. Pp. 131-151.

Brickell, H.M. *Organizing New York State for educational change: A study of the dynamics of instructional change in the elementary and secondary schools of New York State with recommendation for improved organization.* Albany, N.Y.: State Education Department, 1961.

Brickell, H.M. State organization for educational means, symposium on identifying techniques and principles for gaining acceptance of research results of use of newer media in education. In W.C. Meierhenry (Ed.), *Media and educational innovation: Preliminary report.* Lincoln, Nebraska: U.S. Office of Education and University of Nebraska, 1964. Pp. 195-213. ERIC No. ED003134. (a)

Brickell, H.M. State organization for educational change: A case study and a proposal. In M.B. Miles (Ed.), *Innovation in education.* New York: Teachers College, Columbia University, 1964. Pp. 493-531. (b)

Brickell, H.M. Local organization and administration of education.

In E.L. Morphet & C.O. Ryan (Eds.), *Implications for education of prospective changes in society.* Denver, Colo.: Designing Education for the Future: An Eight-State Project, 1967. Pp. 215-235. (a)

Brickell, H.M. Role of research in the innovative process. In E.G. Guba (Ed.), *The role of educational research in educational change.* Bloomington, Indiana: National Institute for the Study of Educational Change, 1967. (b)

Brickell, H.M. Two change strategies for local school systems. In *Rational planning in curriculum and instruction: Eight essays.* Washington, D.C.: Center for the Study of Instruction, National Education Association, 1967. (c)

Bruner, J.S. *The process of education.* New York: Random House, 1960.

Bruner, J.S. *Toward a theory of instruction.* New York: W.W. Norton, 1968.

Bruner, J.S. *On knowing: Essays for the left hand.* New York: Atheneum, 1969.

Bruner, J.S. The skill of relevance or the relevance of skills. *Saturday Review,* 1970, 53 (14): 66-68, 78-79.

Bruner, J.S. & Dow, P.B. *Man: A course of study, a description of an elementary social studies curriculum.* Cambridge, Mass.: Education Development Center, 1967.

Bruner, J.S., Goodnow, J.J., & Austin, G.A. *A study of thinking.* New York: John Wiley & Sons, 1956.

Bruner, J.S., Olver, R.R., Greenfield, P.M. *et al. Studies in cognitive growth.* New York: John Wiley & Sons, 1966.

Burns, R.W. Objectives and content validity of tests. *Educational Technology,* 1968, 8 (23): 17-18.

Casey, J.J. New light on the reliability of indicators of quality. *IAR-Research Bulletin.* New York: Teachers College, Columbia University, 1969, 9 (3): 1-3.

Charters, W.W., Jr. & Gage, N.L. *Readings in the social psychology of education.* Boston: Allyn & Bacon, 1963.

Chesler, M. & Fox, R. *Role playing methods in the classroom.* Chicago: Science Research Associates, 1966.

Chin, R. & Benne, K.D. General strategies for effecting changes in human systems. In W.G. Bennis, K.D. Benne, & R. Chin (Eds.), *The planning of change.* New York: Holt, Rinehart & Winston, 1969. Pp. 32-59.

Clark, D.L. Educational research and development: The next decade. In E.L. Morphet & C.O. Ryan (Eds.), *Implications for education of prospective changes in society.* Denver, Colo.: Designing Education for the Future: An Eight-State Project, 1967. Pp. 156-175.

Clark, D.L. & Guba, E.G. An examination of potential change roles in education. In *Rational planning in curriculum and instruction: Eight essays.* Washington, D.C.: Center for the Study of Instruction, National Education Association, 1967.

Clark, J.W. On facing the crisis of intellectual poverty. *Journal of Creative Behavior*, 1969, 3 (4): 260-270.

Cole, H.P. Process curricula and creativity development. *Journal of Creative Behavior,* 1969, 3 (4): 243-259.

Cole, H.P. Curriculum augmentation and validation. In *Research into process curricula.* Syracuse, N.Y.: Eastern Regional Institute for Education, 1970. Pp. 70-105. (a)

Cole, H.P. One laboratory's attempts at transforming educational practice. Invited paper presented at the Annual Meeting of the Association for Education of Teachers in Science and the National Science Teachers Association, Cincinnati, Ohio, March 13, 1970. (b)

Cole, H.P., Andreas, B.G., & Archer, N.S. A program to establish preservice and inservice education for the effective installation and dissemination of *Man: A course of study.* Proposal funded by the National Science Foundation, Eastern Regional Institute for Education, Syracuse, N.Y., 1969.

Cole, H.P., Bernstein, S., Seferian, A. *et al. Report on the analysis of some process-oriented curricula: An annotated listing.* Program Report 101. Syracuse, N.Y.: Eastern Regional Institute for Education, 1969.

Cole, H.P. & Herlihy, J.G. *Implementation of a process curriculum by the campus team strategy.* Report to the National Science Foundation on a 1969-70 Grant awarded for "A program to establish preservice and inservice education for the effective installation and dissemination of *Man: A course of study.*" Syracuse, N.Y.: Eastern Regional Institute for Education, 1971.

Cole, H.P. & Seferian, A. Analysis of process curricula. In *Research into process curricula.* Syracuse, N.Y.: Eastern Regional Institute for Education, 1970. Pp. 15-69.

Combs, A.W. (Ed.) *Perceiving, behaving, becoming. Yearbook 1962.* Washington, D.C.: Association for Supervision and Curriculum Development, 1962.

Covington, M.V. The cognitive curriculum: A process-oriented approach to education. In J. Hellmuth (Ed.), *Cognitive studies.* New York: Bruner-Mazel, 1970.

Covington, M.V., Crutchfield, R.S., & Davies, L.B. *Teacher's guide to the productive-thinking program, series one: General problem-solving.* Berkeley, Calif.: Educational Innovation, 1967.

Cronbach, L.J. How can instruction be adapted to individual differences? In R.M. Gagné (Ed.), *Learning and individual differences.* Columbus, Ohio: Charles E. Merrill, 1967. Pp. 23-39.

Crutchfield, R.S. Nurturing the cognitive skills of productive thinking. In L.J. Rubin (Ed.), *Life skills in school and society. Yearbook 1969.* Washington, D.C.: Association for Supervision and Curriculum Development, 1969. Pp. 53-71.

Daniels, A.K. The captive professional: Bureaucratic limitations in the practice of military psychiatry. *Journal of Health and Social Behavior,* 1969, 10 (4): 255-265.

Davis, G.A., Manske, M.E., & Train, A.J. *Training creative thinking.* Occasional paper #6, Research and Development Center for Learning and Reeducation, University of Wisconsin, Madison, Wisconsin, 1967.

Dewey, J. *Experience and education.* New York: Macmillan, 1944.

Dow, P.B. Man: A course of study—An experimental social science course for elementary schools. In *Man: A course of study, talks to teachers.* Cambridge, Mass.: Education Development Center, 1968. Pp. 3-16.

Flanders, N.A. *Teacher influence, pupil attitudes and achievement.*

Cooperative Research Monograph No. 12, OE-25040. Washington, D.C.: U.S. Printing Office, 1965.

Flavell, J.H. *The developmental psychology of Jean Piaget.* New York: D. Van Nostrand, 1966.

Fox, R., Lippitt, R., & Girault, E. Social science for the secondary school. Unpublished paper, School of Education, University of Michigan, Ann Arbor, Michigan, 1969.

Fox, R., Luszki, M.B., & Schmuck, R. *Diagnosing classroom learning environments.* Chicago: Science Research Associates, 1966.

Gage, N.L. (Ed.) *Handbook of research on teaching.* Chicago: Rand McNally, 1964.

Gagné, R.M. A psychologist's counsel on curriculum design. *Journal of Research in Science Teaching,* 1963, 1: 27-32.

Gagné, R.M. *The conditions of learning.* New York: Holt, Rinehart & Winston, 1965. (a)

Gagné, R.M. Psychological issues in *Science–A process approach.* In *Psychological bases of Science–A process approach.* Washington, D.C.: American Association for the Advancement of Science, 1965, Pp. 1-8. (b)

Gagné, R.M. Varieties of learning and the concept of discovery. In L.S. Shulman & E.R. Keislar (Eds.), *Learning by discovery: A critical appraisal.* Chicago: Rand McNally, 1966. Pp. 135-150.

Gagné, R.M. Contributions to human development. *Psychological Review,* 1968, 75 (3): 177-191. (a)

Gagné, R.M. Learning hierarchies. Presidential Address, Division 15, American Psychological Association, San Francisco, August, 1968. (b)

Gagné, R.M. Instruction based on research in learning. Paper presented at the Annual Meeting of the American Society for Engineering Education, Columbus, Ohio, June 22-25, 1970. (a)

Gagné, R.M. Some new views of learning and instruction. *Phi Delta Kappan,* 1970, 51 (9): 468-472. (b)

Gesler, H.L. Concerns of school people. *Educational Leadership,* 1970, 28 (1): 27-30.

Getzels, J.W. A psychological framework for the study of educational administration. *Harvard Educational Review,* 1952, 22: 234-246.

Getzels, J.W. Conflict and role behavior in the educational setting. In W.W. Charters, Jr. & N.L. Gage (Eds.), *Readings in the social psychology of education.* Boston: Allyn & Bacon, 1963. Pp. 309-318.

Goodlad, J.I. The schools vs. education. *Saturday Review,* 1969, 52 (16): 59-61, 80-82.

Greenberg, H.M. *Teaching with feeling.* New York: Pegasus, 1969.

Guba, E.G., Jackson, P.W., & Bidwell, C.E. Occupational choice and the teaching career. *Educational Research Bulletin,* 1959, 38 (1): 1-28.

Guba, E.G., Jackson, P.W., & Bidwell, C.E. Occupational choice and the teaching career. In W.W. Charters, Jr. & N.L. Gage (Eds.), *Readings in the social psychology of education.* Boston: Allyn & Bacon, 1963. Pp. 271-278.

Guilford, J.P. *The nature of human intelligence.* New York: McGraw-Hill, 1967.

Haber, R.N. (Ed.) *Current research in motivation.* New York: Holt, Rinehart & Winston, 1967.

Hanley, J.P., Whitla, D.K., Moo, E.W., & Walter, A.S. *Curiosity/competency/community, an evaluation of Man: A course of study.* (Preliminary ed.) Cambridge, Mass.: Education Development Center, 1970. (a)

Hanley, J.P., Whitla, D.K., Moo, E.W., & Walter, A.S. *Curiosity, competency, community. Man: A course of study.* An evaluation. A summary of the original two-volume edition. Cambridge, Mass.: Education Development Center, 1970. (b)

Harper, R.J.C., Anderson, C.C., Christensen, C.M., & Hunka, S.M. *The cognitive processes: Readings.* Englewood Cliffs, N.J.: Prentice-Hall, 1965.

Havelock, R.G. *Planning for innovation through dissemination and utilization of knowledge.* Ann Arbor, Michigan: Institute for Social Research, University of Michigan, 1969.

Havelock, R.G. *A guide to innovation in education.* Ann Arbor,

Michigan: Institute for Social Research, University of Michigan, 1970.

Heathers, G. The strategy of educational reform. Unpublished paper, New York University School of Education, 1965.

Heisenberg, W. The relation of quantum theory to other parts of natural science. In R.T. Blackburn (Ed.), *Interrelations: The biological and physical sciences.* Chicago: Scott, Foresman & Co., 1966. Pp. 212-221.

Hellmuth, J. (Ed.) *Cognitive studies.* New York: Bruner-Mazel, 1970.

Herlihy, J.G., Andreas, B.G., & Archer, N.S. *A campus-based installation strategy for Man: A course of study.* Program Proposal 103 funded by the National Science Foundation. Syracuse, N.Y.: Eastern Regional Institute for Education, 1969.

Herlihy, J.G., Cole, H.P., & Herlihy, M.T. The campus team—A change strategy for preservice and inservice teacher education. A paper presented at the annual meeting of the American Educational Research Association, New York, February 6, 1971.

Herlihy, J.G. & Wallace, R.C. Expansion of the campus team *Man: A course of study* network. Program proposal funded by the National Science Foundation. Syracuse, N.Y.: Eastern Regional Institute for Education, 1970.

Holton, G. & Roller, D.H.D. *Foundations of modern physical science.* Reading, Mass.: Addison-Wesley, 1958.

Hoy, W.K. The influence of experience on the beginning teacher. In M.B. Miles & W.W. Charters (Eds.), *Learning in social settings: New readings in the social psychology of education.* (2nd ed.) Boston: Allyn & Bacon, 1970. Pp. 615-623.

Hunt, J.M. The epigenesis of motivation and early cognitive learning. In R.N. Haber (Ed.), *Current research in motivation.* New York: Holt, Rinehart & Winston, 1967. Pp. 355-370.

Indicators of quality, observer instrument. New York: Institute of Administrative Research, Teachers College, Columbia University, 1968.

Indicators of quality, orientation manual. New York: Institute of

Administrative Research, Teachers College, Columbia University, 1968.

Inhelder, B. & Piaget, J. *The growth of logical thinking from childhood to adolescence.* New York: Basic Books, 1958.

Karns, E.A. Politics: A vital force in education. *Educational Leadership,* 1970, 28 (1): 38-39.

Kelley, E.C. The fully functioning self. In A.W. Combs (Ed.), *Perceiving, behaving, becoming. Yearbook 1962.* Washington, D.C.: Association for Supervision and Curriculum Development, 1962. Pp. 9-20.

Kemeny, J.G. *A philosopher looks at science.* Princeton, N.J.: D. Van Nostrand, 1959.

Krathwohl, D.R., Bloom, B.S., & Masia, B.B. *Taxonomy of educational objectives, handbook II: Affective domain.* New York: David McKay, 1964.

Kresse, F.H. *Volume 1: Materials and activities for teachers and children: A project to develop and evaluate multimedia kits for elementary schools. Volume II: Appendices.* Final Report, U.S. Department of Health, Education, and Welfare, Office of Education, Project No. 5-0710. Boston: The Children's Museum, 1968.

Kubiak, D. Political power and the schools—At the state level. *Educational Leadership,* 1970, 28 (1): 26-27.

Lippitt, R. Roles and processes in curriculum development and change. In R.R. Leeper (Ed.), *Strategy for curriculum change.* Washington, D.C. Association for Supervision and Curriculum Development, 1964. Pp. 11-28.

Lippitt, R. Process of curriculum change. In R.R. Leeper (Ed.), *Curriculum change: Direction and process.* Washington, D.C.: Association for Supervision and Curriculum Development, 1966. Pp. 43-59.

Lippitt, R. The neglected learner. *Social Science Education Consortium Newsletter,* 1970, 8: 1-5.

Lippitt, R., Fox, R., & Schaible, L. *The teacher's role in social science investigation.* Chicago: Science Research Associates, 1969.

Lippitt, R. & Havelock, R. Needed research on research utilization. A paper presented at the 1968 National Conference on the Diffusion of Educational Ideas, East Lansing, Michigan, March 26-28, 1968.

Livermore, A.H. The process approach of the AAAS Commission on Science Education. *Journal of Research in Science Teaching,* 1964, 2: 271-282.

Loving, A.D., Sr. Political power, the school, and the culture. *Educational Leadership,* 1970, 28 (1): 7-8.

MacKinnon, D.W. The courage to be: Realizing creative potential. In L.J. Rubin (Ed.), *Life skills in school and society. Yearbook 1969.* Washington, D.C.: Association for Supervision and Curriculum Development, 1969. Pp. 95-110.

Mahan, J.M. Curriculum installation and diffusion strategies. In *Research into process curricula.* Syracuse, N.Y.: Eastern Regional Institute for Education, 1970. Pp. 106-142. (a)

Mahan, J.M. Can teachers use consultants effectively when implementing a new curriculum? Paper presented at the Annual Association for Supervision and Curriculum Development meeting, San Francisco, California, March 16-17, 1970. (b)

Mann, J.S. Political power and the high school curriculum. *Educational Leadership,* 1970, 28 (1): 23-26.

Maslow, A.H. Some basic propositions of a growth and self-actualization psychology. In A.W. Combs (Ed.), *Perceiving, behaving, becoming. Yearbook 1962.* Washington, D.C.: Association for Supervision and Curriculum Development, 1962. Pp. 34-49.

Massialas, B.G. The school in the political socialization of children and youth. *Educational Leadership,* 1970, 28 (1): 31-33.

Meade, E.J., Jr. The changing society and its schools. In L.J. Rubin (Ed.), *Life skills in school and society. Yearbook 1969.* Washington, D.C.: Association for Supervision and Curriculum Development, 1969. Pp. 35-51.

Michaelis, J.U. An overview of the report of the state wide social sciences study committee. Report to the Curriculum Commission and the State Board of Education. Sacramento, Calif.: State Department of Education, October, 1968.

Michaelis, J.U. An inquiry-conceptual theory of social studies curriculum planning. *Social Education,* 1970, 34 (1): 68-71.

Miles, M.B. *Innovation in education.* New York: Teachers College Press, 1967. (a)

Miles, M.B. Educational innovation: The nature of the problem. In M.B. Miles (Ed.), *Innovation in education.* New York: Teachers College, Columbia University, 1967. Pp. 1-48. (b)

Miles, M.B. On temporary systems. In M.B. Miles (Ed.), *Innovation in education.* New York: Teachers College, Columbia University, 1967. Pp. 437-490. (c)

Miles, M.B. Innovation in education: Some generalizations. In M.B. Miles (Ed.), *Innovation in education.* New York: Teachers College, Columbia University, 1967. Pp. 631-662. (d)

Montessori, M. *The Montessori method.* Cambridge, Mass.: Bentley, 1965.

Newell, A., Shaw, J.C., & Simon, H.A. Elements of a theory of human problem-solving. *Psychological Review,* 1958, 65: 151-166.

Olivero, J.L. The meaning and application of differentiated staffing in teaching. *Phi Delta Kappan,* 1970, 52 (1): 36-40.

Olton, R.M., Wardrop, J.L., Covington, M.V. *et al. The development of productive thinking skills in fifth grade children.* Madison, Wisconsin: Wisconsin Research and Development Center, University of Wisconsin, 1967.

Parnes, S.J. *Creative behavior guidebook.* New York: Scribner's, 1967.

Piaget, J. *Six psychological studies.* Translation edited by David Elkind. New York: Random House, 1967.

Postman, N. & Weingartner, C. *Teaching as a subversive activity.* New York: Delacorte Press, 1969.

Random House dictionary of the English language. (Unabridged ed.) New York: Random House, 1966.

Ritz, W.C., Harty, H., Brown, F.A., & Wallace, C.W. *Evaluation of curriculum installation.* Syracuse, N.Y.: Eastern Regional Institute for Education, 1970.

Roberts, J. Curriculum development and experimentation. *Review of Educational Research,* 1966, 36 (3): 353-361.

Rogers, C.R. *On becoming a person.* Boston: Houghton-Mifflin, 1961.

Rogers, C.R. Toward becoming a fully functioning person. In A.W. Combs (Ed.), *Perceiving, behaving, becoming. Yearbook 1962.* Washington, D.C.: Association for Supervision and Curriculum Development, 1962. Pp. 21-33.

Rogers, C.R. The facilitation of significant learning. In L. Siegel (Ed.), *Instruction: Some contemporary viewpoints.* San Francisco: Chandler, 1967. Pp. 172-182.

Rubin, L.J. (Ed.) *Life skills in school and society. Yearbook 1969.* Washington, D.C.: Association for Supervision and Curriculum Development, 1969. (a)

Rubin, L.J. Prologue: New skills for a new day. In L.J. Rubin (Ed.), *Life skills in school and society. Yearbook 1969.* Washington, D.C.: Association for Supervision and Curriculum Development, 1969. Pp. 1-13. (b)

Rubin, L.J. The object of schooling: An evolutionary view. In L.J. Rubin (Ed.), *Life skills in school and society. Yearbook 1969.* Washington, D.C.: Association for Supervision and Curriculum Development, 1969. Pp. 15-32. (c)

Rubin, L.J. Epilogue: The skills we need. In L.J. Rubin (Ed.), *Life skills in school and society. Yearbook 1969.* Washington, D.C.: Association for Supervision and Curriculum Development, 1969. Pp. 153-164. (d)

Russell, D.H. *Children's thinking.* Boston: Ginn, 1956.

Schmuck, R.A. Helping teachers improve classroom group processes. *Journal of Applied Behavioral Science,* 1968, 4 (4): 401-435.

Schmuck, R.A. Helping teachers improve classroom group processes. In M.B. Miles & W.W. Charters (Eds.), *Learning in social settings: New readings in the social psychology of education.* (2nd ed.) Boston, Mass.: Allyn & Bacon, 1970. Pp. 707-735.

Schmuck, R.A., Chesler, M., & Lippitt, R. *Problem-solving to improve classroom learning.* Chicago: Science Research Associates, 1966.

Seferian, A. & Cole, H.P. *Encounters in thinking: A compendium of curricula for process education.* Buffalo, N.Y.: Creative Education Foundation, Occasional paper #6, 1970.

Segal, S. Social needs and educational reform. *Journal of Creative Behavior,* 1968, 2 (4): 231-238, 292.

Shulman, L.S. & Keislar, E.R. (Eds.) *Learning by discovery. A critical appraisal.* Chicago: Rand McNally, 1966.

Siegel, L. (Ed.) *Instruction: Some contemporary viewpoints.* San Francisco: Chandler, 1967.

Silberman, C.E. *Crisis in the classroom.* New York: Random House, 1970.

Skinner, B.F. *The technology of teaching.* New York: Appleton-Century-Crofts, 1968.

Smith, B.O., Cohen, S.B., & Pearl, A. *Teachers for the real world.* Washington, D.C.: American Association of Colleges for Teacher Education, 1969.

Snygg, D. & Combs, A.W. *Individual behavior.* New York: Harper & Brothers, 1949.

Spindler, G.D. Education in a transforming American culture. *Harvard Educational Review,* 1955, 25 (3): 145-156.

Strang, R. The development or stifling of creativity in the early years of formal education. In F.E. Williams (Ed.), *Creativity at home and in school.* St. Paul, Minn.: Macalester Creativity Project, 1968. Pp. 1-31.

Taba, H. *Teachers' handbook for elementary social studies.* Palo Alto, Calif.: Addison-Wesley, 1967.

Tanner, D. Curriculum theory: Knowledge and content. *Review of Educational Research,* 1966, 36 (3): 362-372.

Torrance, E.P. *Rewarding creative behavior.* Englewood Cliffs, N.J.: Prentice-Hall, 1965.

Torrance, E.P. Must pre-primary educational stimulation be incompatible with creative development? In F.E. Williams (Ed.), *Creativity at home and in school.* St. Paul, Minn.: Macalester Creativity Project, 1968. Pp. 55-73. (a)

Torrance, E.P. A longitudinal examination of the fourth grade slump in creativity. *The Gifted Child Quarterly,* 1968, 12 (4): 195-199. (b)

Torrance, E.P. *Encouraging creativity in the classroom.* Dubuque,

Iowa: Wm. C. Brown, 1970.

Turner, H.E. Mobilizing political power for action. *Educational Leadership,* 1970, 28 (1): 40-41.

Vincent, W.S. Indicators of quality. *IAR-Research Bulletin.* New York: Teachers College, Columbia University, 1967, 7 (3): 1-5.

Vincent, W.S. & Casey, J.J. Statistical report on indicators of quality. *IAR-Research Bulletin.* New York: Teachers College, Columbia University, 1968, 8 (3): 1-3.

Vincent, W.S. (Ed.) *Signs of good teaching.* New York: Columbia University, 1969.

Vincent, W.S. Levels of pupil participation in a sample of the nation's schools. *IAR-Research Bulletin.* New York: Teachers College, 1970, 10 (2): 4-6.

Walberg, H.J. Personality-role conflict and self-conception in urban practice teachers. *The School Review,* 1968, 76: 41-49.

Walberg, H.J. Professional role discontinuities in educational careers. *Review of Educational Research,* 1970, 40 (3): 409-420.

Walberg, H.J., Metzner, S., Todd, R.M., & Henry, P.M. Effects of tutoring and practice teaching on self-concept and attitudes in education students. *Journal of Teacher Education,* 1968, 19 (3): 283-291.

Wallace, R.C. & Shavelson, R.J. Evaluation of curricular programs. In *Research into process curricula.* Syracuse, N.Y.: Eastern Regional Institute for Education, 1970. Pp. 143-164.

Wallen, N.E. & Travers, R.M. Analysis and investigation of teaching methods. In N.L. Gage (Ed.), *Handbook of research on teaching.* Chicago: Rand McNally, 1963. Pp. 448-505.

Webster's seventh new collegiate dictionary. Springfield, Mass.: G.&C. Merriam, 1967.

Williams, F.E. Workshops on the use and adaptation of new media for developing creativity. Washington, D.C.: U.S.O.E. Final Report of National Schools Project, Project #6-1619, 1968. (a)

Williams, F.E. (Ed.) *Creativity at home and in school.* St. Paul, Minn.: Macalester Creativity Project, 1968. (b)

Williams, F.E. Intellectual creativity and the teacher. In F.E. Williams (Ed.), *Creativity at home and in school.* St. Paul, Minn.: Macalester Creativity Project, 1968. (c)

Williams, F.E. Models for encouraging creativity in the classroom by integrating cognitive-affective behaviors. *Educational Technology*, 1969, 9 (12): 7-14.

Williams, F.E. *Classroom ideas for encouraging thinking and feeling.* Buffalo, N.Y.: D.O.K. Publishers, 1970.

Williams, F.E. & Eberle, R.F. *Content, process, practice: Creative production in the classroom.* Edwardsville, Ill.: Creative Concepts Unlimited, 1968.

Wittrock, M.C. The learning by discovery hypothesis. In L.S. Shulman & E.R. Keislar (Eds.), *Learning by discovery: A critical appraisal.* Chicago: Rand McNally, 1966. Pp. 33-75.

Woodruff, A.D. Living behaviors: Their delineation and the educational system necessary to develop them. Paper delivered at the Tenth Annual Phi Delta Kappa Research Symposium, Salt Lake City, Utah, April 11-12, 1969.

Worthen, J.E. Processes in education: Delineation, potential, and realization. Unpublished paper, Harvard University, February, 1963.

SUBJECT INDEX

AUTHOR INDEX